RACE, EQUITY, AND THE
LEARNING ENVIRONMENT

RACE, EQUITY, AND THE LEARNING ENVIRONMENT

The Global Relevance of Critical and Inclusive Pedagogies in Higher Education

Edited by Frank Tuitt, Chayla Haynes, and Saran Stewart

Foreword by Lori D. Patton

1996-2016 20TH ANNIVERSARY

Stylus

PUBLISHING, LLC.

STERLING, VIRGINIA

Published by Stylus Publishing, LLC.
22883 Quicksilver Drive
Sterling, Virginia 20166-2102

Library of Congress Cataloging-in-Publication Data
Names: Tuitt, Frank (Franklin A.), editor. |
Haynes, Chayla, editor. | Stewart, Saran, editor.
Title: Race, equity and the learning environment :
the global relevance of critical and inclusive pedagogies in higher
education / edited by Frank   Tuitt, Chayla Haynes, and Saran
Stewart ; foreword by Lori D. Patton.
Description: First edition. | Sterling, Virginia : Stylus Publishing,
LLC, 2016. | Includes bibliographical references and index.
Identifiers: LCCN 2015042808 (print) |
LCCN 2016004251 (ebook) |
  ISBN 9781620363393 (cloth : alk. paper) |
  ISBN 9781620363409 (pbk. : alk. paper) |
  ISBN 9781620363416 (library networkable e-edition) |
  ISBN 9781620363423 (consumer e-edition)
Subjects: LCSH: Critical pedagogy. | Multicultural education. |
Education, Higher--Social aspects. |
Minorities--Education (Higher) | Educational equalization.
Classification: LCC LC196 .R327 2016 (print) |
LCC LC196 (ebook) | DDC 370.11/5--dc23
LC record available at http://lccn.loc.gov/2015042808

13-digit ISBN: 978-1-62036-339-3 (cloth)
13-digit ISBN: 978-1-62036-340-9 (paperback)
13-digit ISBN: 978-1-62036-341-6 (library networkable e-edition)
13-digit ISBN: 978-1-62036-342-3 (consumer e-edition)

Printed in the United States of America

All first editions printed on acid-free paper
that meets the American National Standards Institute
Z39-48 Standard.

Bulk Purchases

Quantity discounts are available for use in workshops and for
staff development.
Call 1-800-232-0223

First Edition, 2016

CONTENTS

FOREWORD   *vii*
Lori D. Patton

ACKNOWLEDGMENTS   *xi*

INTRODUCTION   1
Critical and Inclusive Pedagogy: Why the Classroom *Is All* It's
Cracked Up to Be
Chayla Haynes

PART ONE: HOW WE THINK ABOUT OUR WORK

1. ADVANCING A CRITICAL AND INCLUSIVE PRAXIS   9
   Pedagogical and Curriculum Innovations for
   Social Change in the Caribbean
   Saran Stewart

2. PURSUING EQUITY THROUGH DIVERSITY   23
   Perspectives and Propositions for Teaching and
   Learning in Higher Education
   Liza Ann Bolitzer, Milagros Castillo-Montoya, and Leslie A. Williams

3. A DEMOCRATIC PEDAGOGY FOR A
   DEMOCRATIC SOCIETY   44
   Education for Social and Political Change (T-128)
   Eileen de los Reyes, Hal Smith, Tarajean Yazzie-Mintz, Yamila Hussein,
   and Frank Tuitt
   With José Moreno, Anthony De Jesús, Dianne Morales, and
   Sarah Napier

PART TWO: HOW WE ENGAGE IN OUR WORK

4. RADICAL HONESTY   71
   Truth-Telling as Pedagogy for Working Through
   Shame in Academic Spaces
   Bianca C. Williams

5. USING THE BARNGA CARD GAME SIMULATION TO
   DEVELOP CROSS-CULTURAL THINKING AND EMPATHY   83
   David S. Goldstein

6. CAMPUS RACIAL CLIMATE AND EXPERIENCES
   OF STUDENTS OF COLOR IN A MIDWESTERN COLLEGE   98
   Kako Koshino

7. HUMANIZING PEDAGOGY FOR EXAMINATIONS OF
   RACE AND CULTURE IN TEACHER EDUCATION   112
   Dorinda J. Carter Andrews and Bernadette M. Castillo

PART THREE: MEASURING THE IMPACT OF OUR WORK

8. DEHUMANIZING AND HUMANIZING PEDAGOGIES   131
   Lessons From U.S. Latin@ and Undocumented
   Youth Through the P–16 Pipeline
   Lisa M. Martinez, Maria del Carmen Salazar, and Debora M. Ortega

9. DE-RACIALIZING JAPANESENESS   149
   A Collaborative Approach to Shifting Interpretation and
   Representation of "Culture" at a University in Japan
   Ioannis Gaitanidis and Satoko Shao-Kobayashi

10. UNSUNG HEROES   170
    Impact of Diverse Administrators on the Creation of
    Transformative, Affirming, and Equitable Learning Environments
    Stella L. Smith

11. CRITICAL PEDAGOGY AND INTERSECTIONAL SEXUALITY   186
    Exploring Our Oppressions and Privileges Through
    Reflexivity, Responsibility, and Resistance
    *Haneen S. Ghabra, Sergio F. Juarez, Shanna K. Kattari,
    Miranda Olzman, and Bernadette Marie Calafell*

    CONCLUSION   205
    Inclusive Pedagogy 2.0: Implications for Race, Equity, and
    Higher Education in a Global Context
    Frank Tuitt

    EDITORS AND CONTRIBUTORS   223

    INDEX   227

FOREWORD

Race, equity, and higher education, when stated together, have a nice ring. The concepts are undoubtedly linked and mutually shaping. However, when it comes to the enactment of critical and inclusive pedagogies (CIPs), race, equity, and higher education fail to reflect the racist, inequitable structures embedded in most higher education classrooms. Regardless of educational context or social location, the conversations about race that occur in the classroom are limited, if existent at all. When we dare to broaden the context in which learning occurs, and the extent to which race plays a significant role, several factors become abundantly clear (at least to me):

1. Most conversations about race are doomed and ineffective because they often occur as isolated events, with few if any long-term efforts toward authentic engagement.
2. Conversations often begin with "good" intentions that lead to few accomplishments, the greatest being that someone lacking initial awareness exits the conversation with a small clue about why race matters.
3. Conversations about race may unintentionally cause participants to engage in unwarranted self-congratulatory behavior, coupled with their failure to demonstrate a raised consciousness through substantive behavioral changes.
4. Such conversations may begin with race but can easily shift to other forms of oppression that make race invisible or deemphasize its importance.
5. Although most institutions of higher education espouse commitments to diversity, inclusive of race, the enactment of such commitments have done little to move higher education toward more global, progressive racial understandings.

In this foreword, I argue that educators must be holistically (mind, body, spirit) committed to developing more global, progressive racial understanding toward equity in higher education, particularly as it pertains to the enactment of CIPs. We must acknowledge that racism is a transnational problem. The capacity to acknowledge the deeply entrenched inequities that exist in society and are reflected on our campuses and in learning spaces is critical. In my book (with University of Pennsylvania professor Shaun Harper) *Respond-ing to the Realities of Race on Campus*, we asserted:

> It is entirely possible for students to graduate from college without critically reflecting on their racist views, never having engaged in meaningful conver-sations about race, and using racially offensive language unknowingly. In this way . . . educators share responsibility for the reproduction of racially oblivious corporate executives, government and political leaders, and other college graduates who continue to enact laws and manage structures and institutions that maintain White supremacy. (Harper & Patton, 2007, p. 1)

To be sure the "race conversation" is not new, and it is apparently ineffective. I can think of two reasons to explain this phenomenon. First, the conversations are there, but the content is lacking. People are neither interested in discomfort and risk-taking nor do they wish to engage in the horrible truths that threaten to dismantle their safe (albeit racist) worldviews. Colorblindness and race neutrality represent the safer route. Second, people refuse to acknowledge that racism is permanent. This reality might be better digested by reading the work of the late critical race scholar Derrick Bell, who wrote a thesis entitled "Racism Is Here to Stay: Now What?" He stated:

> My thesis is jarring, I think, because for too long we have comforted our-selves with the myth of "slow but steady" racial progress. . . . You will note a seeming inconsistency that plagues my argument. On the one hand, I urge you to give up the dream of real, permanent racial equality. . . . On the other hand, I urge you to continue the fight against racism. One experi-ences an understandable desire to choose one or the other as valid . . . but it is not a question of pragmatism or idealism. Rather . . . it is a question of both recognition of the futility of action . . . *and* the unblinking conviction that something must be done, that action must be taken. (1991, p. 79)

Bell exposed a deeper and more complex response to dismantling racism and fighting for racial equity while demanding deeper reflection, especially for those who avoid dealing with race. More important, his words should resonate with those of us who are committed to ending systemic oppression, even as we fight to disrupt it, even as we acknowledge our own complicity in fueling inequities.

Educators, as an extension of the institution in which they work, are coimplicated in the oppression of others. Conversely, those who employ CIPs realize the power they have to resist traditional modes of teaching and learning that marginalize the voices and experiences of racially minoritized students. Educators must possess critical self-awareness, realizing we cannot effectively engage others in the practice of liberation until we have engaged ourselves in working toward equity via an enhanced understanding of racism. Critical self-awareness requires that we abandon imperialistic notions of teaching and learning and gravitate toward CIPs that name and disrupt racism and White supremacy in higher education.

This volume bridges the gap from thought to action, providing the necessary context for educators around the world to either embrace or recommit to centering race in postsecondary classrooms and engage in necessary conversations to ensure that students do not leave our institutions the way they came. I applaud the editors of this book as they dare to move beyond the conversation to engage in teaching and learning that reflects how progressive racial understandings promote equity in higher education.

Lori D. Patton
Associate Professor
Higher Education and Student Affairs
School of Education
Indiana University–Purdue University Indianapolis

Reference

Bell, D. (1991). Racism is here to stay: Now what? *Howard Law Journal, 35*(1), 79–93.

Harper, S. R., & Patton, L. D. (Eds). (2007). *Responding to the realities of race on campus: New directions for student services* (No. 120). San Francisco, CA: Jossey-Bass.

ACKNOWLEDGMENTS

Curiosity as restless questioning, as movement toward the revelation of something hidden, as a question verbalized or not, as search for clarity, as a moment of attention, suggestion, and vigilance constitutes an integral part of the phenomenon of being alive. There could be no creativity without the curiosity that moves us and sets us patiently impatient before a world that we did not make, to add to it something of our own making. (Freire, 1998, p. 38)

We wish to honor all of the transformative intellectuals who have inspired us to create spaces of curiosity as we strive to foster critical and inclusive learning environments in our classrooms. Additionally, we send much love and our greatest appreciation to the many scholars, educators, and practitioners (our partners in the struggle) who continue to provoke and have courageous conversations about race and equity in higher education, as they accept the challenge to teach, to transform, to engage, to respect, and to care for the souls of their students. To the contributors in this project, who authentically shared their lived experiences and provided insightful testimonies of their efforts to advance critical and inclusive pedagogies, we thank you. Finally, we genuinely acknowledge Kawanna Bright (graduate assistant, University of Denver) for her contribution, support, and assistance in bringing this project to completion.

Reference

Freire, P. (1998). *Pedagogy of freedom: Ethics, democracy and civic courage.* Lanham, MD: Rowman & Littlefield.

INTRODUCTION

Critical and Inclusive Pedagogy:
Why the Classroom *Is All* It's Cracked Up to Be

Chayla Haynes

Despite growing racial and ethnic diversity on university campuses, institutions across the globe struggle to resolve systemic challenges that contribute to inequitable educational outcomes among students. There is no greater indicator of educational outcomes than evaluations of academic persistence. Graduation rates among college students remain low, but they are particularly low among racial and ethnically diverse students: In 2013, only 20.5% of African Americans and 15.7% of Hispanics between the ages of 25 and 29 earned a bachelor's degree or more, compared to 40% of Whites (U.S. Department of Education, 2015). These types of gaps in achievement are consistent with academic persistence trends globally.

The Organisation for Economic Co-operation and Development (OECD, 2013) found that less than 60% of students who enter tertiary programs, from across its 34 member countries, actually graduate with a first degree. Further, the advent of online education has removed the bounds of the classroom and fueled a critique of the ivory tower's traditional modes of delivery. Presumably, its popularity has signaled a shift in expectations, where students function as consumers and higher education is seen as a product that ought to be mass produced (Berrett, 2012). The circumstances of this predicament have forced institutions, both at home and abroad, to rethink how to place emphasis back on the classroom and saturate the market.

Gumport (2000) underscored this notion when she posited that higher education's faculty and administrators no longer have the luxury to expect financial returns from increases in enrollment based on institutional legacies, histories, and prestige alone. Her conclusions suggest that in order to maintain a competitive edge, institutions of higher education must respond to the growing cultural, ethnic, and racial diversity of today's college student through innovations in teaching. Faced with the possibly of becoming obsolete, institutions are realizing it is the *how,* rather than the *what,* that is being taught that actually matters, as they learn how to perform as multicultural organizations (Jackson, 2005). With a focus on the classroom, this volume illuminates the global relevance of critical and inclusive pedagogies (CIPs), while exposing how its application can transform the teaching and learning process and promote more equitable educational outcomes among *all* college students, but especially racially minoritized students.

Critical and Inclusive Pedagogies

CIPs are not a new phenomenon in the field of education. However, their prevalence has had much more to do with exploring the impact of teaching in U.S. secondary education rather than postsecondary education. And though evaluations of CIPs impact have evolved beyond that of race, gender, and class to include ability, language, and even religion, the existing literature neglects to substantively address their global relevance. Drawing on the works of Paulo Freire (1973, 2000), Henry Giroux (1988, 1994), bell hooks (1994), and Peter McLaren (1998), critical and inclusive pedagogues have asserted that teaching and learning are deeply interrelated. Moreover, they have contended that the knowledge construction process must confront dominant ideologies and stimulate praxis. In considering their applicability, instructors are prompted to evaluate who is being included in and excluded from the learning process when teaching fails to consider the varying social, psychological, physical, and/or emotional needs of students (Danowitz & Tuitt, 2011; Florian & Black-Hawkins, 2011; hooks, 1994; Tuitt, 2003, 2010).

Moreover, CIPs encourage teaching practice that creates an oppositional ontology of history to expose the relationship between knowledge and lived experience. Entering into the field of comparative education, this edited volume addresses the current gaps in the discourse by bringing together higher education scholars across academic disciplines and countries to explore how CIPs not only promote deep learning among students but also better equip instructors to attend to the needs of diverse students. Specifically, CIPs seek to create inclusive learning environments by doing the following: (a) prioritizing the intellectual and social development of students, (b) fostering classroom climates that challenge each student to achieve academically at high levels, (c) recognizing and cultivating the cultural and global differences that learners bring to the educational experience, and (d) engaging the "whole" student (e.g., intellectually, spiritually, and emotionally) in the teaching and learning process (Danowitz & Tuitt, 2011).

Volume Contents

This edited volume has been organized into three sections to make clear how CIPs can transform both the teaching and learning process for all who are involved: *the students and the instructor(s)*. Part one, aptly titled "How We Think About Our Work," presents a discourse on the philosophical underpinnings that inform a critical and inclusive pedagogue's approach to instruction and course design. In their chapters, contributors reveal how they create conditions in their classrooms for students to develop critical, theoretical, and practical understandings of power to expose the impact of race, ethnicity, gender, sexual orientation, religious affiliation, and other social identities on students' individual and collective learning. Further, contributors in this section critique their teaching effectiveness as measured by CIPs' aim to produce transformative intellectuals acting as critical agents who question how knowledge is produced and distributed, have the courage to explore new ways of thinking and being, and have a willingness to take risks without fear of failure.

Consisting of three chapters, this section begins with an autoethnographic evaluation of teaching by Saran Stewart, who details how critical-inclusive pedagogy allowed her to embrace the role of instructor as activist through the personal and political act of curricular change at the University of the West Indies. The next chapter is a thoughtful examination of the educational benefits of diversity by Liza Ann Bolitzer, Milagros Castillo-Montoya, and Leslie A. Williams, who argue that greater access and equity depend on a systematic adoption of a more expanded definition of *diversity* that incorporates the multiple diversities students bring with them to our classrooms. In part one's concluding chapter, Eileen de los Reyes, Hal Smith, Tarajean Yazzie-Mintz, Yamila Hussein, and Frank Tuitt, with contributions from José Moreno, Anthony De Jesús, Dianne Morales, and Sarah Napier, tackle the complexities of democracy in the creation of academic learning spaces to promote the type of social and political change not intended to remain inside the classroom.

In part two, entitled "How We Engage in Our Work," we are reminded that race still matters; therefore, neither our classrooms globally nor the knowledge constructed within are void of a sociopolitical context. Through their reflections, contributors discuss how CIPs enabled them to serve simultaneously as teacher and student (Freire, 2000) to accurately reflect the history and composition of the world. Through their adoption of CIP, we discover how teaching can translate to deep learning, allowing students to (a) connect their personal experiences to theoretical principles under study in a course and (b) live life more fully and deeply (Freire, 2000; hooks, 1994) by linking their desire to learn with their desire to become who they are meant to be: critically conscious global citizens.

Beginning with Bianca C. Williams, part two has a total of four chapters. Williams prompts us to rethink our teaching with a compelling and thought-provoking narrative about her use of *radical honesty as a truth-telling pedagogy*. Rooted in Black feminist anthropology and African American studies, *radical honesty* underscores the value of personal narrative and self-authorship in disrupting racist and patriarchal institutional cultures and influences the construction of academic spaces.

Also included in part two are chapters by David S. Goldstein and Kako Koshino. Goldstein exposes the pedagogical power of experiential learning through an evaluation of the classroom simulation game Barnga, which leads students to deeper empathy for individuals with different cultural backgrounds. Classroom simulations like Barnga, Goldstein argues, enact a critical pedagogy that enables students to relinquish mistaken preconceptions and to adopt a deeper social justice orientation. In her chapter, Koshino presents research findings that illuminate the relationship between culture and education through an exploration of culturally responsive teaching. Positing that educational equity for students of color begins with the educator, Koshino's findings indicate that learning environments that accurately reflect the history and composition of the world also contribute to retention and satisfaction.

Part two concludes with Dorinda J. Carter Andrews and Bernadette M. Castillo, who assert that students are rendered colorblind, colormute, and culturally deficient when schooling fails to adequately educate them about race, culture, and power. An illustration of how theory informs teaching practice, their chapter explores how they embraced humanizing pedagogy to foster a critical consciousness among the preservice teachers who are their students.

Part three, "Measuring the Impact of Our Work," makes explicit how CIPs enable the knowledge constructed in our classrooms to transform not only an institution but also the community in which it resides. Powerful reflections are presented that reveal how teaching that emphasizes shared power, inequality, race and ethnicity, class, and gender promotes increased understanding of lived experience among students. Containing four chapters, part three begins by challenging our operating assumption that educational institutions are culturally, politically, and racially neutral. Lisa M. Martinez, Maria del Carmen Salazar, and Debora M. Ortega use a life history approach to present illustrations of dehumanizing and humanizing pedagogy. They conclude that early intervention, support, and emphasis on the whole student promote academic success among Latin@ and undocumented youth in the P–16 pipeline. Next, Ioannis Gaitanidis and Satoko Shao-Kobayashi focus on evaluating the process and product of instructor–student interactions. They applied a collaborative learning framework to their design and instruction of a course they cotaught at a university in Japan, where race, ethnicity, language, citizenship, and culture are readily conflated. Gaitanidis and Shao-Kobayashi found that de-racializing Japaneseness required that students continuously engage in curriculum that rebuilt their knowledges, a difficult task when racial dominance and homogeneity of both course content and classroom composition are used to assimilate and normalize students.

Stella L. Smith adds to this discourse in the chapter that follows, which explores what is at risk when we presume that learning is restricted to the classroom. Rooted in the lived experiences of African American senior university administrators, Smith's findings reveal that an engaged pedagogical (hooks, 1994) approach to professional practice has both inspired students' development and aided in disrupting systemic institutional structures that have inhibited the fostering of truly transformative learning environments. Rounding out part three, Haneen S. Ghabra, Sergio F. Juarez, Shanna K. Kattari, Miranda Olzman, and Bernadette Marie Calafell critique their lived experiences in the classroom to identify inclusive pedagogical strategies that foster spaces of possibility, connection, and resistance in an academy that is often hostile to students who—like themselves—are marked as abject and often undesired in relationship to the White, heterosexual, male norm for whom the academy caters. Using critical pedagogy and intersectional sexuality as a frame, their chapter uses performance writing to evaluate the impact of classroom interactions that are driven by an ethic of care, responsibility, and love, revealing how instructors and students can work together to create inclusive academic spaces.

Finally this volume closes with a thoughtful reflection by Frank Tuitt on inclusive and critical pedagogies' ability to address racial inequities that permeate higher education globally. Drawing on his expertise as an inclusive pedagogy scholar and critical race pedagogue, Tuitt walks readers through how inclusive pedagogy emerged and has evolved through an exploration of his scholarship that aims to recenter race in college teaching, his collaborative partnership with equity-minded educators he has fostered across the globe, and the meaningful interactions he has had with diverse students over the years. We learn through his commentary about the theory, praxis, and outcomes of CIP, while also discovering how teaching and learning, from this vantage point, can inspire the greatest of possibilities for institutional and student transformation. To that end, the editors of this volume contend that only when educators dare to draw upon the tenets of CIP will teaching and learning, as fundamental components of the academic enterprise of higher education, be included as part of the solution to the racial inequity experienced at institutions globally.

References

Berrett, D. (2012). Harvard conference seeks to jolt university teaching. *The Chronicle of Higher Education, 58*, 24.

Danowitz, M. A., & Tuitt, F. (2011). Enacting inclusivity through engaged pedagogy: A higher education perspective. *Equity & Excellence in Education, 44*(1), 40–56.

Florian, L., & Black-Hawkins, K. (2011). Exploring inclusive pedagogy. *British Educational Research Journal, 37*(5), 813–828.

Freire, P. (1973). *Education for critical consciousness.* New York, NY: Seabury.

Freire, P. (2000). *Pedagogy of the oppressed* [Pedagogía del oprimido] (30th anniversary ed.) New York, NY: Continuum.

Giroux, H. A. (1988). *Teachers as intellectuals: Toward a critical pedagogy of learning.* South Hadley, MA: Bergin Garvey.

Giroux, H. A., & McLaren, P. (1994). *Between borders.* New York, NY: Routledge.

Gumport, P. J. (2000). Academic restructuring: Organizational change and institutional imperatives. *Higher Education, 39*(1), 67–91.

hooks, b. (1994). *Teaching to transgress: Education as the practice of freedom* (Vol. 4). New York, NY: Routledge.

Jackson, B. W. (2005). The theory and practice of multicultural organization development in education. In M. L. Ouellett (Ed.), *Teaching inclusively: Resources for course, department and institutional change in higher education* (pp. 3–33). Stillwater, OK: New Forums.

McLaren, P. (1998). *Life in schools: An introduction to critical pedagogy in the foundations of education.* Reading, MA: Addison Wesley Longman.

Organisation for Economic Co-operation and Development. (2013). How many students fail to graduate? In *Education at a Glance 2013: Highlights* (pp. 28–29). doi:10.1787/eag_highlights-2013-en

Tuitt, F. (2003). Afterword: Realizing more inclusive pedagogy. In A. Howell & F. Tuitt (Eds.), *Race and higher education: Rethinking pedagogy in diverse college classrooms* (pp. 243–268). Cambridge, MA: Harvard Educational Review.

Tuitt, F. (2010). Enhancing visibility in graduate education: Black women's perceptions of inclusive pedagogical practices. *International Journal of Teaching & Learning in Higher Education, 22*(3), 246–257.

U.S. Department of Education, National Center for Education Statistics. (2015). Percentage of persons 25 to 29 years old with selected levels of educational attainment, by race/ethnicity and sex: Selected years, 1920 through 2014 [Table 104.20]. In *The condition of education 2015* (NCES 2015-144). Retrieved from https://nces.ed.gov/programs/digest/d14/tables/dt14_104.20.asp

PART ONE

HOW WE THINK ABOUT OUR WORK

ADVANCING A CRITICAL AND INCLUSIVE PRAXIS

Pedagogical and Curriculum Innovations for Social Change in the Caribbean

Saran Stewart

Three years ago, I booked a one-way ticket to Jamaica, my "foreign-homeland." The term *foreign-homeland* represents how I view Jamaica as an adult, as opposed to how I viewed it as a child. Some customs and practices I once found normative and comforting I now view as oppressive and intolerable. Upon my arrival, I made several conscious decisions to renegotiate how I operated within the social structures and governance of life at home. To reacclimatize, I had to unlearn privileges, as explained by Spivak (1988, 2004), and understand that I operated within an identity as a knowledge elite. Having earned a doctoral degree, I had become a "power broker" (Gaventa, 1980, p. 28) and had to rationalize how I navigated within that role. I found myself struggling with the term *knowledge elite* as it represented "the control of knowledge in the hands of the few, in a manner that exercises power over the lives of many" (Gaventa, 1980, p. 30). The power dynamic between student and professor can often be off-balance and result in an exclusive learning environment.

I knew returning to my foreign-homeland, armed with a global perspective of teaching and learning, would challenge the "traditional modes of instruction, which serve to exclude rather than include students" (Danowitz & Tuitt, 2011, p. 43). These challenges echo Freire's (2005) concept of banking education, which I believe reverberates through the halls of the university where I currently teach:

The teacher teaches and the students are taught; . . . the teacher talks and the students listen—meekly; . . . the teacher chooses the program content, and the students (who were not consulted) adapt to it; . . . the teacher is the subject of the learning process, while the pupils are mere objects. (p. 73)

The difficulty in disrupting the banking system of education (Freire, 2005) is that both the oppressed (i.e., the students) and the oppressor (i.e., the lecturer) can be resistant to change. For example, a first-year postgraduate student visited my office in the middle of the semester, not to discuss her grades or class assignments, but to relay, on behalf of her classmates, that my style of teaching was too "foreign-minded" (having Eurocentric ideals and expectations) and was not welcomed at the university. She said, "Doc, why can't you be like the other lecturers; just come to class, run through the power point, and give us notes? All these questions, questions about what we think, and group work activities in class; we are not use to that" (personal communication, September 2013). After she left, I reflected on the words of my mentors: "Expect and be prepared to engage student resistance in teaching and learning" (Danowitz & Tuitt, 2011, p. 52).

Despite the research on the benefits and gains of student-centered learning and engaging pedagogical models, lecture-style instruction continues to be the de facto style of higher education teaching around the world (Brown & Atkins, 2002; Chisholm, 2008). Lecture style, although not equated to banking education (Freire, 1993), is reminiscent of shared similarities, such as one-directional learning in which the lecturer (i.e., faculty member, instructor, or teacher) is the subject of knowledge and the students, the objects.

The lectureship instructional design is the customary choice of content delivery in Jamaica's higher education institutions, in which students attend class with little exchange of ideas or expectation to co-construct knowledge. In the United States, many researchers have debated the need for a more inclusive shift in pedagogy (e.g., Darder, 1996; hooks, 1994; Knefelkamp, 1997; Tuitt, 2003). The debate is further compounded in postcolonial and neocolonial societies, such as Jamaica, in which inherited customs of higher education practice reflect conflicting power dynamics aimed at continuing colonial traditions. Inherited customs, such as the dominance of a patriarchal climate amongst senior administrators and faculty, a lecture–tutorial learning system, and an examinations-driven culture resemble some of the political and ideological struggles of the colonial era. This is the context in which I returned to teach in Jamaica.

Within that context, this chapter examines how I employed a critical and inclusive pedagogy (CIP) framework (Stewart, 2013) to develop pedagogical and curriculum innovations for social change. It is intended as a critical reflection of my experiences teaching at a public regional research university in the Caribbean, which is referred to as the Caribbean University hereafter. I present a hybridized framework to describe how I apply and practice CIP in postgraduate educational research and higher education courses. In doing this, I employ both Alvesson's (2003) self-ethnography, "to draw attention to one's own cultural context" (p. 175), and Ellis and Bochner's (2000) autoethnography in which the researcher–author's method is to "tell stories about their [his or her] own lived experiences, relating the personal to the cultural" (Richardson, 2000, p. 931). Thereafter, I outline what I believe are movements of social change in my students and conclude by addressing some of the implications for educators who seek to apply the CIP framework (Stewart, 2013) in higher education institutions.

Applying CIP

Being trained and prepared for academia by transformative intellectuals, I understood that scholarship should not be devoid of a social and political context. I recognized the need to develop a conceptual and theoretical base in which to engage students in higher education, as co-constructors in the teaching–learning process. It was not enough to develop an inclusive learning environment for my students. I also needed to create a classroom experience that would enable them to attain a heightened awareness for social change. During my doctoral studies, I developed the CIP framework as a guide in which to map core competencies onto a set of teaching practices aimed to foster both critical consciousness and a more inclusive learning environment. My conceptual mapping of a CIP framework centered on the use and application of Tuitt's (2003) five tenets of inclusive pedagogy to attain Freire's (2005) ideal of *conscientização,* or critical consciousness. The framework is highly adaptive to regional context and dependent on the respectful relationship between student and faculty (see Figure 1.1).

Developing Critical Consciousness

I understand *critical consciousness* as "learning to perceive social, political, and economic status contradictions and to take action against the oppressive elements of reality" (Freire, 2005, p. 35). Freire (2005) suggested that in order for oppressed persons to truly be liberated, dialectical, and dialogical, they must be able to read the world and not just the word. They must "recognize themselves as the architects of their own cognitive process" (p. 112). In attempting to help my students develop critical consciousness, I expect them to not only learn how to critically view, understand, and debate social, political, and economic contradictions, but also see the *self*

Figure 1.1 Critical–inclusive pedagogical framework.

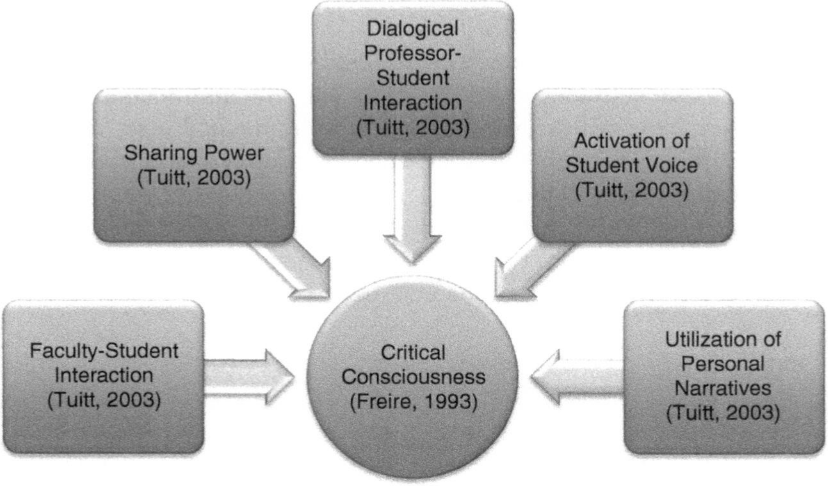

Note. Adapted from *Everything in di Dark Muss Come to Light: A Postcolonial Examination of the Practice of Extra Lessons at the Secondary Level in Jamaica's Education System,* by S. Stewart, 2013 (Doctoral dissertation). Retrieved from ProQuest (Order No. 3597983).

through the *self* and as the *other* (adapted from Ellis, 2004). This meta-awareness involves self-reflection and critical pedagogy to guide the process. Furthering this approach, critical reflection is necessary and "is a requirement of the relationship between theory and practice" (Freire, 1998, p. 30). As the lecturer, I am also the oppressor with the assumed sole power to construct knowledge in the class. I control the direction of my students' learning and can either encourage or diminish inclusion and social change activism. However, the instructor as oppressor must first acknowledge and accept the status of oppressor, even one who may have been oppressed previously, and use authority to facilitate learning, not control it. Additionally, as Freire (1998) explained, "the educator with a democratic vision or posture cannot avoid in his teaching praxis insisting on the critical capacity, curiosity and autonomy of the learner" (p. 33). The educator must be the facilitator of knowledge to guide self-efficacy and respect what students know entering the classroom.

Freire (1993) problematized systems of banking education, revealing the inequities, injustices, and misappropriation of teaching and learning in the classroom. He went further in stating, "A characteristic of the ideology of oppression negates education and the knowledge as processes of inquiry" (p. 72). In unveiling the inequities in the education system, Freire then revealed new concepts of pedagogy, homing in on the need for "problem-posing" education that truly transforms rather than transfixes men and women into becoming dialogical (Stewart, 2013). In this regard, Freire acknowledged that the "teacher's thinking is authenticated only by the authenticity of the student's thinking" (1993, p. 77). Accordingly, I am accountable for my students' learning and, in that, also responsible for how we, together, co-construct knowledge in the classroom. By developing critical consciousness, students develop agency when they leverage their voices to speak out and purposely act against oppressive systems of society, including education. In my experience, developing critical consciousness has no timeline and can resemble an oscillating pendulum, because in any given moment, one's critical consciousness can shift according to recognition of himself or herself in society amid revolving societal changes.

Inclusive Pedagogy at the Caribbean University

In the first couple of months as a newly minted lecturer, I realized that if I were to navigate the roles of bureaucratic authority, I had to tactically infuse the framework without disrupting the norm completely. I set out not to demand and overhaul years of banking education (Freire, 1993), but to demonstrate, as a "tempered radical" (Meyerson, 2003), the subtle inclusion of problem-posing education (Freire, 1993). Unfortunately, my subtle attempts to infuse the CIP framework were not met with open arms. In meetings, any suggestions I made as a new hire in academia were dismissed as being "foreign-minded" and juvenile. I was reminded of being a young woman in a patriarchal environment, led by men but operated by women. The very women who were oppressed had become oppressive. Women who had been overlooked for promotions and/or paid less than their male counterparts had arguably internalized years of oppression. Seemingly, the internalized oppression was unleashed on young and naïve hires like myself. In the first year, my suggestions for pedagogical and curriculum improvements were constantly overlooked. I was told that the majority of my students were classroom teachers in local primary and secondary schools, that they would remain that way after graduating with their master's degrees, and that further aspirations to doctoral work or employment outside of the country and industry were unrealistic.

As a means to disrupt these forms of "academic orthodoxy" (Chisholm, 2008, p. 328), I employed Tuitt's (2003) concept of inclusive pedagogy derived from an amalgamation of critical and transformative pedagogical models—for example, Banks and McGee's (1997) equity pedagogy, Freire's (1993) pedagogy of the oppressed, Giroux's (1992) border pedagogy, and hooks' (1994) engaged pedagogy and transformative education. Inclusive pedagogy includes the following key tenets: (a) faculty–student interaction,

(b) sharing power, (c) dialogical professor–student interaction, (d) activation of student voice, and (e) utilization of personal narratives (Tuitt, 2003). It is transformative as a holistic concept and a methodological approach because it provides key principles to guide teaching practices to make the learning environment inclusive and engaging. In practicing the CIP framework (Stewart, 2013), I made conscious decisions not to dictate the class, but to facilitate and guide learning at the students' pace, so as to foster an inclusive learning environment where all voices were respected and encouraged. I asked more questions than time allowed and did not provide finite answers, but let students question alternatives to answers. I allowed multiple pathways to arrive at an answer so as to encourage divergent thinking. In the next section, I explain how Tuitt's (2003) tenets manifest in my teaching, which is informed by the CIP framework (Stewart, 2013).

Realizing a Critical and Inclusive Praxis

The first tenet of inclusive pedagogy, *faculty–student interaction,* promotes positive relationships between student and faculty in which trust is earned and reciprocated. The interaction between faculty and student is encouraged inside and outside the classroom to foster "positive social interactions" (Tuitt, 2003, p. 247). Throughout my tenure at Caribbean University, I found constant and consistent communication to be key factors in promoting this level of interaction. I found myself engaging with students using various forms of instant messaging, live video chats, and social media, which resulted in mini-advising sessions. Being available to students in various modes of communication allowed for increased access to mentoring and advising.

The second tenet, *sharing power,* debunks the role of the professor as the sole constructor of knowledge. Instead, both student and faculty are expected to co-construct knowledge and are equally responsible to contribute to the process of teaching and learning in the classroom. As part of the course assessment, I used interactive group-led class activities in which students were required to take sections of the core topics of the course and develop classroom activities to teach said topics. This allowed students to demonstrate their teaching styles and helped to foster a sense of ownership of the course material. Students were guided to assess their individual learning styles and incorporate techniques to demonstrate each. Moreover, students were expected to coteach course content as part of the assignments and peer-review other students' work. Each semester, there was resistance and rejection of the newly required responsibilities of the students in co-constructing the learning environment and knowledge generated in my courses. The students were initially resolved to engage minimally, take notes, and do what they were told. I was transparent about having them recognize their learned behavior as a legacy of banking education by having them read excerpts from Tuitt's (2003) and Freire's (1993) works (to name a few). In the past, I hosted video-conference sessions with Tuitt on inclusive pedagogy, as well as invited him to speak in-person on campus. Demystifying scholarly research and making it applicable and embedded in lived experiences cements to the students a greater responsibility for their own learning.

The third tenet, *dialogical professor–student interaction*, is often challeng-ing to implement in learning environments where knowledge is disseminated in formal lecture styles and regulated by top-down institutional policies. This tenet advocates for constant, reciprocal dialogue and discourse that is both respectful and problem posing. The discourse thereby allows for differing perspectives and multiple "truths," with an aim of creating "collaborative learning environments" (Tuitt, 2003, p. 248). I encouraged my students to interrogate my views and respectfully challenge course content and literature by delving even deeper into the literature to propose counterarguments. I found that the organizational culture of the institution often made it dif-ficult for students to be comfortable with disagreeing with the professor and contributed to accepted silence.

To disrupt the silence, my aims were to create trusting learning environ-ments in which students were free to express their varying and opposing opinions and engage in critical discourse. To do this, the students and I col-laboratively set the norms and aims of the class at the start of the semester. Thereafter, we held each other accountable to those aims throughout the course. This disruption essentially led to the development of the fourth tenet, *activation of student voice*, which Tuitt (2003) explained: "By having a voice, students can bring into the classroom the world as they have experienced it" (p. 250). The deliberate inclusion of students' experiences and encour-agement of experiential learning allows students to bring their whole selves into the learning environment. I found this to be the most difficult tenet to actualize with my students, because my students entered higher education from their years of silence in primary and secondary schooling. Some of the teaching techniques used to undo the silencing were social blog assignments and self-reflexive journaling. Both proved to be effective. Students on the social blog sites were able to voice their opinions in a community setting that allowed for creativity and expressive thought. The self-reflexive journal allowed for a fusion of guiding literature and personal narratives to merge and layer. The *utilization of personal narratives* is Tuitt's fifth tenet, wherein reflexiveness is evoked and critical thought, through experiential knowledge, is written as a response to required readings (Beynon & Dossa, 2010; Tuitt, 2003). The underlying assumption is that "one's own experience is central to understanding and developing knowledge" (Danowitz & Tuitt, 2011, p. 49).

These five tenets of inclusive pedagogy were used as a guiding framework with a central aim to develop students' critical consciousness. My decision to focus on developing students' critical consciousness was attributed to wanting my students to be able to fully understand their circumstance and their place in the world and to recognize that they can be empowered to change that circumstance and place.

Promoting Critical Consciousness: Curriculum Innovations for Social Change

The CIP framework (Stewart, 2013) supports the movement toward not only pedagogical innovation but also curriculum innovation: to better develop, align, and sequence courses that are critical in theory and praxis. After what I viewed as several levels of tempered radicalism and a proficiency in research methodology, I was given the opportunity to better streamline the postgraduate research courses and with that make decisive changes to the curriculum. I made a conscious decision to increase the use of technology, thereby reducing the paper trails of assignments and allowing access to course materials and delivery of assignments asynchronously, using course management systems. Although the use of course management systems was practiced prior to my arrival at the university, it was arguably not frequently or effectively utilized.

In addition, the curriculum I inherited was mostly outdated, and the delivery mechanism remained lecture style. My first cohort had no prior experience with statistics or educational research, but was expected by the end of a semester to present three comprehensive chapters simulating a research proposal, complete with a literature review, framework, and methodology section. In many ways, I believed the curriculum was not intended for or designed with the students in mind, and they were therefore faced with many challenges, such as not having the proper sequencing of courses or requisite skills for each course. In the first year, I infused additional lessons and resources to provide students with the foundation necessary to succeed in the course. I purposefully looked at ways to better align the course content with the course objectives and respective assessments.

Hargreaves (1998), "Pushing the Boundaries of Educational Change" encouraged academics and practitioners to "attend more closely to the societal forces that drive educational change and to move beyond images of change as a linear, predictable, means-to-an-end process in favor of models of change as a complex and even 'chaotic' process" (as cited in Waks, 2007, p. 278). Like Hargreaves, I strongly believe that the means-to-an-ends approach is outdated and that any reform in education cannot be devoid of the social and political context. And even though the model of change might be chaotic, it is necessary to have a philosophical foundation to guide the process. As such, I developed my teaching philosophy to be more culturally relevant and sociopolitically contextual within the parameters of the CIP framework (Stewart, 2013). I made a conscious decision to include it in the syllabus so that my students would know *why* and *how* I teach. It was important to create a space for my students to reflect on how I use the critical–inclusive pedagogical framework to undergird my approach to teaching and design of the curriculum. It reads as follows:

> I approach teaching as a transformative process: believing that my students and I should leave the course changed from when we entered. I am interested in how students can develop critical consciousness and activate their voice to transform their educational experiences. Although I cannot create "safe" learning environments, my aim is to create inclusive spaces where opinions and ideas are valued and respected. I will challenge my students to understand their role and responsibility in the social and political context in education. I will be transparent and authentic in delivering the course and at times make learning uncomfortable. Hold me accountable to co-construct knowledge and change the curriculum as needed. Recognizing that students learn differently, I will engage the various learning styles using multiple techniques to facilitate dialogical discourse. Although I am the lecturer, I do not possess the sole power to control the direction of the course and welcome shared responsibilities with my students. hooks (1994) said it best, "The classroom, with all its limitations, remains a location of possibility. In that field of possibility we have the opportunity to labor for freedom, to demand of ourselves and our comrades, an openness of mind and heart that allows us to face reality even as we collectively imagine ways to move beyond boundaries, to transgress. This is education as the practice of freedom." (Stewart, p. 207)

I close the philosophy with a few challenges, reminding students that *learning occurs when you are most uncomfortable.* To subliminally include aspects of the framework in the curriculum, I looked at the selection of readings, learning objectives, and respective assignments and updated sections where necessary and applicable.

Depending on the course, I complement the required texts and readings with more current and transformative literature to assist with activation of student voice. For example, I select readings that are written by local and regional authors first and then look internationally to add to the list. Thereafter, I layer the expected learning outcomes to reflect engagement and change in the understanding, respect, and practice of the course content. The assessment rubric is altered to include scaffolding techniques in which assignments are separated and given a sequential order, building from the previous. Before any new sections are to be submitted for a grade, students receive feedback on the previous sections of the assignment. This provides students with constant feedback and, more importantly, examples of my expectations of work submitted. The assignments also map onto the expected learning objectives and where applicable include assignments that utilize personal narratives such as the social blogs or reflexive journals. The course content or modules are written to provoke and entice dialogical discourse. The sequencing of units in each course module is purposefully ordered to increase shared power of knowledge construction and delivery of course content.

In my experience, the CIP framework provides a catalyst for social activism and change to occur through the development of critical consciousness. However, implementing the framework in pedagogy and curriculum requires an initial interrogation of the self to completely understand, first, how to recognize and then navigate the roles of oppressed and oppressor and, second, how to develop inclusive learning environments to transform students.

Empowering Students Using the CIP Framework

The critical–inclusive pedagogical framework (Stewart, 2013) provides techniques and strategies where instructors and their students become agents of change, unlearning normative ideologies of teaching and learning and becoming architects of their own understanding. Since implementing the framework at Caribbean University, I have seen the pendulum swing for some of my students and, for them, it was a frightening process and at times an overwhelming responsibility—to be armed with a higher level of meta-awareness and knowledge of change but sometimes unable to act. Through their writing and expressions of critical thought, they began to interrupt hegemony and heterogeneous normativity and started to question their social and political repositioning. They themselves were recognizing their compounding roles as the oppressor and the oppressed: the oppressor in their individual work-related roles and the oppressed as students at the university.

However, there was more to be done; the work had just started. Following the completion of the first semester, I purposefully requested to teach the same cohort of students throughout its remaining time in the postgraduate program to continue to embed the principles of inclusive pedagogy and gauge students' development of critical consciousness. Each semester, the change became more evident, but the group became smaller. At the end of the second semester in my first year, I urged the students to submit aspects of their course assignments to academic conferences. I wanted the students to position their work and own their scholarship amongst fellow educational academics. Seven of my students were invited to present their research at an international academic conference. Those seven students had the most notable development of critical consciousness and activation of agency; not because they were accepted to present at the conference but arguably because they became more self-aware of their roles in society as educators. They rejected prevalent notions of banking education and actively engaged in transformative learning. They started to question the sociopolitical and historical context of their own educational journeys and current roles in society. They began to peer-teach their classmates and change their individual classroom practice. They started to advocate for research that was meaningful to their communities and change oriented. They began discussions of social policy for public good. They recognized themselves as researchers, ethically responsible for systemic change. Four of them completed applications for doctoral degrees and changes in employment. The remaining three sought to develop and include tenets of inclusive pedagogy in their practice and now mentor other teachers, thereby creating their own legacy of advancing CIP.

Implications for Practice

My experience using the critical–inclusive pedagogical framework has taught me that the lecturer must engage in critical self-work in developing critical consciousness and be vulnerable in the process in order to have courageous conversations with his or her colleagues and students. In this process, the work and learning environment may become hostile and isolating but may become an axis point for social change. I view the university as a microcosm of society, one that produces the leaders of the country and has the ability to make systemic change for the public good. Envisioning the graduates of the twenty-first century means looking at the possibility for radical social change to occur and developing critically conscious students to recognize the contradictions of social, economic, and political policies to create that change. In order to envision these changes, students must be developed to be equally responsible to co-construct knowledge, activate their voices, and engage in critical discourse. It further means debunking the social elitism of the university structure and recognizing ourselves (i.e., lecturers, faculty members, professors) as the oppressor. Thereafter, I believe the pendulum will begin to swing, and change agents will be developed.

I caution those who want to engage in CIP to first start with the self-work needed and the recognition of being the oppressor, with the responsibility to constantly question and act against systems of oppression. Embedded systems of bureaucratic traditions, rooted in colonial principles, are difficult to dismantle and disrupt. Acting as a tempered radical within the system allows for "more good by staying within the organization, and temper[s] [the] activities and strategies to create change from the bottom up" (Kezar, Gallant, & Lester, 2011, p. 130). Even so, there are risks of being marginalized and labeled as an agitator. These risks can possibly hinder the tenure and promotion process and place the lecturer in a vulnerable state. However, I believe strategies can be put in place to identify the critical changes needed to work within the system to make those changes systemically.

I believe that the individual lecturer (e.g., faculty member, instructor, or professor) must first craft her or his teaching philosophy with the espoused beliefs of developing critical consciousness, and then make it visible and transparent to students. As a tempered radical, the lecturer must learn the system in which he or she operates and understand the cultural organization and value placed on the quality of teaching. Lecturers can then consult with other faculty members and seek mentorship with like-minded change agents, utilizing inclusive pedagogical models. They can expect resistance from both students and colleagues but be prepared to continue the process with the same cohort to encourage reinforcement of like-thought. Also, lecturers can provide a community space for students as well as create a space for fellow lecturers who embark on developing critical consciousness in themselves and their students, to disrupt feelings of isolation in the process.

Teaching cannot be viewed as a silo practice devoid of the social and political context of the larger society. It must impact, question, and take on an activism approach for social change to occur. I continue to straddle the line between native and foreigner in my homeland, with a heightened awareness of my position of power as an academic. It is a struggle at times to resist normative ideologies and conventional practices and remain true to the theoretical underpinnings of the CIP framework. However, I recognize the challenges and continue to be a work in progress as I crystalize my own understanding of what it means to be critically conscious.

References

Alvesson, M. (2003). Methodology for close up studies: Struggling with closeness and closure. *Higher Education, 46*(2), 167–193.

Banks, J., & McGee, C. M. (1997). *Educating citizens in a multicultural society.* New York, NY: Teachers College Press.

Beynon, J., & Dossa, P. (2010). Mapping inclusive and equitable pedagogy: Narratives of university educators. *Teacher Education, 14*(3), 249–264.doi:10.1080/1047621032000135168

Brown, G., & Atkins, M. (2002). *Effective teaching in higher education.* London, UK: Routledge.

Chisholm, M. (2008). Curricular transformation in higher education and the role of a cross-disciplinary WAC approach. *Caribbean Journal of Education, 30*(2), 323–344.

Danowitz, M., & Tuitt, F. (2011). Enacting inclusivity through engaged pedagogy: A higher education perspective. *Equity & Excellence in Education, 44*(1), 40–56.

Darder, A. (1996). Creating the condition for cultural democracy in the classroom. In C. Turner, M. Garcia, A. Nora, & L. I. Rendon (Eds.), *Racial and ethnic diversity in higher education* (pp. 134–149). Needham Heights, MA: Simon & Schuster.

Ellis, C. (2004). *The ethnographic I: A methodological novel about teaching and doing autoethnography.* Walnut Creek, CA: AltaMira.

Ellis, C., & Bochner, A. P. (2000). Autoethnography, personal narrative, reflexivity. In N. Denzin & Y. Lincoln (Eds.), *Handbook of qualitative research* (2nd ed., pp. 733–768). Thousand Oaks, CA: Sage.

Freire, P. (1993). *Pedagogy of the oppressed* (new rev. 20th anniversary ed.). New York, NY: Continuum Books.

Freire, P. (1998). *Pedagogy of freedom: Ethics, democracy and civic courage.* Lanham, MD: Rowman & Littlefield.

Freire, P. (2005). *Pedagogy of the oppressed* (new rev. 30th anniversary ed.). New York, NY: Continuum Books.

Gaventa, J. (1980). *Power and powerlessness: Quiescence and rebellion in an Appalachian valley.* Urbana: University of Illinois Press.

Giroux, H. A. (1992). *Border crossings: Cultural workers and the politics of education.* New York, NY: Routledge.

hooks, b. (1994). *Teaching to transgress: Education as the practice of freedom.* New York, NY: Routledge.

Kezar, A., Gallant, T., & Lester, J. (2011). Everyday people making a difference on college campuses: The tempered grassroots leadership tactics of faculty and staff. *Studies in Higher Education, 36*(2), 129–151.

Knefelkamp, L. (1997). Effective teaching for the multicultural. *Diversity Digest, 2*(1), 11–12.

Meyerson, D. E. (2003). *Tempered radicals: How everyday leaders inspire change at work.* Boston, MA: Harvard Business School Press.

Richardson, L. (2000). Writing: A method of inquiry. In N. Denzin & Y. Lincoln (Eds.), *Handbook of qualitative research* (pp. 923–948). London, UK: Sage.

Spivak, G. (1988). Can the subaltern speak? In C. Nelson & L. Grossberg (Eds.), *Marxism and the interpretation of culture* (pp. 271–313). Basingstoke, UK: Macmillan.

Spivak, G. (2004). Righting wrongs. *The South Atlantic Quarterly, 103*, 523–581.

Stewart, S. (2013). *Everything in di dark muss come to light: A postcolonial examination of the practice of extra lessons at the secondary level in Jamaica's education system* (Doctoral dissertation). Retrieved from ProQuest (Order No. 3597983).

Tuitt, F. A. (2003). Afterword: Realizing a more inclusive pedagogy. In A. Howell & F. A. Tuitt (Eds.), *Race and higher education: Rethinking pedagogy in diverse college classrooms* (pp. 243–268). Cambridge, MA: Harvard Educational Review.

Waks, L. (2007). The concept of fundamental educational change. *Educational Theory, 57*(3), 277–295. doi:10.1111/j.1741-5446.2007.00257.x

2

PURSUING EQUITY THROUGH DIVERSITY

Perspectives and Propositions for Teaching and Learning in Higher Education

Liza Ann Bolitzer, Milagros Castillo-Montoya, and Leslie A. Williams

Access to higher education in the United States has grown dramatically over the last half-century, particularly for students from racial and ethnic minority, low-income, and immigrant backgrounds (Bowen & Bok, 1998; Howard, 1997; Karabel, 2005; Karen, 1991, 2002). Consequently, college classrooms across the United States are increasingly becoming sites of global contact for a diverse student population in terms of race, ethnicity, class, country of origin, and religion, as well as other identity categories. However, researchers have revealed that significant inequities in learning and persistence exist among this increasingly diverse population of college students, with White and upper-income students experiencing greater gains and outcomes than racial/ethnic minority and lower-income students (Arum & Roksa, 2011; Bowen, Chingos, & McPherson, 2009; Kugelmass & Ready, 2011).

In response to these inequities, scholars and practitioners continue to study and implement policies to increase retention and support for underrepresented students (Bensimon, 2007; Berger, Ramirez, & Lyon, 2012; Harper & Quaye, 2009). In addition to efforts focused on admissions and support services, we posit that the college classroom is also likely a critical location from which to pursue the goals of equity in higher education (Dowd & Bensimon, 2015). Access is about ensuring not only that all people have the means and opportunities to go to college, but also that all students have opportunities to learn within it (Brief for American Educational Research

Association [AERA], 2012; Castillo-Montoya, 2013; *Fisher v. University of Texas at Austin,* 2011; Neumann, 2014).

Toward making college classrooms sites of access to academic learning for all students, in this chapter we present three perspectives on diversity and consider how these perspectives may lead college faculty to create equitable learning environments where students may collectively engage their identities toward learning academic subject matter. We emphasize the importance of students' identities, given that higher education scholars and educators increasingly agree that students' learning and holistic development is supported through pedagogies that draw on their cultural knowledge (Bensimon, 1994; Lee, 2007; Meeuwisse, Severiens, & Born, 2010; Tuitt, 2003). Moreover, some scholars have found that interacting with peers from diverse backgrounds can lead to improvements in students' cognitive abilities, critical thinking, and self-confidence, as well as increased cross-racial understandings that counter prejudice (Brief for AERA, 2012). Yet research supporting the educational benefits of diversity has also shown that not all students benefit equally from interacting with diverse peers. For instance, several studies have found that White students experienced greater educational benefits from classroom diversity and interaction than students from racialized backgrounds (Bowman, 2009; Gurin, Dey, Hurtado, & Gurin, 2002; Milem, 2003). The question that this research raises, and that we aim to address in this chapter, is how faculty can engage their students' identities toward creating equitable learning environments—spaces where diverse groups of students have the opportunity to experience the cognitive and emotional gains of learning academic subject matter.

Perspectives on Diversity

Diversity in higher education has come to be understood as the inclusion of historically underrepresented groups, primarily women and racial and ethnic minorities, as a result of the legal and social fight for these groups' inclusion in higher education (Chang, Witt, Jones, & Hakuta, 2003; *Fisher v. University of Texas,* 2013; Glazer-Raymo, 2001, 2008; *Gratz v. Bollinger,* 2003; *Grutter v. Bollinger et al.,* 2003; *University of California Regents v. Bakke,* 1978). However, we believe that to engage students' identities, it is important to include but go beyond gender, race, and ethnicity and consider broader perspectives on diversity that embrace the multiplicity and complexity of identities within an individual or group. To explore how college faculty may facilitate the learning of all students, particularly those who have been and continue to be marginalized in their college learning experiences, we, therefore, begin by presenting three perspectives for thinking about students' identities relative to teaching and learning: diversity as the intersection of identities and power, diversity as fostering individual and collective growth, and diversity within subject-matter learning.

Diversity as the Intersection of Identities and Power

Individuals and communities have multiple aspects of their identities that interact with the larger society in which they are situated. Unitary approaches to identity, for either groups or individuals, which focus on a single category of diversity (e.g., race or gender) can mask additional, significant areas of diversity within people and groups (e.g., how race and gender, as well as other aspects of identity, may inform group and individual identity) (Crenshaw, 1991; Davis, 2008). To explore the multiple dimensions of individual and community identity, we draw on the following ideas: *superdiversity*, from sociolinguistic studies of immigrant communities, and *intersectionality*, from critical legal studies. Together, these concepts allow us to see the complexity of diversity as a lived experience, as both communities and individuals navigate complex processes of identity and power.

Superdiversity is a descriptive term for the complexity of communication and representation within communities of "multiple-origin, transnationally connected, socio-economically differentiated and legally stratified immigrants" (Vertovec, 2007, p. 1024). The adjective *super* is applied to *diversity* to emphasize the multiplicity of variables that constitute diversity in such communities, including but not limited to racial, ethnic, linguistic, national, cultural, and socioeconomic factors (Blommaert, 2010; Vertovec, 2007).

Originated by European scholars, the term emphasizes the large variety of origins for people living within communities of immigrants, as well as the diversity within the individuals themselves. It is used to describe how immigrants often settle in multilayered communities comprising many generations of immigrants, often from diverse regions of the world. Immigrants who settle in these types of communities develop "multilingual repertoires" consisting of both linguistic and cultural elements of diverse groups that they interact with (Blommaert, 2010, p. 7). For example, a Chinese immigrant to the Flushing section of Queens, New York, which has a large proportion of immigrants from Asia and South America, may come to adopt aspects of the language and culture of other immigrants to that area. In interacting with people from Korea or Ecuador, the immigrants may come to adopt new styles of action or ways of speaking. Likewise, this Chinese immigrant's cultural practices may also be adopted by earlier generations of Chinese immigrants to Flushing, resulting in alterations in the culture of the Chinese immigrants in this area as a subgroup. The continual development of culture within this area is likely to contribute new modes of communication, which may in turn be carried into other parts of the borough of Queens and elsewhere in New York City.

Furthermore, through technology, people maintain extensive connections with their countries of origin and with immigrants in other locations, allowing them to operate simultaneously in multiple spaces (Blommaert, 2010). All of these connections—across people and locations—can give rise to new cultural practices and changes in language use. Blommaert (2010) and Vertovec (2007) posited that these conditions—a multiplicity of host countries and sustained connections—gave rise to the need to employ *superdiversity* as a new term to describe the hybridity of both these communities and the identities of the people within them.

The term *superdiversity* has limits when applied to diversity within the United States and other countries that have long histories of immigrants arriving and settling into communities occupied by different racial, ethnic, national, and religious groups. We question how Vertovec (2007), in originating the term, simplified Europe's own history of immigration. For example, he described "Jews from throughout Eastern Europe" (p. 1027) as a single group of immigrants, overlooking the large varieties of language—German, Russian, Yiddish, Hebrew, to name a few—as well as the even larger number of countries and cultures from which Jews emigrated. Moreover, by focusing exclusively on immigrant communities, Blommaert (2010) and Vertovec (2007) ignored the diversity within populations that are native to those countries. Even within a nation that is relatively racially homogenous, there is likely to be a diversity of gender, sexual orientation, class, and ethnicity, as well as other aspects of identity. We reject, therefore, the notion that such superdiversity is limited to immigrant communities. As such, we propose that all communities, and the individuals within them, likely possess multiple identities and ways of communicating that merit consideration when thinking about what diversity means.

The concept of *intersectionality* expands the idea of superdiversity by providing a critical perspective that focuses on how the multiplicity of identities within individuals and groups is shaped by social structures that determine the individual's power and position in society (Ball, Rollock, Vincent, & Gillborn, 2013; Crenshaw, 1991; Hancock, 2007b). This perspective, which originated in critical legal studies and feminist criticism, has theorized how power differentials can be identified in order to counter the suppression of individuals and communities (Crenshaw, 1991; Delgado, 2000; Hancock, 2007a; Simien, 2007).

Intersectionality comprises five central features. First, multiple categories of identity (including but not limited to race, class, nationality, gender, language, sexuality, ethnicity, and culture) interact within individuals and social groups as well as across groups to produce unique experiences (Crenshaw, 1991; McCall, 2005; Settles, 2006). Second, the complex identities of individuals and social groups are constructed in a particular social, historical, political, and economic context, locally and globally, where power is a central factor (Brah & Phoenix, 2004; Choo & Ferree, 2010; Crenshaw, 1991). Third, individuals and groups can simultaneously experience oppression and marginalization as well as agency and empowerment (Crenshaw, 1991; Davis, 2008; Nash, 2008). Fourth, recognizing the intersectional nature of identities gives political and intellectual voice to multiply marginalized individuals and social groups whose experiences would otherwise be excluded from mainstream society (Choo & Ferree, 2010; Crenshaw, 1991). Fifth, highlighting experiences of subordination and privilege is valuable but not sufficient. It is also necessary to promote justice and change by implementing concrete practices in communities and institutions, such as at colleges and universities (Torres, Jones, & Renn, 2009).

Taken together, these five aspects of intersectionality draw attention to the ways that multiple aspects of identity may interact and provide a framework for countering the social, political, and institutional structures that marginalize individuals and groups. Yet how intersectionality may apply to a college classroom remains uncertain. Some scholars question whether intersectionality applies to those who are not marginalized (e.g., Nash, 2008), thus raising concerns about how it can be applied in college classrooms where students are diverse and possess some privileged as well as marginalized identities. Although this issue remains unsettled, we view intersectionality as a tool for revealing both multiple levels of subordination as well as privilege that individuals and groups experience as they navigate the multiple aspects of their identities.

By recognizing diversity operating at the intersection of identity and power, we highlight the complexity of diversity at the national and community levels, as well as within individuals and social groups. This view of diversity gives attention to the benefits and the power differentials that can arise within such communities. This perspective, however, does not illuminate how such benefits and tensions of power can be engaged at either an individual or collective level within the specific context of education. To consider how people can position themselves to engage positively with difference, we turn to the philosophy of cosmopolitanism.

Diversity as Fostering Individual and Collective Growth

We now turn from looking at diversity as an attribute of individuals or groups to considering how people may relate to one another within communities of diverse individuals. In so doing, we respond to a central question raised by the previous perspective: How might we engage the inherent tensions between an individual and the group to build inclusive communities where all can thrive? To respond, we draw on the philosophy of *cosmopolitanism*, which posits that people can both join others in diverse communities and still maintain and develop within their own cultures and identities (Dharwadker, 2001; Hansen, 2011).

Cosmopolitanism is based on the idea that diverse groups of people can come together as a community by recognizing both their inherent connections and their unique identities (Hansen, 2009). Individuals may position themselves to connect with "others" by recognizing the universal humanity that binds all people and serves as the basis for their common moral duty to one another (Hansen, 2009; Lu, 2000; Quinn, 2010). Simultaneously, they can rejoice in the great diversity within any given group: "While cosmopolitanism is indeed about seeing yourself as belonging to a world of fellows, the cosmopolitan fellows are living lives in their own style, and . . . rejoices in the fact that 'their' style need not be 'ours'" (Appiah, 2001, p. 202). To live and flourish in such a community is facilitated by developing what Hansen (2011) called a "cosmopolitan compass," which guides people in responding to "incessant change and . . . endless human diversity" (p. 48). Such a compass enables people to orient themselves to be both open to change and still rooted in their own identities. The basis of such a compass within individuals is the intertwined practices of *hospitality* and *reflection*.

Hospitality is the idea that welcoming another into one's home, be it physically, emotionally, or intellectually, is a mutual act of entanglement: "It is not one party offering a service to the other, which in all its kindness would still imply an outstanding obligation for compensation, but rather an open gesture in which both find recognition" (Papastergiadis, 2007, p. 146). Applied to education, students may be hosted not only in the physical space of the classroom but also in the intellectual realm of subject matter. This is a contrast to a receptacle approach to education, where the teacher gives subject matter to the student; instead, knowledge becomes a place for mutual recognition and potential change for teachers and students alike (Freire, 1996). Papastergiadis (2007) described a host as exhibiting cosmopolitan hospitality not through grand actions but by small gestures, thereby existing "only in the act of relating to the other" (p. 146). For example, hospitality may happen through students and teachers carefully listening to one another and asking questions that facilitate each other's understandings.

In conjunction with hospitality, reflection is an important component of engaging with new ideas, people, and one's own primary affiliations. To reflect is to engage in the world with wide-awakeness of who you are and what you encounter (Greene, 1977, 1995). To reflect, people need "the capacity to fuse reflective openness to the new with reflective loyalty to the known" (Hansen, 2009, p. 151). As such, reflection can be understood as the action of moving between oneself and the other, whether it be an idea or a person, with consciousness and respect for each. Such reflective processes support individuals to simultaneously be part of communities that are inclusive of diverse people and to develop their own sense of themselves, as rooted in their own cultures.

The cosmopolitan practices of hospitality and reflection have the potential to facilitate teachers' understandings of their students as individuals, as well as pedagogical practices that engage their students' identities. Additionally, by thinking deeply about their students, faculty may be called to deepen their understanding of the broader social context in which they and their students are situated and where power and privilege are unequally distributed. Reflection may lead to faculty being good hosts who welcome all students' knowledge into the classroom space. In teaching diverse groups of students, hosting may include acknowledging the differences in students' power and privilege and taking steps to prevent the re-creation of those asymmetries within the classroom.

By engaging in hosting and reflection, faculty may also help students develop awareness of their power and privilege as well as marginalization that are derived from the intersection of their various identities (Maxwell, Nagda, & Thompson, 2011). For example, a White female student may come to simultaneously better understand the privileges she experiences as a White person and the discrimination she faces as a woman. Or a Muslim man in the United States may come to understand how his power is shaped by both his gender and by being part of a religious minority. Both students may also, at the same time, come to recognize additional aspects of their identities, such as their particular passions or abilities, through which they may identify themselves in addition to identifications based on race, gender, or religion. Whereas each student's learning is likely to be distinct, the hope is that by collectively learning together, all students would come to recognize the potential to work against the power differentials in society. Furthermore, students will hopefully develop a deeper sense of the collective responsibility of caring for others and not just those within local or national boundaries (Benhabib, 2004; Hansen, 2011).

Thinking about diversity as potentially fostering individual and collective growth supports our exploration of how people may position themselves to engage with others. The next question this raises is: How might such an equitable learning environment, where diversity is a present and central feature of the classroom, foster students' learning of academic subject matter?

To respond, in the following section we explore the role of students' identities in subject-matter learning.

Diversity Within Subject-Matter Learning

We propose that to create equitable learning experiences, faculty members may bring aspects of their own and students' lives into conversation with academic subject matter. To consider how professors may create opportunities for students to enhance their learning of subject matter, we focus on prior knowledge and how it can scaffold students' learning. We also consider the likely dissonance that students may experience when their existing ways of knowing themselves, others, and the world around them confront different perspectives from their own (Gurin et al., 2002; Maxwell et al., 2011).

Students' Prior Knowledge as a Base for Learning Academic Subject Matter

Prior knowledge may seem like a rather simple idea—all people have things they already know. Yet it is important to unpack this idea to consider its elements and their implications for teaching and learning. The sources of a student's prior knowledge can vary widely, including what has been previously learned from school (Bransford, Brown, & Cocking, 2000) or personal experiences outside of formal education (González, Moll, & Amantí, 2005; Lee, 2007; Vygotsky, 1978). This suggests that students have many types of prior knowledge they can bring to bear on their academic learning.

Scholars have suggested that to build on students' prior knowledge, instructors need to be mindful that students with a variety of diverse backgrounds (e.g., race, ethnicity, class, religion, gender, etc.) may share some characteristics with like individuals, yet they may also have individual histories that differentiate their experiences (Castillo-Montoya, 2013; Gutiérrez & Rogoff, 2003; Irizarry, 2007). They urge scholars and practitioners to view students' ways of knowing as flexible—changing with time and experiences and their identities as hybrids, including a mix of backgrounds (e.g., race, class, and religion *in* urban environment versus race, class, and religion *or* urban environment) (González et al., 2005; Irizarry, 2007). Thus, unearthing students' prior knowledge means paying attention to the many social realities that historically may be informing teachers' and students' experiences and ways of knowing.

Because college students may enter the classroom with a breadth of experiences, instructors may want to consider which aspects of students' prior knowledge to surface and use for the purpose of enhancing academic learning. Given the value that researchers have found in teachers' purposefully incorporating identity into the learning process (Delgado-Bernal, 2002;

Gutiérrez, Baquedano-López, & Tejada, 1999; Sealey-Ruiz, 2007), one type of prior knowledge that teachers can surface is that which is based on students' multiple identities. Within this knowledge set, it is important for instructors to consider whether and how students' prior knowledge can be related to the subject-matter ideas being taught (Lee, 2007).

As an example of how a faculty member may engage students' prior knowledge to teach academic subject matter, we turn to a teaching moment from a study of first-generation college students' development of sociopolitical consciousness as they learned sociology (Castillo-Montoya, 2013, 2014). The sociology professor, who identified as White, Jewish, and middle class, was seeking to teach the sociological idea of family and marriage as social institutions to his undergraduate students, who were diverse by race, ethnicity, age, social class, religion, and other identities. He began teaching this idea by sharing his own experiences and then invited students to do the same. The teacher and the students, drawing from their experiences, then collaborated in thinking about what these social institutions mean and considered how they could question and even critique those terms, given what they knew from their own lived experiences.

The professor began the class by providing students with the formal definition of *family* used by the U.S. Bureau of the Census. He stated that blood, marriage, or adoption determined who is legally recognized in the United States as being a member of a family. He shared that as a Jewish man without children, he is viewed by members of his community as not fulfilling the major responsibility of having a family. The professor explained that although it is now much more acceptable not to have children, family as including children is still a dominant idea in our society.

The professor then used the class discussion of the difference between the U.S. Census definition of *family* and more modern perspectives to introduce a modified definition that emphasized people in a relationship who live together and have a shared commitment to one another. This definition prompted an African American Muslim student from a low-income background and neighborhood to state that although some kids have legal parents, those parents may not be in a position to care for them, and so people outside of the "family," including staff members of a school, end up taking care of them. A Latina student, also from a low-income background and a neighborhood with a concentration of low-income families, joined the discussion and said that some teachers are like parents because they see children who are hungry or being abused. The professor then shared a personal story of receiving some support from a school member at some point in his childhood.

To continue exploring the idea of family, the professor then raised the topic of polygamy to consider additional constraints placed on the definition of *marriage*. The African American Muslim student then contributed again by sharing that she married by law instead of through a Muslim ceremony because she wanted legal rights as a wife and for her husband to commit to not having several wives. The professor and students listened carefully to her and inquired gently about her experience. That is, they did not press her to share things she was not prepared to share, but instead inquired to the extent that she was comfortable and interested in sharing—an important feature of engaging in intergroup dialogue (Maxwell et al., 2011). It is important to note that this occurred in a university in the New York City metropolitan area post-9/11 where many people had limited and perhaps misinformed understandings of Muslim traditions.

In this example, several things seemed to be happening. First, the discussion between the professor and the students was anchored mutually in the subject matter and in their lives. That is, the subject matter and their relevant lived experiences were present and equally drawn upon for learning the sociological idea being taught, families and marriages as social institutions. Further, both the professor and the students allowed themselves to be vulnerable in sharing their own experiences of family and were therefore both positioned as learners, sharing the responsibility of applying the subject-matter idea to lived experiences.

Conflict and Tension in Equitable Learning Environments

Thus far, we have considered opportunities to enhance learning in classrooms with diverse students without delving deeply into the challenges that may exist. We have stressed how equitable learning environments may promote cognitive gains because students are in classrooms with diverse peers who are likely to bring differing perspectives (Chang, Denson, Sáenz, & Misa, 2005; Hurtado, Milem, Clayton-Pedersen, & Allen, 1999). Given the diversity of students' perspectives based on their various understandings of themselves and the subject matter, it is important to also recognize that within these equitable learning environments, conflict and tension may emerge (Cochran-Smith, 2003; Gutiérrez et al., 1999; hooks, 1994; Kumashiro, 2003). These tensions can be both expected and welcomed, by faculty and students alike, in classrooms that seek to have the "speculation, experiment and creation" which Justice Powell identified as "essential to the quality of higher education" (*University of California Regents v. Bakke*, 1978, p. 313). For students, coming into contact with ideas or people who challenge their prior conceptions of themselves or the world may provoke uneasiness or even anger. Although research has shown that students experience cognitive growth when they encounter a certain level of dissonance between what they know and what they are learning, that does not mean that the learning is always pretty or easy (Gurin et al., 2002; Milem, 2003). It also does not mean that students are responsible for managing these moments of tension or conflict on their own. Instead, faculty can take great care in making the tension part of the learning (Maxwell et al., 2011). As such, conflict and tension that arise in such a learning space can be understood as part of rather than in contradiction with the learning space itself (Gutiérrez et al., 1999; hooks, 1994; Kumashiro, 2003).

Propositions for Engaging Diversity Within Equitable Learning Environments

The three perspectives on diversity we have presented explore the complex, multiple meanings of diversity and their potential application to teaching and learning in higher education. Drawing from these perspectives, we conceptualize diversity as the multiple historical and socially situated identities that individuals and groups possess. These identities inform how individuals view themselves and interact with others, as well as the power they have within their communities and the larger society. Moreover, the multiple aspects of identity, which can include and also reach beyond race, ethnicity, class, religion, gender, and sexuality, are inseparable within peoples' unique conceptions of themselves. All of the aspects of students' identities, as well as what they form, together present opportunities for teachers to engage their students' prior knowledge within the study of academic subject matter.

Drawing from these perspectives, we now return to the question with which we began this chapter: How can faculty engage their students' identities toward creating equitable learning environments—spaces where diverse groups of students have the opportunity to experience the cognitive and emotional gains of learning academic subject matter? To create an equitable learning environment within their own classrooms, it is important for faculty to consider who their students are and use their prior experiences to engage their identities within classroom learning. This may include helping all students to recognize aspects of their lives in which they are privileged as well as those where they are marginalized. It is important for instructors to also engage students who are multiply marginalized in ways that facilitate their participation and learning of subject matter at levels comparable to their more privileged peers. To consider how college faculty may create such an equitable learning environment for a diverse group of students, we present the following three propositions.

Proposition 1: Engage Diversity as a Collective Resource

To create an equitable learning environment, faculty may consider engaging diversity as a collective resource wherein both the teachers' and students' identities are sites for learning. When diversity is a collective resource, students are called on to bring forward their experiences and understandings of the world, and the class collectively engages with them within subject-matter learning. It is the role of the instructor to facilitate the students' bringing forward of their prior knowledge, recognizing that members of any classroom can have unique ways of understanding an academic topic (Castillo-Montoya, 2013; Neumann, 2014). A valuable part of this process entails instructors taking great care to facilitate classroom dialogue so that students feel encouraged to participate and are open to the multiple perspectives that may exist. Diversity cannot be engaged as a collective resource when individuals, or aspects of individuals' identities, are excluded from the collective. It is important that faculty carefully consider whose prior knowledge is at the center of the room and work to help students engage with one another, recognizing that not all students will be able to share at all times. If diversity is a collective resource, students can be exposed to a range of viewpoints from their peers, thus reducing their reliance on stereotypes and prejudice that disrupt the ability to engage with one another (Maxwell et al., 2011).

Furthermore, by facilitating the active participation of all class members, instructors work to counter the pressures to assimilate to a dominant norm that arises when diverse peoples come together (e.g., Maher & Thompson Tetreault, 2003). For diversity to become a collective resource for subject-matter learning, it is important that faculty and students counteract the privileging of certain identities and knowledge (Maxwell et al., 2011). This approach calls for faculty to consider whose voices and what knowledge is being included and excluded in designing curricula and writing syllabi, as well as in classroom teaching. It also suggests that instructors make time and space for students to confront the tensions among different individuals, as well as the tensions students may experience within themselves among different aspects of their identities (Maher & Thompson Tetreault, 2003; Maxwell et al., 2011).

One pedagogical method for publicly and collectively unearthing students' prior knowledge, and therefore making students' diversity a collective resource, is discussion-based teaching (Castillo-Montoya, 2014). For example, Black and Mills (1984) described how within discussions, "each individual's experiences or perception adds to the total understanding of the question at hand, [which leads students to be] active learners who can question and challenge, inquire and research, discover and invent" (p. 101). It is essential to note that the kinds of deep engagement that Black and Mills described come from discussions where deep listening and questioning by both students and faculty are at the center. For example, a professor in a core curriculum at Saint Joseph's College described the openness that can be part of discussion-based teaching:

> I have to listen to my students, and they to one another as well as to me, as we wrestle with the content. And not infrequently, one or the other of them knows a lot more about the topic under discussion than I do. . . . It becomes a topsy-turvy world; one feels inept and threatened, humiliated and frustrated. If one does not despair and surrender, it all becomes very salutary after a time. I find that I tend to respect and trust, have faith in and hope for, and downright love students far more than I used to. And I even believe that these feelings are mutual. (Black & Mills, 1984, p. 105)

The desire to teach in this "topsy-turvy" way for this professor came from realizing that his normal way of teaching where he was the "sole arbiter of truth and justice" (p. 105) did not work when he was assigned to teach in a core curriculum that required interdisciplinary teaching. Through this assignment, he realized the limits of his own knowledge as well as the rich understandings that students can carry from their lives into the study of literature. The opening up on the part of a faculty member can, therefore, be an important first step in engaging the diversity of a class as a collective resource. Furthermore, the rewards for such a positionality may lead to not only increased student learning, but also the engagement and love that this faculty member describes. Such feelings are one of the potential rewards of teaching and learning within a diverse classroom in which people open themselves up to engaging with one another (Hansen, 2011).

Proposition 2: Facilitate Students' Self-Representation of Their Intersecting Identities

To foster equitable learning environments, faculty may consider how to create opportunities for students to share their own representations of who they are and help students recognize the multiplicity and complexity of their intersecting identities. Students' intersecting identities may include religion, language, gender, sexual identity, or aspects of their identity that do not fit into any preexisting categories. The intersectional perspective recognizes that people may identify at both an individual level (e.g., I am a Garifuna male immigrant from Belize who grew up in New York City) as well as with larger social groups (e.g., I identify with Afro-Caribbean/West Indian immigrants to the United States). This social and individual identification is likely to vary as students move between contexts that pull forward certain aspects of their identities (e.g., In my home, I am a Garifuna son, brother, and uncle who is an educator, whereas on the street, I am a Black male with dread-locks). It is the role of the instructor to help the student recognize and draw on these multiple aspects of his or her identity and relate them to subject matter in order to foster personal and academic learning.

Facilitating students' self-representation of their identities may need to be an ongoing activity wherein students are supported in both engaging and developing the multiple aspects of themselves, some of which may not always be readily apparent. This proposition calls on faculty to leave behind unitary and preconceived ideas of their students' identities. We propose that students themselves are best able to express the varied aspects of their identities and that such self-representation is a critical starting point to the learning of sub-ject matter when it is encouraged, facilitated, and engaged by faculty.

For an example of how faculty may teach subject matter through engag-ing students' intersectional identities, we turn to an example of a secondary schoolteacher who breaks from a unitary view of identity in an urban, mul-tiethnic/multiracial school context. Irizarry (2007) described Mr. Talbert, a history teacher in an urban vocational school, who incorporated students' individual identities as youth with varying ethnic identities by encouraging them to speak and write in their authentic voices. One student described how he completed an assignment for Mr. Talbert by writing in tag, an urban art form and writing style. In this same class, students spoke in Ebonics, some wrote in Spanish and English, and others relied on their knowledge of rap music to complete assignments. These varied representations of knowing engaged multiple aspects of students' varied identities and offered them the opportunity to represent different aspects of themselves. They also developed a sense of community with the teacher:

> Both groups of students and the various ways they expressed their identi-
> ties, coupled with the teachers' cultural identity, influenced the class culture
> as a whole. The culture of the classroom was socially constructed and nego-
> tiated by all of the participants. (Irizarry, 2007, p. 24)

This example points to the possibility of creating an equitable learn-ing environment through facilitating students' own representations of their intersecting identities.

Proposition 3: Engage Diversity to Advance Subject-Matter Learning

To create equitable learning environments, faculty can engage students' prior knowledge to advance their learning of academic subject matter (Bransford et al., 2000; Castillo-Montoya, 2013, 2014; Neumann, 2014). Recognizing diversity as a collective resource and facilitating students' representation of their identities are important first steps for faculty in fostering such a process. Yet within a classroom of diverse students, multiple prior knowledges are likely present and these different ways of knowing may also conflict with one another. When students' and professors' different perspectives are engaged, tensions may arise that disrupt students' familiar ways of thinking. We, therefore, suggest that advancing students' subject-matter learning by incorporating their multiple diversities is not only instrumental—as a means to teach—but also an emotional experience for students and faculty in which they experience significant tensions and joys. The potential for diversity to advance subject-matter learning calls for professors to be attentive to students' emotional as well as cognitive processes of learning (Maxwell et al., 2011). Such work requires both wide-awakeness and intentionality on the part of faculty as they both open themselves up to the multiple aspects of their students' identities as well as bring them into dialogue with subject matter.

College teachers are rarely taught how to help students see the potential connections between their identities and academic subject matter. hooks (1994) described how professors aiming to engage diversities in their classrooms need to learn how to do so and allow themselves to be vulnerable in the classroom:

> Few of us [professors] are taught to facilitate heated discussions that may include useful interruptions and digressions, but it is often the professor who is most invested in maintaining order in the classroom. Professors cannot empower students to embrace diversities of experience, standpoint, behavior, or style if our training has disempowered us, socialized us to cope effectively only with a single mode of interaction based on middle-class values. (p. 187)

hooks posited that professors need flexibility in their thinking and in their emotions while teaching to engage their students. She added that students also need flexibility in their thinking as they hear and consider alternative perspectives that conflict with their own experiences or that promote changes in how they view their own thinking.

Educational research has found that having teachers and students who are vulnerable, who listen to others, and who engage and listen to emotions in order to work through conflict can support learning and growth (Gurin et al., 2002; Maxwell et al., 2011). Thus, to engage diversity as a resource for subject-matter learning calls on both professors and students to be willing to share aspects of who they are with each other and be open to the learning that may occur in such sharing.

Conclusion

Within this chapter, we have brought together three distinct views of diversity for teaching and learning by drawing from multiple disciplines, including critical legal studies, feminist criticism, sociolinguistics, philosophy, history, cultural studies, and education. These disciplines include theories of education, community, and identity that come from the United States, Europe, Latin America, and ancient Greece. In examining perspectives on diversity, it is clear that just as there are multiplicity and complexity in individual and collective identities, a variety of disciplines can contribute toward understanding the pedagogical role of diversity in higher education. Bringing these disciplines together leads us to propose ways in which faculty may work toward creating an equitable learning environment, where all students' knowledge is engaged in subject-matter learning.

For faculty to be able to create the opportunity for all their students to learn necessitates a model of faculty support that recognizes the need for faculty to continually learn within their teaching. This learning may include deepening their understanding about themselves—their beliefs and practices—at the same time that they are learning about their students. Support may include faculty development sessions but also other institutional support so that faculty have the time and space needed to develop as teachers.

Furthermore, the perspectives on diversity presented previously offer a basis from which to launch research into institutions and individual professors' efforts to realize the educational benefits of student diversity. Researchers concerned with equitable student experiences and outcomes could focus on students' multiple intersecting identities to examine classroom learning in small-, medium-, and large-scale studies.

In conclusion, we view understanding diversity, and the application of that understanding within the college classroom, to be an essential part of providing more equitable learning opportunities and outcomes in higher education. Just as college recruitment or student advisement is a place where students can come to understand that they belong in college, so too are college classrooms potential sites of access and persistence. We hope the perspectives on diversity presented here, as well as the propositions for teaching and learning that we draw from them, serve as a preliminary step in guiding the teaching practices of faculty who seek to reach all of their students, thereby elevating the learning of all.

References

Appiah, K. (2001). Cosmopolitan reading. In V. Dharwadker (Ed.), *Cosmopolitan geographies: New locations in literature and culture* (pp. 197–227). New York, NY: Routledge.

Arum, R., & Roksa, J. (2011). *Academically adrift: Limited learning on college campuses.* Chicago, IL: University of Chicago Press.

Ball, S. J., Rollock, N., Vincent, C., & Gillborn, D. (2013). Social mix, schooling and intersectionality: Identity and risk for Black middle class families. *Research Papers in Education, 28*(3), 265–288.

Benhabib, S. (2004). *Another cosmopolitanism.* New York, NY: Oxford University Press.

Bensimon, E. M. (Ed.). (1994). *Multicultural teaching and learning: Strategies for change in higher education.* University Park, PA: National Center for Postsecondary Teaching, Learning, and Assessment.

Bensimon, E. M. (2007). The underestimated significance of practitioner knowledge in the scholarship on student success. *The Review of Higher Education, 30*(4), 441–469.

Berger, J. B., Ramirez, G. B., & Lyon, S. C. (2012). Past to present: A historical look at retention. In A. Seidman (Ed.), *College student retention: Formula for student success* (2nd ed., pp. 7–34). Lanham, MD: Rowman & Littlefield.

Black, N., & Mills, M. (1984). Inspiring teachers to revitalize teaching. In Z. Gamson (Ed.), *Liberating education* (pp. 95–112). San Francisco, CA: Jossey-Bass.

Blommaert, J. (2010). *The sociolinguistics of globalization.* New York, NY: Cambridge University Press.

Bowen, W., & Bok, D. (1998). *The shape of the river: Long-term consequences of considering race in college and university admissions.* Princeton, NJ: Princeton University Press.

Bowen, W., Chingos, M., & McPherson, M. (2009). *Crossing the finish line: Completing college at America's public universities.* Princeton, NJ: Princeton University Press.

Bowman, N. A. (2009). College diversity courses and cognitive development among students from privileged and marginalized groups. *Journal of Diversity in Higher Education, 2*(3), 182–194. doi:10.1037/a0016639

Brah, A., & Phoenix, A. (2004). Ain't I a woman? Revisiting intersectionality. *Journal of International Women's Studies, 5*(3), 75–86.

Bransford, J. D., Brown, A. L., & Cocking, R. R. (Eds.). (2000). *How people learn: Brain, mind, experience, and school.* Washington, DC: National Academy Press.

Brief for American Educational Research Association (AERA), American Association for the Advancement of Science, the American Sociological Association, the American Statistical Association, the Association for the Study of Higher Education, the Law and Society Association, the Linguistic Society of America, and the National Academy of Engineering as Amici Curiae Supporting Respondents, Fisher v. University of Texas at Austin, No. 11-345 (argued October 10, 2012).

Castillo-Montoya, M. (2013). *A study of first-generation African American and Latino undergraduates developing sociopolitical consciousness in introductory sociology classes* (Doctoral dissertation). Retrieved from ProQuest Dissertations and Theses. (Order No. 3590255)

Castillo-Montoya, M. (2014, November). *Teaching toward learning: Practices in diverse classrooms that help first-generation college students connect their learning of subject matter to their own lives.* Paper presented at the Association for the Study of Higher Education (ASHE) Annual Conference, Washington, DC.

Chang, M. J., Denson, N., Sáenz, V., & Misa, K. (2005). *The educational benefits of sustaining cross-racial interaction among undergraduates* (Research and Occasional Paper Series: CSHE.2.05). Berkeley: University of California Center for Studies in Higher Education.

Chang, M. J., Witt, D., Jones, J., & Hakuta, K. (Eds.). (2003). *Compelling interest: Examining the evidence on racial dynamics in colleges and universities.* Stanford, CA: Stanford University Press.

Choo, H. Y., & Ferree, M. M. (2010). Practicing intersectionality in sociological research: A critical analysis of inclusions, interactions, and institutions in the study of inequalities. *Sociological Theory, 28*(2), 129–149.

Cochran-Smith, M. (2003). Blind vision: Unlearning racism in teacher education. In A. Howell & F. Tuitt (Eds.), *Race and higher education: Rethinking pedagogy in diverse college classrooms* (pp. 157–190). Cambridge, MA: Harvard University Press. (Reprinted from *Harvard Educational Review*, 2000, *70*(2), 157–190)

Crenshaw, K. (1991). Mapping the margins: Intersectionality, identity politics and violence against women of color. *Stanford Law Review, 43*(6), 1241–1299.

Davis, K. (2008). Intersectionality as a buzzword: A sociology of science perspective on what makes a feminist theory successful. *Feminist Theory, 9*(1), 67–85.

Delgado, R. (2000). Rodrigo's sixth chronicle: Intersections, essences, and the dilemma of social reform (pp. 250–260). In R. Delgado & J. Stefancic (Eds.), *Critical race theory: The cutting edge.* Philadelphia, PA: Temple University Press.

Delgado-Bernal, D. (2002). Critical race theory, Latino critical theory, and critical raced–gendered epistemologies: Recognizing students of color as holders and creators of knowledge. *Qualitative Inquiry, 8*(1), 105–126.

Dharwadker, V. (2001). *Cosmopolitan geographies: New locations in literature and culture.* New York, NY: Routledge.

Dowd, A., & Bensimon, E. (2015). *Engaging the "race question": Accountability and equity in U.S. higher education.* New York, NY: Teachers College Press.

Fisher v. University of Texas at Austin, 631 F.3d 213 (5th Cir. 2011)

Fisher v. University of Texas at Austin, 133 S. Ct. 2411, 570 U.S., 186 L. Ed. 2d 474 (2013).

Freire, P. (1996). *Pedagogy of the oppressed* (20th anniversary ed.). New York, NY: Continuum. (Original work published in 1970)

Glazer-Raymo, J. (2001). *Shattering the myths: Women in academe.* Baltimore, MD: Johns Hopkins University Press.

Glazer-Raymo, J. (2008) *Unfinished agendas: New and continuing gender challenges in higher education.* Baltimore, MD: Johns Hopkins University Press.

González, N., Moll, L. C., & Amantí, C. (2005). *Funds of knowledge: Theorizing practices in households, communities, and classrooms.* Mahwah, NJ: Lawrence Erlbaum.

Gratz v. Bollinger, 539 U.S. 244, 123 S. Ct. 2411, 156 L. Ed. 2d 257 (2003).

Greene, M. (1977). Toward wide-awakeness: An argument for the arts and humanities in education. *Teachers College Record, 79*(1), 119–125.

Greene, M. (1995). *Releasing the imagination.* San Francisco, CA: Jossey-Bass.

Grutter v. Bollinger et al., 539 U.S. 306 (2003).

Gurin, P., Dey, E. L., Hurtado, S., & Gurin, G. (2002). Diversity and higher education: Theory and impact on educational outcomes. *Harvard Educational Review, 72*(3), 330–367.

Gutiérrez, K. D., Baquedano-López, P., & Tejada, C. (1999). Rethinking diversity: Hybridity and hybrid language practices in the third space. *Mind, Culture, and Activity, 6*(4), 286–303.

Gutiérrez, K. D., & Rogoff, B. (2003). Cultural ways of learning: Individual traits or repertoires of practice. *Educational Researcher, 32*(5), 19–25.

Hancock, A. M. (2007a). Intersectionality as a normative and empirical paradigm. *Political Science and Politics, 37*(1), 41–45.

Hancock, A. M. (2007b). When multiplication doesn't equal quick addition: Examining intersectionality as a research paradigm. *Perspectives on Politics, 5*(1), 63–79.

Hansen, D. (2009). Chasing butterflies without a net: Interpreting cosmopolitanism. *Studies in Philosophy of Education, 29*(2), 151–166.

Hansen, D. (2011). *The teacher and the world: A study of cosmopolitanism as education.* New York, NY: Routledge.

Harper, S. R., & Quaye, S. J. (2009). Beyond sameness, with engagement and outcomes for all: An introduction. In S. R. Harper & S. J. Quaye (Eds.), *Student engagement in higher education: Theoretical perspectives and practical approaches for diverse populations* (pp. 1–15). New York, NY: Routledge.

hooks, b. (1994). *Teaching to transgress: Education as the practice of freedom.* New York, NY: Routledge.

Howard, J. (1997). Affirmative action in historical perspective. In M. García (Ed.), *Affirmative action's testament of hope: Strategies for a new era in higher education* (pp. 19–45). Albany: State University of New York Press.

Hurtado, S., Milem, J., Clayton-Pedersen, A., & Allen, W. (1999). *Enacting diverse learning environments: Improving the climate for racial/ethnic diversity in higher education.* Washington, DC: George Washington University Press.

Irizarry, J. G. (2007). Ethnic and urban intersections in the classroom: Latino students, hybrid identities, and culturally responsive pedagogy. *Multicultural Perspectives, 9*(3), 21–28.

Karabel, J. (2005). *The chosen: The hidden history of admissions and exclusion at Harvard, Yale and Princeton.* Boston, MA: Houghton Mifflin.

Karen, D. (1991). The politics of class, race, and gender: Access to higher education in the United States, 1960–1986. *American Journal of Education, 99*(2), 208–237.

Karen, D. (2002). Changes in access to higher education in the United States: 1980–1992. *Sociology of Education, 75*(3), 191–210.

Kugelmass, H., & Ready, D. D. (2011). Racial/ethnic disparities in collegiate cognitive gains: A multilevel analysis of institutional influences on learning and its equitable distribution. *Research in Higher Education, 52*(4), 323–348.

Kumashiro, K. K. (2003). Against repetition: Addressing resistance to anti-oppressive change in the practices of learning, teaching, supervising, and researching. In A. Howell & F. Tuitt (Eds.), *Race and higher education: Rethinking pedagogy in diverse college classrooms* (pp. 45–68). Cambridge, MA: Harvard University Press. (Reprinted from *Harvard Educational Review*, 2002, *72*(1), 67–92)

Lee, C. D. (2007). *Culture, literacy, and learning: Taking bloom in the midst of the whirlwind.* New York, NY: Teachers College Press.

Lu, C. (2000). The one and the many faces of cosmopolitanism. *The Journal of Political Philosophy, 8*(2), 244–267.

Maher, F. A., & Thompson Tetreault, M. K. (2003). Learning in the dark: How assumptions of whiteness shape classroom knowledge. In A. Howell & F. Tuitt (Eds.), *Race and higher education: Rethinking pedagogy in diverse college classrooms* (pp. 69–96). Cambridge, MA: Harvard University Press. (Reprinted from *Harvard Educational Review*, 1997, *67*(2), 321–349)

Maxwell, K. E., Nagda, B. A., & Thompson, M. C. (Eds.). (2011). *Facilitating intergroup dialogues: Bridging differences, catalyzing change.* Sterling, VA: Stylus.

McCall, L. (2005). The complexity of intersectionality. *Signs, 30*(3), 1771–1800.

Meeuwisse, M., Severiens, S. E., & Born, M. H. (2010). Learning environment, interaction, sense of belonging and study success in ethnically diverse student groups. *Research in Higher Education, 51*(6), 528–545.

Milem, J. (2003). The educational benefits of diversity: Evidence from multiple sectors. In M. J. Chang, D. Witt, J. Jones, & K. Hakuta (Eds.), *Compelling interest: Examining the evidence on racial dynamics in college and universities* (pp. 126–169). Stanford, CA: Stanford University Press.

Nash, J. C. (2008). Re-thinking intersectionality. *Feminist Review, 89*(1), 1–15.

Neumann, A. (2014). Staking a claim on learning: What we should know about learning in higher education and why. *The Review of Higher Education, 37*(2), 249–267.

Papastergiadis, N. (2007). Glimpses of cosmopolitanism in the hospitality of art. *European Journal of Social Theory, 10*(1), 139–152.

Quinn, M. (2010). "Ex and the city": On cosmopolitanism, community and the "Curriculum of Refuge." *Transnational Curriculum Inquiry, 7*(1), 77–102.

Sealey-Ruiz, Y. (2007). Wrapping the curriculum around their lives: Using a culturally relevant curriculum with African American adult women. *Adult Education Quarterly, 58*(1), 44–60.

Settles, I. (2006). The use of intersectional frameworks to understand black women's racial and gender identities. *Sex Roles: A Journal of Research, 54*(9–10), 589–601.

Simien, E. M. (2007). Doing intersectionality research: From conceptual issues to practical examples. *Politics & Gender, 3*(2), 264–271.

Torres, V., Jones, S. R., & Renn, K. A. (2009). Identity development theories in student affairs: Origins, current status, and new approaches. *Journal of College Student Development, 50*(6), 577–596.

Tuitt, F. (2003). Afterword: Realizing a more inclusive pedagogy. In A. Howell & F. Tuitt (Eds.), *Race and higher education: Rethinking pedagogy in diverse college classrooms* (pp. 243–268). Cambridge, MA: Harvard University Press.

University of California Regents v. Bakke, 438 U.S. 265, 98 S. Ct. 2733, 57 L. Ed. 2d 750 (1978).

Vertovec, S. (2007). Super-diversity and its implications. *Ethnic and Racial Studies, 30*(6), 1024–1054.

Vygotsky, L. S. (1978). *Mind in society: The development of higher psychological processes* (M. Cole, S. John-Steiner, E. Scribner, & E. Souberman, Eds.). Cambridge, MA: Harvard University Press.

3

A DEMOCRATIC PEDAGOGY FOR A DEMOCRATIC SOCIETY

Education for Social and Political Change (T-128)

Eileen de los Reyes, Hal Smith, Tarajean Yazzie-Mintz, Yamila Hussein, and Frank Tuitt

With José Moreno, Anthony De Jesús, Dianne Morales, and Sarah Napier

> *Teaching is not a profession that requires a uniform, and then I take it off and I go home and I'm somebody else. It's a way of living, a way of being—in a similar way that I always thought of being an activist—if I want to call myself politically involved, it becomes a way of living, not something that I do.*
>
> —Member of the T-128 Teaching Community

Reintroduction

This chapter was originally written (but not published) in 1998, a transformative year in teaching T-128 (Education for Social and Political Change). T-128 was a course originally designed by students at the Harvard Graduate School of Education (HGSE). Over time, the course attracted between 80 to 100 students each year and had a teaching community (professor and teaching assistants) that included 11 members. This was one of the largest and most popular courses at HGSE.

Together with our students we, as a teaching community, reenvisioned teaching and learning in higher education by focusing on the following key areas: (a) establishing the theoretical foundation of the course, (b) rethinking power, (c) engaging in dialogue across differences, (d) building interlocking communities, and (e) committing to *praxis*—the process of reflection and action. We were guided by public intellectuals who modeled for us the intersection of theory–practice–action. These included Paulo Freire, Myles Horton, Antonia Darder, Cornel West, Haunani-Kay Trask, and others. We sought to model how social and political change is possible by making the theoretical framework of the course explicit to students and ourselves and linking it to practice/action. Through our practice, we made the case that social change requires a deep historical and theoretical analysis and disciplined action and that social and political movement and change require an iterative process guided by constant reflection and action.

As the teaching community moved to projects of change elsewhere, T-128 remained for many of us a valuable personal, political, and intellectual compass. The current national context related to racism, immigration, and the continued search for access and equity both highlights the pressing necessity for and reopens the possibility of local and national conversations on race and power. Our hope is to gather again and engage with a new generation of students in the process of reenvisioning social and political change in the age of Ferguson. Thus revisiting this chapter and sharing it in this volume is a first step in our own process of reflection and action. Accordingly, we invite others interested in creating transformative, affirming, and equitable learning environments for all to join us in this collective project of change.

A Democratic Pedagogy for a Democratic Society: Education for Social and Political Change (T-128)

Teachers committed to democratic theory and practice need to "develop a theory by theorizing the practice" (Hernández, 1997, p. 14). If we speak of democracy in society and in the classroom, then we need to practice it and avoid being what Freire called "revolutionaries in the abstract" (Freire, Freire, & Macedo, 1998, p. 211). As he explained, "Revolution begins precisely with revolution in our daily lives" (p. 211). Our understanding of democratic practice is informed through our daily work—the ways in which we teach, the ways in which we learn—in short, the ways in which we live. Through our daily practice, we continually inform our understanding of a theory of democracy. The course, Education for Social and Political Change (T-128), which we taught at HGSE in 1998, was the result of a commitment to democracy in the classroom and in society.

The content and pedagogy of T-128 were grounded in critical and feminist theory and pedagogy. Consequently, we understood that "the intrinsic link between feminist pedagogy and organizing for social change reflects the connection between the classroom and the world outside it" (Briskin, 1990, p. 23). By establishing clear and transformative links between the classroom and the world outside, we argue that education and social and political change are inextricably linked: The world outside informs our understandings and action inside the classroom; likewise, the classroom informs our understandings and actions outside.

A seminal year during which this confluence of pedagogy and action became explicit prompted us to ask, *How does Education for Social and Political Change (T-128) prepare educators for active participation in a democratic society? How do we prepare educators to become agents of social and political change in our classroom, at our institution, and in society?*

After 4 years of teaching the course with an implicit theoretical and pedagogical framework (1994 to 1997), we decided in 1998 to make this framework explicit by explaining to students that a democratic theory guided us in terms of both the content as well as the pedagogy. At the time, we felt prepared to synthesize what we had learned teaching the course. This synthesis became a coherent and transparent framework, which we presented in the first class. By making it public in this manner, we hoped to transform the course (content and pedagogy) into an ongoing unit of analysis and action for both teachers and students.

We then observed in 1998 that significant changes had occurred, particularly in how students developed a language to critique the course, evaluating it against the standard of democratic practice that we had announced in the first class, studied through the texts, and experimented with in the classroom. Furthermore, students began speaking a language of transformation in our classroom and at the school—creating a dialectical relation between the inside and the outside. Realizing that we had taken a significant step in transforming how we taught, we decided to analyze how the process had evolved. This chapter examines how our decision to define and articulate a theoretical and pedagogical framework led to the transformation of our course and the institution. We discuss what we chose to include in this framework and why, and how students spoke about, experienced, and critiqued the framework. We also explain some of the problems we encountered and how we tried to resolve them.

The objective of this chapter is to contribute to the discussion about democracy both in the classroom and in society. Like Lather (1991), we believe that "feminism has much to offer in the development of practices of self-interrogation and critique, practice-based theorizing, and more situated and embodied discourses about pedagogy" (p. 131). We are particularly interested in sharing what we learned with faculty and students who are struggling to transform their classrooms into democratic spaces conducive to dialogue, co-construction of knowledge, and social and political change.

Who We Are

We described ourselves as a teaching community, where each member was responsible for all aspects of the course. Decisions regarding T-128 included all of us in intense and often lengthy discussions. The decision to write this chapter emerged out of one such discussion, where we decided to stop and analyze our work so as to understand better what we should do in the future. Because the course fluctuated between 80 to 100 students each year, 6 teaching fellows (TFs) worked with the professor, Eileen de los Reyes. In 1998, the teaching fellows were Hal Smith, Tarajean Yazzie-Mintz, Yamila Hussein, Frank Tuitt, José Moreno, and Anthony De Jesús. Smith, Yazzie-Mintz, Hussein, and Tuitt collaborated in coauthoring this chapter with me, de los Reyes.[1]

The collective knowledge generated from our different research projects and our shared understanding of the connections among education, democracy, and social change informed our teaching of the course. I began teaching Education for Social and Political Change in 1994. At that time, I was a faculty member at Salem State College. I taught courses in the Women's Studies Program, which meant having an understanding of feminist theory and pedagogy. My research focused on understanding "pockets of hope," classrooms in communities and schools engaged in democratic practice and social change (de los Reyes & Gozemba, 2002). Smith's research dealt with the application of education in social movements, as well as in community development programs and practice. Smith envisioned the African American struggle for liberation as a large-scale community education process. Yazzie's contribution to the course emerged from research in the field of American Indian education. In particular, she offered insights into theory and practice, drawing upon her work on the role of the federal government in the "invention" of an education system for American Indian students. Tuitt's research examined how African American graduate students described and experienced the learning conditions and pedagogical practices they identified as most beneficial for academic success. Hussein studied the role of education in popular movements, specifically the popular education in the Palestinian occupied territories during the 1987 Intifada when schools were closed by military order until further notice. The diversity of our backgrounds and interests influenced the texts and the theories we used in the course as well as the ways we practiced those theories.

Analysis of the Course

A discussion of T-128 requires that we present its radical beginnings, a legacy of student activism at HGSE. The history helps explain why T-128 found firm grounding in a tradition of student struggle and contestation. After describing this history, we analyze the course by using the theoretical and pedagogical framework we introduced the first day of class. In this manner, we hope to show how it provided students with a frame, language, and standard against which to make sense of the course as well as critique it. Our analysis was informed by course evaluations available at the HGSE Gutman Library, a series of two interviews with a random sample of students who took the course in 1998, and interviews of the teaching fellows and faculty members previously associated with the course.

Radical Beginnings

The course appeared in its initial form 11 years before the 1998 course under investigation in this chapter. Before that, in 1983, a group of students created a course with links in both content and pedagogy to the 1998 course. In 1992, Education for Social and Political Change was taught as a module.[2] Unlike other courses where faculty chose the topic, curriculum, and pedagogy, the idea for T-128 came from students, who designed and carried it out. Faculty members attended the class as participants. The creators of T-128 had hoped to create a space where students and interested faculty could do the intellectual and political work they felt was not happening at the school. Our emphasis on the redistribution of power and dialogue as part of maintaining a democratic classroom had clear historical links to these earlier versions of the course.

Evident to anyone teaching or taking the course between 1994 and 1997, as shown in the evaluations from those years, was our attempt to make sure that how we taught reflected the course's fundamental theories. For example, if we were speaking of transforming authoritarian practices in education, "the banking method" Freire (1993) spoke about in a dialogical classroom, the obvious questions would be, *How could we reconceptualize the classroom in ways that were conducive to dialogue? How could we create the conditions for a dialogue that redistributed power between teachers and students to develop?*

Until 1998, these attempts at democratic pedagogy were not made explicit to students. Instead, students only knew that they were entering a "different" classroom. The numbers of students attending the course, as well as the evaluations, indicated that we were, for the most part, successful in our attempts. Yet we were dissatisfied with what we perceived to be our insufficient political clarity. Of particular concern was how democratic theory remained decoupled from its practice, unnamed and hidden from students.

Transforming T-128: Power, Dialogue, Community, and Action

Divulging to students that a democratic theory informed the course involved developing the framework that we presented in the first class. We focused on the key areas noted previously: (a) establishing the foundation of the course, (b) rethinking power, (c) engaging in dialogue across differences, (d) building interlocking communities, and (e) committing to the process of reflection and action. Our previous experiences teaching the course had enabled us to identify these areas as necessary to creating and articulating a coherent framework.

I used the format of a reflective journal to present the course's framework. Using three theoretical lenses—personal, political, and intellectual—I modeled the idea that to engage in coherent, transparent, and effective social and political action, one needs to reunite these ways of understanding the world. In the next section, we focus on the analysis of the course's framework and its impact on the students' analyses and experiences. The passages in italics come from the reflective journal I referred to previously. The voices and analyses of students come from the interviews we conducted.

Establishing the Foundation of the Course: Practicing What We Preach and Proposing a Language of Democracy

We established the foundation of the course by making a commitment to practicing what we preached. This commitment to practicing democracy served as the standard against which we understood and measured all aspects of the course.

> *Practicing What We Preach. The course seeks to link theory and practice. The most important commitment this course makes is to democratic practice. This means that the course (teachers and students) seeks to create and re-create a vision that supports the practice of democracy in the classroom. The difficulty in engaging in democratic practice stems from our lack of education in a participatory democracy. Through our collective practice in this classroom, we hope to contribute to our education in democracy.*

By making a commitment to practicing democracy in the classroom, we shared with students our ideology, or the beliefs and values that sustained the course. We came to realize that making our ideology explicit was essential. We remembered from our own education that trying to figure out what a professor believed in and what he or she stood for often required that we become detectives. As teachers, we realized that this is a comfortable and powerful state of affairs. Shrouded in mystery and folklore, we could avoid any challenges to our ideology, pedagogy, or curriculum. For too many students, the force of tradition and low expectations for their teachers has anesthetized them to the educational potential inherent in questioning and critical analysis. This "domestication" of students creates "passive receptacles for official knowledge. Domesticated students are no threat to inequality; they tolerate and celebrate the status quo" (Shor, 1992, p. 99). Given that their success as students has to some extent come as a result of mastery and strict adherence to inert school practices, their "celebration" can be implicitly understood as the social contract between the professor and the captive audience. Silence is the price of a student's success. Our commitment to political clarity opened the class up to the possibility of authentic accountability: We held ourselves to a democratic standard, and students held us accountable to using this standard.

Students' responses to our commitment to "practicing what we preach" reflected what they heard in our class and aided them in drawing comparisons to their previous experiences in higher education, as one student explained:

> That's when she sold the class to me. She [de los Reyes] says that she's going to be real, as I understood, and that she's going to hold us to the same standard, it's going to be difficult and I was a little bit scared, wondering oh my God, what am I going to be expected to do, but it was completely exciting.

Another student said, "When I heard her talk like this, I was like 'Wow! You're a brave lady.' I was really scared for her, if she really meant it." Sadly, in the eyes of this student, simply explaining our ideology made us seem brave. What was for the most part a new experience for students, a brave act, generated a powerful energy in the class. It was both excitement and fear of the unknown.

Asking students to measure us by both our theories and our actions represented a risk. The temptation to revert to authoritarianism when things go wrong never disappears. However, contrary to what one might expect, the more transparent we made our thinking and our practice, the more trust, care, and compassion we found in the students' participation, analysis, and feedback. This reciprocity between teachers and students became the foundation on which we built the democratic classroom.

Proposing a Language of Democracy. My research, which focuses on studying democratic spaces in formal and informal education, helps me come up with a working definition of democratic practice: Democratic practice means that once teachers and students reconsider and redistribute power in the classroom, there is a process whereby everyone can speak and be heard (speak with responsibility and listen with respect), construct knowledge, dissent, and share in an equitable and responsible manner in the decision-making process.

The definition of *democracy* that we proposed in the first class immediately signaled that we were not speaking of what Unger and West (1998) described as "low-energy democracy" (p. 28), requiring only superficial engagement from citizens. Clearly, we were not educating students to simply vote in elections every 2 to 4 years. We were raising the bar and asking that students join us in preparing for a democracy, such as the one described by Lummis (1996): "Radical democracy describes the adventure of human beings creating, with their own hands, the condition of their freedom" (p. 19). By believing in the ability of citizens to create the conditions of their own freedom, we assumed that we have the will and capacity to determine all aspects of our individual and collective lives, ranging from how we govern ourselves to how we lead our daily lives, both in public and in private. To reach this goal, we believed that we needed to prepare intensively and extensively. In our vision, education is responsible for the social function of preparing students to participate in a high-energy democracy, requiring deep engagement from citizens.

An exchange among students reflecting on the first class shows their reaction to the project of creating a democratic classroom:

[Student 1]: I was trying to conceptualize what did that mean in the classroom of 80-some people with six TFs and a professor. . . . How does that work?
[Student 2]: If we're really going to try this . . . we would need much more than just a semester to do it in, and more than once a week.
[Student 3]: To me it was a turn-on, an opportunity to engage in learning in a way that I like to do. I didn't really think about logistics.
[Student 2]: Don't quite know what that means, nor have I thought about it in that way—that I hadn't put the two definitions [*democracy* and *education*] together for myself.

This range of opinions illuminates where we started. Prevalent in the students' comments was the notion of this being a new experience and of never having "put the two definitions together." For a significant number of students, the logistics seemed to make this attempt at democracy difficult if not impossible. However, the comment of the student who thought this was a "turn-on," where learning would be done in a way students liked, reflected a widespread feeling.

Students took a risk by giving us the benefit of the doubt; they were not familiar with the concept of democracy we proposed, nor what was expected of them in this kind of classroom. Similarly, we also took a risk by attempting to do something we, as a teaching community, had seldom, if ever, experienced. A member of the teaching community acknowledged that "we're talking about something and none of us really knows what it is. We have imagined what we think it might look like, and then we try it on. We put it in practice to see what it looks like."

Rethinking Power

Creating the conditions for a democratic classroom to emerge hinged on the systematic rethinking of power in the classroom and in society. Horton (1990) guided us:

> If we are to have a democratic society, people must find or invent new channels through which decisions can be made. . . . The problem is not that people will make irresponsible or wrong decisions. It is, rather, to convince people who have been ignored or excluded in the past that their involvement will have meaning and that their ideas will be respected. The danger is not too much, but too little participation. (p. 134)

If we wanted our students to engage in "too much participation" and grab hold of their individual and collective power, then we needed to rethink how power was distributed in the classroom. The course provided us, both teachers and students, with a language for understanding the manifestations and consequences of power over people, as well as the use of collective power—power with others—so as to transform society (Gaventa, 1980; Kreisberg, 1992; Starhawk, 1987).

In the framework, we addressed the power of the teacher and the teaching community and challenged students to rethink power in the classroom and at the institution.

> *The Power of the Teacher. I do not see democracy and leadership as mutually exclusive, and I am fully aware of my responsibilities in this classroom. Given the institutional power and, most importantly, the moral authority that I see in teaching, I believe I am accountable for making decisions and charting a path. For me, teaching is a mission, and I take it seriously. I have not capitulated to the capitalist notion that education is a consumer item that can be purchased in the supermarket of knowledge. For me, education is about freedom, liberation, possibility, and hope.*

The role of the faculty in a democratic classroom and in the teaching community needed to be articulated with great clarity because a democratic classroom often gets interpreted as a teacherless classroom where students gather to express their individual opinions. Teachers caught in the wave of this assumption are swept away by the tide of their own students. Even when students may think it is good to talk about how they feel whenever they so desire, these kinds of classrooms often end in chaos and discord. Such teachers, allowing themselves to be rendered powerless, cannot recover and transform the classroom into an environment conducive to serious and sustained dialogue.

As a faculty member at HGSE, I did not attempt to conceal or disregard the institutional power of the position. To do so would have been to pretend that entering that classroom made null and void the power of the institution and of my position. That was not the case. However, it was the moral authority of the teacher that I chose to invoke as the ground I stood upon when speaking of learning and teaching.

If education is to be about freedom, liberation, possibility, and hope, then teaching becomes a moral and ethical mission with serious implications for both the present and the future. Understanding education in this manner means the teacher is responsible and accountable for creating the conditions for learning to take place. To allow the classroom to drift aimlessly would be seen as an unethical act. But even in those instances when teachers make unilateral decisions, they remain accountable to their students for the outcome of such decisions.

For a Puerto Rican woman without tenure at Harvard, speaking from a position of strength and positioning the role of the teacher in this manner was quite difficult. Yet I realized that by not creating a framework for serious discussion in previous years, I had left enough room for students to engage in what I perceived to be sexist and racist challenges to my power in and outside the classroom. Particularly in the first years of teaching the course, I had to remind myself constantly that I did believe in democracy and that there had to be a way to claim the power to teach in a democratic manner. Importantly, students of color and women who understood the fragility of my power at HGSE protected me in significant ways. Students spoke in the interviews of "protecting her outside of class," which meant not tolerating any public criticism of the course or of me. In turn, I tried to protect those students who I believed faced the same situation.

There was a cost involved in having to function in this manner. For both students and me, this resulted in what I labeled a "siege mentality," where we felt all too often at risk of being disrespected and trivialized. Public spaces were seen as "critique-free" environments that inevitably resulted in truncated conversations and superficial analyses. Our challenge, however, required that we both protect each other and create the course we envisioned and needed. Importantly, we were trying to protect something more precious and indescribable: the possibility of transforming our vision of democracy into the practice of democracy in our classroom. The framework functioned as a way of gaining clarity, resolve, and strength.

Students seeking to define the role of the teacher in a democratic classroom spoke of the teacher as "the ideological leader" with the mission of guiding the dialogue and "present[ing] her hope for the class and not something set in stone." Because "democracy [means] that you propose, you don't impose," then the role of the teacher becomes explaining the "agenda" of the class and trying to "invest other people enough in it so that they join you." However, "if no one does anything, it's not going to happen."

A successful classroom is one where the teacher–leader is not always needed. As one student explained, "If Eileen hadn't been there one day . . . I would have noticed, but I don't get the sense that the class would have fallen apart." Another student added,

> I think the class could still go on because of the structure that she facilitates. . . . I don't know how many of you went to hear Mandela speak, and he was talking about, the good shepherd is like leading from behind, it's kind of . . . how I see her. Even when she's not there, she's there.

> *Rethinking Power in the Classroom and at the Institution. I want you to look around and reflect on what you see. This space produces an illusion: that in this classroom there is a shift in power and those who are normally powerless out there have a space of power in here. I want to remind you that this class is inextricably linked to the institution and to the society in general. As I have mentioned before, HGSE provides the context in which we work and the text we examine. Beware of thinking that this is a protected space and that we do not reproduce what is out there in here.*

The composition of our class created possibilities and challenges seldom found in higher education. For example, in 1998, approximately 57% of the students taking the course were students of color (Latina/o, African American, Asian American, Native American, and international). That led a student to comment that although HGSE was diverse, T-128 was "really diverse." By speaking directly about our "really" diverse classroom, we sought to dispel the illusion that given the racial and ethnic composition of the class, our ideology, and the topics we discussed, there was a shift in power in the classroom that favored students of color, women, gays and lesbians, and working-class students. Simultaneously, it seemed to represent a moment of powerlessness for Whites, men, heterosexuals, and middle- and upper-class students. This, we argued, was an illusion: Struggle and contestation outside the classroom continued inside our walls. To dispel this potential illusion, we examined the connection between the outside (i.e., HGSE, Harvard, and the larger society) and the inside (i.e., the classroom).

We recognized that it was often taboo to turn the microscope inward, which in our case meant looking at HGSE and Harvard, when typically our students were trained to solve problems "out there." We also recognized that this was a political choice on the part of the teaching community. We let students know that we embraced the fact that we were located at Harvard and at the School of Education. We proposed that we analyze how we existed within Harvard and asked, *Where do we stand as individuals and as a collective within the context in which we work and study?*

To produce this kind of analysis, HGSE became the context in which we taught and the text we analyzed. A very concrete example was our use of the orientation readings that all incoming students had read and discussed during their first week at Harvard. We asked students to reconsider the readings and ask themselves what messages the institution was trying to convey. We hoped this engagement with the institution would provide students with a model for thinking and acting in other institutions and in society.

Students in T-128 found a fundamental flaw in the prevalent notion that academic work and political and social work were separate, even sequential spheres. In other words, first we learn in one sphere what we then do in another. As a result of T-128, a student decided,

> I no longer felt like here I am; I need to learn as much as possible to do the work that I want to do. No, this is part of my work, too. So not only am I here to learn; I'm also here to work. . . . So it made the democratic process seep into other classes for me.

Students began to feel responsible for analyzing their courses' ideology, content, and pedagogy, as well as expressing their opinions and becoming active through their feedback and suggestions. This process proceeded to "seep" into the rest of the institution, providing students with the experience of feeling responsible for their education and their school.

This feeling of responsibility for the school moved the discussion of the issues raised in the class to the outside, continuing after the course was over. As a student observed, "I can honestly say [the dialogue] is going to go beyond [commencement] for myself. I have engaged in this and I don't choose to ever leave it." These dialogues planted the seeds for actions that the students undertook surrounding the issue of diversity at the school. Dialogues in the course also allowed students to identify and establish close relations with those peers whom they believed shared similar beliefs and commitment to social action. One student explained, "I found that I could pinpoint my allies after that course . . . and those who were possible allies who needed a little work, but possibly people who were willing to dialogue." As a result of the energy and focus provided by the dialogues and alliances emanating from the course, students from T-128 were overrepresented as leaders and participants in school-wide dialogues on diversity and in students' organizations demanding change and accountability for the diversity initiatives undertaken by HGSE.

Engaging in Dialogue

Dialogue was the central pedagogy that sustained the course. We thought it was necessary that teachers and students in the democratic classroom constitute themselves into a body of people capable of discussing topics that affect their daily lives. Young (1996) explained that "the model of deliberative democracy conceives of democracy as a process that created a public, citizens coming together to talk about collective problems, goals, ideals, and actions" (p. 121). We believed that learning about the obstacles and the possibilities in a radical, deliberative, democratic classroom, where a diverse group of students and teachers engage in dialogue about concrete questions, provided students with an education for responsible participation in society.

A member of the teaching community explained the process of coconstructing knowledge through dialogue:

> When I think about community, it seems to me that there's all these individuals looking for a way in which to find out more. And you learn from one person and that person becomes then a part of your community. And then you both find out together that you don't know something. And you find another person who adds to that conversation and they become a part of the community.

At the center of a democracy, and therefore a democratic classroom, are citizens looking for ways to "find out more." They expand the circle of knowledge to include others who, through their experiences and ideas, bring new wealth to the community. Empowered by their shared knowledge, citizens gather to learn and then prepare to act.

In the framework, we focused on the diversity in the classroom, describing it as a source of possibilities as well as obstacles to our creation of a deliberative community.

Invitation to Dialogue. The culture of silence in which we live, where we know which topics are dangerous, where we make sure that we are safe and don't take the risks necessary to advance the dialogue, insures that we will not experience democracy. Instead, we will continue supporting the silence. This culture of silence, as Freire (1993) put it, supports the continuation of things as they are: the status quo.

I will now make a series of observations that we have gathered after 4 years teaching the course. I am sure we will be able to add after the experiences of this year, but for now, this is what we have seen. Other communities may see themselves represented in these observations.

We want to invite the women in the classroom to occupy the intellectual space and to speak about gender issues. We hope to hear your voices because this issue must be brought out of silence and into the public sphere.

We want to invite students of color to occupy the intellectual space in the classroom, and I want to share an insight I had 3 years ago. Often as people of color, we are allowed to occupy the space and to say whatever we want to say. But, we are seldom challenged. We find that the result of this interaction is devastating. We want to invite you to participate in the dialogue with the certainty that we are here to listen and to challenge you with the understanding that to simply affirm you would be, in our opinion, to engage in the most insidious form of miseducation and disrespect.

Two years ago, a male White student had the honesty to share with us a feeling that I want to articulate. He told us it was okay for him to feel powerless in the course because he knew that given who he was, this feeling of powerlessness would end the minute he left the room. I want to invite those of you who may feel it is okay to let the balance of power shift in this course, as it may seem to, who feel that it is okay to become an impartial observer, knowing that the course is finite—that it ends at 7:30 and in January, to take the risk, speak, listen, and be challenged.

Like Freire, we believed "dialogue is meaningful precisely because the dialogical subjects, the agents in the dialogue, not only retain their identity, but actively defend it, and thus grow together" (Freire et al., 1998, p. 248). We understood that a diverse classroom intent on growing together will face significant obstacles, which must be recognized and addressed if we are to uncover what is possible. We named gender and racial differences, which have had a significant impact on our ability to engage in dialogue.

We looked once more to the work of Young (1996) to help us frame the connection between power and dialogue, problematizing further what may appear to be a simple engagement among a number of people under conditions of equality:

In many formal situations the better-educated White middle-class people, moreover, often act as though they have a right to speak and that their words carry authority, whereas those of other groups often feel intimidated by the argument requirements and the formality and rules of parliamentary procedure, so they do not speak or speak only [in] a way that those in charge find "disruptive." (p. 124)

We sought to dispel any illusions that a democratic classroom ignored differences or the connection between power and diversity. We made the commitment to deal with these issues openly, without shying away from what would inevitably be tense and uncomfortable moments.

Our experience throughout the years has been that what may be seen as a divisive opening message, breaking up the big group into distinct communities and making separate invitations, is actually heard and received as a very personal invitation that acknowledges the obvious: We do not enter as a homogenous group sharing the same needs, expectations, modes of speaking, or ways of dreaming.

Repeatedly, students commented, "The most valuable thing I have gained from this course was the opportunity to engage in dialogue with a diverse group of students." The opportunity to hear diverse voices proves invaluable to many students but, as some students explained eloquently, this process comes at a price.

T-128 did not disconnect completely from the consistent critique that students of color, women, and gays and lesbians make of their experiences at predominantly White, male, and heterosexual institutions of higher education. We heard constantly of the exhaustion of having to teach about race, gender, and sexual orientation. We also heard of the unfairness of being constantly asked to teach but not having the opportunity to learn. Even when we recognized the injustice of this situation, we still found it very difficult to create a space where each and every student was a learner and a teacher. A conversation during the interview reflects the range of experiences in our classroom:

[Student 1]: The White students were invited more.
[Student 2]: And they were invited to engage and reinvited and coddled.
[Student 3]: I like that word.
[Interviewer]: Talk about that.
[Student 3]: Go, girl.
[Student 2]: I just felt [it] became a moment to teach them, those that have not ever experienced this, those that have not ever considered the impact of this, those that will be affecting others in teaching or in leadership: Here's the space in order for us to really, you know, make you become this politically and socially aware person. And in the process, many of us were robbed.

Expressing the same views but giving a different reading, other students of color explained:

[Student 1]: I would venture to say that this is the one place I didn't feel like I had to teach . . . and sort of relinquishing power to the TFs and to Eileen. Because I felt like that was their job and they were doing it pretty well.
[Student 2]: You had no need to call somebody out.
[Student 3]: You could be a learner.

Another student of color embraced her role as an educator but acknowledged that this was a new experience for her:

But you know what? To me [the dialogue] is worth it. Because if they asked that question, then that's important; there's learning going on. . . . And I never had to do this back home. Here, I've had to do this several times. And that's fine, and I'll keep doing it.

This range of positions captured our experiences and observations. Each year we entered with a commitment to create a classroom where everyone could speak, listen, and be heard—where everyone could be a learner and a teacher. Yet creating the conditions for that to happen in a diverse classroom was the most serious challenge we faced. Our approach was to name the problem and struggle to address it with students. This approach led to high tension in the classroom. We chose tension over silence even when at times the classroom became extremely uncomfortable and unpredictable.

Even if for 3 hours, once a week, during one semester we tried to create new possibilities for all students to become learners and teachers—to receive an education in democracy—a student of color reminded us of the world outside our doors:

At the end of the class, I get to leave and walk into their world, not my world. Like that is . . . the White world, [T-128] is not reality. And then you leave, it's like their world and you have to make it your reality.

Creating Distinct Yet Interlocking Communities

Serious and sustained dialogue focused on the co-construction of new knowledge necessary for social and political change requires a cohesive community of students and teachers. Without a community, dialogue often remains at a superficial level. Furthermore, living and working in community reclaims the humanity of participants, providing them with much-needed care and compassion. As Wolk and Peake (1998) explained,

Rarely does school see community as people getting together as a regular part of their daily lives to enjoy one another's company, grow from one another, share perspectives and experiences, care for one another, and engage in important conversation. These are the requirements for a deep and thoughtful democracy. (p. 10)

In an effort to create the conditions for a deep and thoughtful democratic classroom, we created a series of interlocking communities that began with the teaching community and continued with the *big group* (consisting of approximately 80 to 100 students and the teaching community) and the *small groups* (consisting of 10 students).

> *The Big Group and the Small Groups. Recognizing that there are a lot of people in this classroom, I want to invite each and every one of you to contribute to the dialogue. This invitation is open to many different ways of contributing. You can contribute through your comments in the big group, you can contribute through your written work, you can contribute by identifying additional resources that support the course, you can contribute through art or through your contributions in the small groups that are brought to the big group.*
>
> *Our experience is such that we recognize that the most difficult space is the big group. In a democratic classroom, each and every one of you needs to feel responsible and be challenged to make this space one of meaningful dialogue. I want to let you know that we may or may not succeed. The concept of failure, which we view as a learning moment, does not scare us. In other words, in an effort to make this work, we will not dismiss the concept of democracy. Each and every person needs to step in to support the possibility of democracy in the classroom.*

The Big Group

The big group, which met for the first half of the class and included the teaching community and all students in the course, created significant challenges. A space where individual students engage in dialogue with other students and with the professor and occasionally the teaching community, it represented the most difficult space to access. The amphitheater-style classroom, the need of a microphone to be heard, and the topics of the discussions created an environment where students felt tremendous pressure to say the "right" thing. Our objective was to think of the big group in ways that addressed the obstacles presented by the space, the number of students, and the nature of the dialogue. Central to this attempt was our rejection of the model where students enter and leave the classrooms as individuals who have little or no contact with their peers; instead, T-128 strove to become a series of interlocking communities intent on co-constructing knowledge together.

Students analyzed the big group experience as being based on the decision of whether to speak or remain silent. For example, a student described the difficulty of speaking and listening in a democratic classroom:

What became clear to me was that . . . the democracy of the classroom was dependent on individual participation. . . . I kept getting stuck in the large group setting. . . . I kept always weighing whether . . . it was important for me to say something, or it was not.

Another student offered an interesting measure of when to speak and when to listen:

For the group of people, [this was] their first time engaging in this kind of discussion. It was really urgent for them [general agreement among interviewees]. . . . I think it takes a lot of courage . . . and also . . . takes a lot of support and I think it speaks to everyone in the class.

According to this student, there was an unspoken agreement in the class where those who had an "urgent" need to speak were the ones who were given the floor.

Although we agree with this analysis, we also see a further explanation. The sense of urgency shifted in the class depending on the topic of discussion. For example, a discussion of the social construction of race and racism may have been perceived to create a sense of urgency for students of color to speak, whereas a discussion of the social construction of gender may have shifted the sense of urgency to women. This particular student was impressed with this unspoken collective agreement to listen to the urgent voices. In this particular interview, everyone signaled their agreement with this analysis. Yet an alternative explanation may be that although some students were yielding the floor because they recognized the courage of those speaking out, there was also a significant number of students who were unwilling to take the risk of challenging students of color in their analysis of racism, or women in their analysis of sexism.

Recognizing the fear and the difficulties associated with speaking in this very public and problematic space, we reassured students that there were other means of contributing. Two means of accessing the big group evolved throughout the years and allowed more students to make their presence felt: announcements and art. In 1997, a ritual developed where students took the floor to announce different activities taking place at the school and in the community. Announcements ranged from relevant lectures at the university to attempts at mobilizing students for collective action against high-stakes testing in Massachusetts. Other announcements were more personal, such as the surprise in-class birthday party organized by students for one of the teaching fellows. These moments transformed the big group into an open and familiar space accessible to all.

Another attempt at building community in the classroom was our decision to open the classroom for students to bring art, asking them to explain why it was important to them and how it connected with the class. As one student commented about art in the classroom: "Having that space, before we started any type of dialogue, that was incredible. That made me feel like that was my class." The proliferation of paintings, sculptures, and photographs with political messages transformed the big group into an open space that attended to the imagination and the spirit of the students.

Even when we opened up other means of contributing to the big group and reconceptualizing how we saw the space, we made clear in that first class that we were willing to see failure as a means of learning. This meant that long silences would happen and that we would not call on students in an effort to fill the silence. In our vision, we shared with them the responsibility of contributing to the dialogue. Failure, we argued, is to be not only tolerated but also understood as a powerful moment of learning. For anyone hoping to work for social change, learning to learn from failure is essential. After all, breaking new ground and moving in new directions necessarily involve taking risks, which, in turn, provide a source for new learning and new actions.

The Small Groups

One of the critical structures in the course were the small groups. For the second half of each class, students met in small groups of 10 to discuss readings, continue dialogues that had begun in the large group, and get to know one another as they struggled to make sense of the course in relationship to their identities and life experiences. Although the teaching fellows participated in the small groups by providing support and direction, the students took on significant responsibility. The mission of the teaching fellow was to help the groups chart their own path, trying not to overpower them by telling them how they must do things.

Over the years, the majority of students expressed their comfort in being members of their small groups, but that was not always the case. We saw the obstacles, even the failure of a group to become a cohesive community capable of engaged dialogue as learning moments and not as a crisis needing to be resolved by the teaching community. One experience in particular reaffirmed our trust in the students' commitment to their groups and their ability to struggle with difficulties. One group declared at the end of the semester that they had failed miserably and disbanded. Failure meant that none of the participants was satisfied with the quality of the dialogue or their ability to collaborate with each other. We were proud to hear that they had decided to regroup in the spring with a renewed commitment to continuing their work.

Reflecting and Acting

Learning to think about democracy involves learning to take action. Consequently, learning to plan and organize is essential in a democratic classroom. As Unger and West (1998) argued, "A disorganized society cannot generate conceptions of its alternative futures or act upon them. Organization is power, a power essential to a vigorous democracy. Disorganization is surrender to drift, to accident, to fate" (p. 79). Our expectation was that students be prepared for thinking and acting individually and collectively, now and in the future. We argued and presented evidence that collective action requires that people reflect and then act in multiple contexts and using a variety of strategies (Agosin, 1993; Alinsky, 1989; Horton, 1990; Piven & Cloward, 1979).

> *Introspection, Reflection, and Action. The course makes the argument that for us to become compassionate and effective agents of change, we need to engage in the process of introspection, reflection, and action. We add to the concept of praxis (reflection and action) the concept of introspection. We define* introspection *as the systematic and careful linking of the personal, the political, and the intellectual in a system of beliefs and values that allows us to know what we are able to do and what contradicts our deeply held beliefs. By being clear about who we are, what political principles and theories support our vision, and what our dreams are, we insure that we remain firm in our practice and that our principles are not compromised. We believe that to disconnect the practice from theory—the personal from the political and the intellectual—is a very dangerous approach to social change leading to confusion, vacillation, reaction, and mistakes.*

Action in a high-energy, deep democracy is the result of introspection and reflection, processes that are further strengthened by renewed action. The challenge for us was to capture the complexity of these processes in a way that allowed students to actually experience the arguments we were making. We met this challenge with two course assignments: the political autobiography and the project of change.

The political autobiography asked students to reflect on their system of personal, intellectual, and political beliefs and values. Through this process, we tried to provide a mechanism for reuniting these three separate spheres of knowledge. We argued that we in the academy have been trained to accept that intellectual or academic knowledge is to be valued above personal experiences. Political understandings and actions within the prevalent model are seen as functioning separately, often without any explicit connection to the personal or intellectual. As educators engaged in liberatory education, we believed this disintegration is a fundamental problem, which the course attempted to address. The process of relearning and reintegrating knowledge continued with the political autobiography.

Because we began the course by sharing our own political autobiographies, students had a general idea of what we were hoping to accomplish. We encouraged students to think about themselves in terms of the history, background, and principles that informed their views on, for example, race, class, gender, sexual identity, immigration, and language, and how these views affected their beliefs about education. We also asked that students reflect on their hopes and dreams.

Throughout the years, we were inspired by our students who struggled during the semester with drafts of their political autobiographies. The overwhelming response was that this was a powerful exercise, often life changing. Advising incoming students, a former student said in the course's evaluation, "Don't be surprised if you scrap your first draft of the political autobiography and start over." Moved by the opportunity to reflect on her political history and hopes for the future, one student wrote a 150-page autobiography; another continued working through the second semester and produced a 300-page document that he hoped to publish. Students described the experience of writing their political autobiographies as an "emotional" and often "painful" undertaking as well as an intellectual and political exercise.

Students then linked their political autobiographies with projects of change, where each person examined either a project already undertaken or one that was planned. In our vision, students needed to be clear on how their political autobiographies (who they are and what they believe in) informed their projects of change (what they do).

After preparing their proposals for a project of change, students gathered in their small groups for intense discussions, often lasting four to six hours, to help each other think about the personal, intellectual, and political implications of their projects. Examples of projects included encouraging and enabling high school librarians to make certain there is literature on gay and lesbian issues at their schools, a proposal for a program seeking to engage teenage Latinas in political study through arts education, and a high school curriculum that examined social issues using math. A significant number of projects were implemented, such as the college-level course titled Poetry and Political Discourse, which was taught at Tufts University, and a discussion group at HGSE to deconstruct "Whiteness." In 1998, Ana Tavares and Rebeca Burciaga, two students from T-128, edited a collection of poetry and essays by 47 HGSE students titled *Meet Us at the River: An Anthology in Progress.* This anthology was dedicated to "incoming students of color and underrepresented students, class of 2000, to take with you on your journey through HGSE." This group of students left a powerful legacy and, as they had hoped, their work became cyclical: In 1999, the next generation of students wrote an anthology titled *Journey Up the River: The Struggle Continues* (Banerjee, 2000).

We saw the projects of change undertaken by our students as the measure of success for the course. Once students bring together their personal, intellectual, and political beliefs, values, and knowledge into a democratic project of change, they have conceptualized and experienced the high-energy, deep democracy we worked and hoped for in the course.

Conclusion

We end our presentation of T-128's framework by sharing our feelings about the course.

> *Passion and Dreams. Having said all of this, we want to reassure you that none of us takes ourselves so seriously that we will not make the essential connections among having fun, remaining healthy, and having a sense of humor. The great discussions, the fun, the passion, and the dreaming that happens in the class are part of the reason that we work together.*

The framework that we presented on the first day of class in 1998 allowed us to create a firm foundation from which to explore with our students education for social and political change. We committed to practicing what we preached and began speaking a new language of democracy with our students. We then proposed an understanding of power, dialogue, community, and social change that would guide us throughout the semester. Students studied, discussed, critiqued, and then proposed their own understandings and visions for the course. Together we engaged in a long and often frustrating journey, trying to understand whether democracy was possible in a diverse classroom.

We believe we were able to take the first steps in preparing educators for active participation in a democratic society. Students tested their knowledge and capacity to become active participants in a democracy in our classroom, and then tested what they had learned in the classroom at the school and the institution. They recognized the obstacles as well as the possibilities of working with a diverse group of people intent on social and political change.

By creating the framework, T-128 (content and pedagogy) became a dynamic unit of analysis. Students analyzed and critiqued the course, joining with us in the commitment to create a democratic classroom not only for themselves but also for the next generation of students. When we strayed from our path, the students were compassionate but firm about realigning us with the course's fundamental principles. Signaling the never-ending work that choosing democracy entails, a student reminded us that T-128 "was not reality." Our challenge was to transform a momentary reality for some into a permanent reality for all.

As a result of this chapter, we identified new challenges and developed new actions with the understanding that a democratic classroom committed to education for social and political change needs to reenergize individual and collective hope through concrete actions. Each year we entered the T-128 classroom with great hope. Students who brought possibilities we had never envisioned have kept this hope alive. In creating T-128, we hoped to provide teachers and students with a space where together we could practice the art of teaching and learning, have fun, support and care for each other, and change the world. For us, T-128 is a way of living.

Notes

1. Sarah Napier, who became part of the teaching community in 1999–2000, joined us as a contributor. Dianne Morales, a doctoral student at HGSE, conducted the interviews for this research project and joined us the following year as a teaching fellow.

2. A module was a short course lasting 9 weeks. Modules were often taught by doctoral students and were designed to introduce newer ideas in the field of education into the Graduate School of Education course offerings and give doctoral students experience designing and teaching a class.

References

Agosin, M. A. (1993). *Surviving beyond fear: Women, children, and human rights in Latin America.* New York, NY: White Pine Press.

Alinsky, S. (1989). *Rules for radicals.* New York, NY: Vintage Press.

Banerjee, K. (2000). *Journey up the river: The struggle continues.* Cambridge, MA: Harvard University Graduate School of Education.

Briskin, L. (1990). *Feminist pedagogy: Teaching and learning liberation.* Ottawa, Canada: Canadian Research Institute for the Advancement of Women.

de los Reyes, E., & Gozemba, P. A. (2002). *Pockets of hope: How students and teachers change the world.* Westport, CT: Bergin & Garvey.

Freire, P. (1993). *Pedagogy of the oppressed.* New York, NY: Continuum.

Freire, P., Freire, A. M. A., & Macedo, D. P. (1998). *The Paulo Freire reader.* New York, NY: Continuum.

Gaventa, J. (1980). *Power and powerlessness: Quiescence and rebellion in an Appalachian valley.* Urbana: University of Illinois Press.

Hernañdez, A. (1997). *Pedagogy, democracy, and feminism: Rethinking the public sphere*. Albany: State University of New York Press.

Horton, M. (1990). *The long haul: An autobiography*. New York, NY. Doubleday.

Kreisberg, S. (1992). *Transforming power: Domination, empowerment, and education*. Albany: State University of New York Press.

Lather, P. (1991). *Getting smart: Feminist research and pedagogy with/in the postmodern*. New York, NY: Routledge.

Lummis, C. D. (1996). *Radical democracy*. Ithaca, NY: Cornell University Press.

Piven, F. F., & Cloward, R. A. (1979). *Poor people's movements: Why they succeed, how they fail*. New York, NY: Vintage Books.

Shor, I. (1992). *Empowering education: Critical teaching for social change*. Chicago, IL: University of Chicago Press.

Starhawk. (1987). *Truth or dare: Encounters with power, authority, and mystery*. San Francisco, CA: Harper & Row.

Tavares, A., & Burciaga, R. (1999). *Meet us at the river—An anthology in progress*. Cambridge, MA: Author.

Unger, R. M., & West, C. (1998). *The future of American progressivism: An initiative for political and economic reform*. Boston, MA: Beacon Press.

Wolk, S., & Peake, L. (1998). *A democratic classroom*. Portsmouth, NH: Heinemann.

Young, I. M. (1996). Communication and the other: Beyond deliberative democracy. In S. Benhabib (Ed.), *Democracy and difference* (pp. 120–137). Princeton, NJ: Princeton University Press.

PART TWO

HOW WE ENGAGE IN OUR WORK

4

RADICAL HONESTY

Truth-Telling as Pedagogy for Working Through Shame in Academic Spaces

Bianca C. Williams

Since I started teaching Africana Studies and Cultural Anthropology, in all my courses during every semester, I conclude the first class session with an introductory monologue. I think about this monologue as a first step in my pedagogical practice of "radical honesty."[1] The monologue sets the tone for the semester and provides students with a sense of the type of truth-telling that will be encouraged as we educate one another about race, gender, power, difference, and oppression:

> I am Professor Bianca Williams. You may call me "Doctor" or "Professor Williams." I identify as both an African American and a Black American. My family is from Jamaica, I was born in the Bronx, and grew up in Orlando, so depending on the day, situation, and political circumstances, I may claim membership in multiple communities. However, it is important for you to remember that *African American* is not always synonymous with *Black American*. *Black American* or *Black person* includes those of Caribbean and African descent and incorporates a variety of experiences that are diverse and sometimes significantly different. Historical and contemporary African American experiences make up a portion of Black experiences, but they do not encompass all of what Blackness is. I identify as a woman, and I prefer the pronouns of *she* and *her*. The people in this room may identify in a variety of ways in relation to gender, and you should ask and use the pronouns they request. I was brought up in a working-class family. As a first-generation college graduate and PhD, I am currently hesitantly middle class, and learning everyday what that means. I am heterosexual and a Christian and live with the sometimes invisible battle of generalized anxiety

disorder. I am a diehard Duke fan, so if you're a Tar Heel fan and want to pass this course, you should probably keep that to yourself (smile).

These are my multiple identities, and I share them with you because I know that they index things that may become significant as I teach you. They act as signifiers for the racialized, gendered, sexualized, religious, and ability-related experiences I've had over the course of my life. These experiences undoubtedly influence the way that I teach, the topics I decide to teach, even the way I choose to organize the syllabus before you. And this is not just the case in this classroom, but in all of your classrooms—even in those so-called "neutral" and "apolitical" disciplines, like biology, math, and English literature. All of your professors are biased, and they bring their prejudices and biases to academic spaces. I choose to be honest with you about how my identities connect to some of the biases I bring to this academic space, while also acknowledging your identities and the stereotypes about me that YOU may bring to this space. As a cultural anthropologist, I don't believe in the fiction of objectivity. I believe that the experiences we have, the identities we embody, and the positions we hold in systems of power impact how we see and navigate the world. This is not only true for me but also for you. Your identities and your biases influence how you will read for this course and the perspectives you choose to share during class discussions. I highlight these issues at the beginning of this course as an effort for us all to constantly be aware of the prejudices we bring into this space, as we attempt to learn from one another, share our cultural knowledge, and engage in dialogue that just might shift and transform our current ways of thinking and being. Thank you and I hope to see you during the next class.

In most courses, thick, heavy moments of silence pervade the classroom as students take in all of this information. In my introductory courses, where freshmen are the majority of the population, mouths hang open with surprise, because some are stunned by this much direct talk, truth-telling, and insight into their professor's life. After class, some students come up to me to introduce themselves and say that they look forward to learning more about power and their identities throughout the semester. Others try to slip out of the classroom unseen, never to be heard from again. The monologue sets the stage for truth-telling, modeling my expectation for the type of deep awareness, reflexivity, and critical thought I expect from myself and my students throughout the semester.

In this chapter, I offer radical honesty as a concept that describes a pedagogical practice of truth-telling that seeks to challenge racist and patriarchal institutional cultures in the academy. In particular, I focus on those cultures and processes that sometimes trigger encounters with shame. Radical honesty emphasizes the significance of personal narratives and opens a space for creating strategies that enable scholars and students to bring their "whole self" to the classroom, while getting rid of the shame that frequently accompanies their bodies in academic settings. Stemming from the teachings of fields such as Black feminist anthropology and African American studies, I envision radical honesty as a teaching practice that concentrates on three key foci:

1. *Truth-telling.* Professors and students are honest about the stereotypes and racialized and gendered assumptions[2] that are brought into the classroom, while examining the histories and processes that brought them there. They tell their own truths about the feelings and emotions they experience when these assumptions are present.
2. *Valuing narrative and personal experience.* Seeing personal experience and narratives as important tools for learning, radical honesty provides space in the classroom for vocalizing these truths and uses them to connect the dots between individual and group experiences of (dis)empowerment to institutional and systemic analyses of racism and sexism.
3. *Acting.* Radical honesty is not simply about truth-telling for the sake of speaking truths (although this is itself a valuable exercise). The use of the word *honesty* emphasizes a critical eye toward analysis, intention, and authenticity, where multiple truths may be taken together to figure out beneficial and effective practices for teaching and learning. Radical honesty provides tools for truth-in-action, understanding that theory influences praxis—that is, acts that shape the world—both inside and outside the ivory tower. In this way, radical honesty is in line with the fundamental teachings of Black feminist scholars, such as Audre Lorde, Barbara Christian, bell hooks, and Beverly Guy Sheftall, who see ideas and knowledge as tools that generate social change.

Shame and the Hauntings of Academic Spaces

Academic institutions, particularly the predominantly White institutions at which I have taught and earned degrees, were created by men who could not fathom that one day I, a woman of African descent, would be standing at the front of the classroom. Even now, over 60 years since school desegregation and with increasing numbers of Black women and men earning doctorates, I am frequently reminded that these spaces of knowledge production and learning were not initially created to nurture Black people's brilliance. These spaces were not made for us. Instead, like many other institutions in the

United States, they were originally designed to miseducate and annihilate the possibility of us—of us as educators critiquing the oppressive systems that make the ivory tower possible. It is inevitable for many, then, that we would continue to experience the effects of what Du Bois (1903/1994) so aptly called "double-consciousness" and all the tensions that come with it.

As I walk through the hallways on my campus or travel to national conferences, I find myself wondering if I deserve to be here. Because my presence frequently disrupts students' and colleagues' notions about the race, gender, and age of people who are traditionally called "Doctor" or "Professor," I sometimes experience anxiety, shame, or other forms of tension as I am consistently made to see that I do not fit that mold. I question whether the material I teach, the articles I write, or the presentations I give will be seen as "real" scholarly work and research. There have been numerous studies about the experiences and effects of this type of Imposter Syndrome; however, much of this work has focused on the gendered experiences of this phenomenon. At times, I prefer to describe my experience as the "psychological battering of racism," a phrase Christian (1996/2007, p. 219) offered, because it emphasizes the role racism plays in Imposter Syndrome. As a Black feminist scholar, I am constantly aware of the ways that my body is read in academic spaces, and the assumptions, stereotypes, and misrecognitions people place on it. I recognize that my teaching, my research, even my service can cause tension in these spaces.

In her book *Sister Citizen*, political scientist Melissa Harris-Perry (2011) described three different forms of shame. First, shame as social, is the notion that "individuals feel ashamed in response to a real or imagined audience. [They] do not feel shame in isolation, [they feel it] only when [they] transgress a social boundary or break a community expectation" (p. 104). Second, shame as global, extending beyond a single incident, causes one to make an evaluation or judgment about one's whole self. In other words, "I *am* shameful" instead of "I did something shameful." And third, shame as psychological triggers a "psychological and physical urge to withdraw, submit, or appease others" (Harris-Perry, 2011, p. 104). Throughout the book, Harris-Perry argued that Blackness is frequently marked by shame in the popular imaginings of the United States, because Black people are portrayed as intellectually inferior and criminalized and represented as hypersexual and inadequate. This is significant because, Harris-Perry argued, "shaming is a profoundly modern exercise of power [where] only the inferior can feel ashamed" (p. 112). In this way, we understand that shame is fundamental to social and institutional forms of oppression, particularly racism.

If the narratives of women-of-color scholars in texts such as *Presumed Incompetent* (Gutierrez y Muhs, Flores Niemann, Gonzalez, & Harris, 2012) and *Telling Histories* (White, 2008) are any evidence, then racism, sexism, and shame are intimately connected in academic institutions. Unfortunately, it seems that racism and sexism are *not* on the decline in this so-called "postracial, postfeminist" United States, but are in fact, pervasive in subtle ways. The forms of racism and sexism that permeate the academy frequently push women and scholars of color to question their sense of worth and belonging, which can lead to feelings of shame about perceived incapabilities. Furthermore, those who choose to speak out about their experiences with microaggressions or other forms of institutionalized racism can be shamed into silence by hierarchal cultures within universities or individuals with more power. Subsequently, participating in radical honesty in the classroom or in other academic spaces can be difficult. Being honest about these experiences while teaching students to be vocal about their own truths requires that I, and other women-of-color faculty, engage in emotional labor that is challenging, as shame continues to rear its ugly head. So we must ask: How do women-of-color faculty engage in healthy transformative teaching and learning when the institutionalized racism of academic spaces is built to trigger a burden of shame among them?

Early on in my career, I decided that instead of finding ways to strategically draw attention away from my body, my experiences, and others' assumptions about me, I would embrace them and use them as a starting point for teaching about power, privilege, and inequality. Hence the introductory monologue I present in my courses and this chapter's opening. The monologue not only helps me deal with Imposter Syndrome, but also is empowering. I see it as a way of facing shame head on, resisting structural and cultural forces that want me to be ashamed of who I am, the way I look, my place in the academy, and the emotional investment I have in my students and the process of educating. I understand that the classroom is a space where I have some autonomy and can feel satisfied and empowered by my labor, especially if I fully embrace the spontaneous and surprising ways discussions about my racialized and gendered experiences can lead to transformative learning. Additionally, the monologue helps establish my authority in the classroom, which students are sometimes hesitant to recognize from women scholars of color.

Truth-Telling as Empowerment in the Classroom

My courses in ethnic studies and anthropology provide space and give voice to alternative narratives and theories that are often left out of other courses. Subsequently, my first-day monologue provides students with a brief introduction to the politics of education and learning. The discussion about my identities, biases, and the ways they may influence the classroom helps students recognize that the classroom—*all* classrooms—are political spaces where histories are told and modified. As students are introduced to Black feminist and antiracist histories, narratives, and voices, they are empowered to turn a critical eye on their own experiences, to move through potential shame, and use these tools to tell their truths. In this way, radical honesty encourages professors and students to recognize that classrooms are important sites for processes that are essential to race-making and gender formation.

I frequently see radical honesty working at its best in my seminar course, Black Women, Popular Culture, and the Pursuit of Happiness. The course is a semester-long interrogation of how race, gender, and systems of racialized and gendered oppression influence one's pursuit of happiness. We examine self-help books, music, films, magazines, and blogs using analytical lenses from Africana studies, anthropology, psychology, and Black feminist thought in order to investigate to what extent historical processes of racism and sexism continue to leave their imprints on an individual's ability to attain and maintain happiness. The classroom can become intense and uncomfortable, because we spend a great deal of time discussing depression, anxiety, shame, and other challenging emotions and disorders frequently connected to Black women's experience of racism and sexism. Throughout the course, students write reflective papers and engage in brief free-writing sessions where they create and modify their personal definitions of *happiness* and identify obstacles that inhibit their pursuit toward realizing this definition. In the final paper, they use these data to find strategies or tools for experiencing happiness on a regular basis, while taking into account their racialized and gendered identities and how these subjectivities influence or inhibit their pursuits of happiness. The end product is a happiness action plan that combines personal narrative and theoretical analysis.

Every year, I receive e-mails and office hour visits from students asking for assistance as they encounter difficulties writing this paper. Many come with questions about grammar, writing clarity, and argument, whereas some express concerns about mental wellness or being overwhelmed with how much they realize they are frequently experiencing unhappiness. Usually, I walk them through the high points in the semester, a moment when they shared an important insight about their positionality in society or connected with another student's argument or an author's experience, and this gets them rejuvenated enough to write a good paper. Other times, I support them as they talk through their difficulties, sharing some of my experiences with unhappiness, therapy, and self-care, and then provide them with information about services on campus. But last spring (Spring 2015), the students seemed to have a more challenging time than usual.

This particular semester was the first time I taught Black Women and Happiness with a class that was composed of all women and mostly women of color. I was delighted when I entered class on the first day. Although the students from previous semesters and I had learned a great deal about happiness, I was excited about this opportunity to see how women of color connected with or critiqued the texts we would examine. The class did not disappoint because the students quickly created a tight, seemingly sacred learning community, connecting the texts in the course to the experiences they were having in their lives, particularly on campus. This community of women of color and White women embraced radical honesty and used it to hear each other's truths and push themselves in critical analyses. Some students were quieter than others, but each showed progress in critical thinking and vulnerability in their reflection papers, classroom discussions, and office visits. However, as the deadline for the final paper rough draft approached, I received numerous complaints about increasing anxiety and/or difficulties getting what was in their heads and hearts onto the page. It was as if the class as a whole had hit a collective moment of analytical paralysis and emotional chaos.

Instead of continuing to meet with students individually, I decided to use class time to have an open discussion about what was impeding their rough draft writing process. I had confidence that they would be comfortable speaking out loud and with one another about what was going on and figured we could collectively come up with some strategies for writing success. The session started with some general comments from a few students about how difficult it was to write openly and honestly about their struggles with maintaining emotional wellness and the power unhappiness could have on academics and relationships. A White woman courageously talked about how she could not find the words to discuss her own struggles with happiness, while simultaneously recognizing that her racialized privilege allowed her to be ignorant about the hurdles the women of color in the class experienced in their own pursuits. After a few more contributions, a student I did not expect to speak raised her hand. I called on her, and she said:

> Last week I tried to commit suicide. I am revealing this to you all because I'm tired of feeling ashamed. Throughout this semester, we've been learning from Professor Williams that we need to speak up, give voice to our stories, and get rid of the shame that keeps us silent. I've decided to start right now, so this is why I'm telling you.

As the student revealed this intimate experience to her peers, I admit that I was struck silent. I knew about her suicide attempt, because she had contacted me for assistance right after, and I had done all I could in the short time since (with the resources on campus) to help with her healing process. I actually had not expected her in class that day and was even more shocked that she wanted to speak about the incident.

In the moments after her radically honest confession, I was temporarily paralyzed by conflicting desires and responsibilities. I wanted to comfort her and the other students who immediately had tears flowing down their faces. A voice in my head screamed that there would be no way to transition to the text we were supposed to discuss during that class session, and my anxiety grew as I remembered a speaker was scheduled to Skype into the class in 20 minutes. I quickly considered canceling class, so we could discuss the impact of her bold confession, but decided that doing so would undermine the learning community we had created and the truth-telling and teachable moments we had all participated in throughout the semester. Most importantly, I wanted to take the student's lead, giving all of us space to speak our truths in response to what we had just heard.[3] I quickly said a silent prayer for guidance and ability, and decided to move forward.

As a woman scholar of color, I have had students (particularly students of color) reveal all types of emotional crises to me after class, on campus sidewalks, and during office hours. Because of my race and gender, students and the institution expect a particular form of affective labor from me. However, in this moment, my humanity felt in conflict with what I knew my institution desired from me. Whereas Bianca, the person, wanted to rush over and hug her and hug the other students who I could tell were rattled, my positionality as a professor at a research institution meant that I was to hold my composure. The notion is that classrooms are spaces where teaching gets done, and this type of emotionally invested teaching is not really valued by one who wishes to be recognized as a scholar. At least not until after they procure tenure.

I could tell the students were also negotiating how to deal with their emotions in the classroom, as they wiped their tears and looked like they wanted to hug one another, but somehow the classroom space restricted their movement. It was as if they knew that physically comforting one another—a human desire—was inappropriate in the classroom. As I processed my own emotions and how I was going to deal with this unexpected moment, I asked the student who shared her truth if she minded if her classmates hugged her. She said no. Slowly, one by one, they each got up, hugging her and each other. Eventually, they ended up in a group of small circles comforting one another.

That particular day I decided that I did not need to participate in the physical comforting taking place. As I watched my students caring for one another, being vulnerable and open about the harsh realities of their experiences with shame, racism, and sexism, I decided that my participation was not necessary. They knew from the tears streaming down my face that I connected and empathized with what they were feeling. And I wanted them to experience the power of each other's strength without the awkwardness or additional layer of translation that can be present when one "in authority" participates. However, the moment demonstrated to me that my dedication to radical honesty matters. It assists in creating a classroom where students can engage in this type of emotional, transformative learning. The truth-telling and brave vulnerability the students and I participated in that semester, and in previous semesters, open up space for educational moments that chip away at cultures of silence and shame. In the next week, I was witness to powerful class presentations and read some of the most provocative final student papers I have ever recieved.

Disciplinary Burdens of Truth-In-Action

As an educator, my goal is to provide students with conceptual tools that allow them to analyze how power and privilege work, and to understand their positionalities within these systems. I believe my role in the classroom is twofold: first, to assist students in acquiring and developing critical thinking and writing skills and, second, to aid in creating a classroom environment and learning community that is empathetic and supportive during the difficult moments we all experience in the development of these skills. It is my belief that my pedagogical approach and philosophy come from a deep love and commitment to the disciplines and fields in which I was trained. For me, fields and disciplines such as ethnic studies, Africana studies, women and gender studies, and Black feminist anthropology were created to trouble oppressive systems of power and provide tools for changing the ways we experience our lives. These are research areas dedicated to connecting praxis and theory and founded on principles of truth-telling, truth-seeking, critique, and transformation. We are here to ask the tough questions and to do the critical work, which means at the basis of our radical honesty must be a commitment to see truth-telling turn into action. This action does not always have to produce large-scale political and social change. Sometimes the transformation is on an individual level and looks like growth in critical thinking or self-definition. But part of our disciplinary burden is that our work should actually do something. Radical honesty is not the only pedagogical practice that can successfully achieve these learning objectives. However, it is the practice I have found most useful in my classroom.

As a cultural anthropologist who sees life experience as a rich object of study, I train my students to use themselves as case studies, bringing their social and institutional experiences into the classroom in order to understand how such systems as racism and sexism operate. As a Black feminist scholar, I value life narrative as a complex and multilayered analytical tool and teach students that it is useful for both understanding and constructing theoretical knowledge. And as a lifelong student of Africana studies, I understand that there is an interrelated relationship between the classroom and the "community." My pedagogical choices result in class discussions that are usually lively. Sometimes they are tense with conflict, as students begin to become aware of the racialized, classed, gendered, sexualized, and nationalized meanings and ideologies embedded in the language they use; in the historical perspectives they have been taught; in their educational, familial, social, and political experiences; and in the popular cultural forms they consume and produce. Over time, however, students usually grow increasingly comfortable with disagreements that arise as they learn that conflict frequently indexes a moment of important learning and transformation. Creating an open and supportive environment is key to growing comfortable with this educational discomfort. Radical honesty encourages the professor and students to cultivate trust in one another and build a community where truth-telling and vulnerability are valued.

In the past, this type of critical, emotional, and transformative labor (particularly in Africana studies and Black feminist thought) actually demanded people put their minds and bodies on the line through protests, teach-ins, and hunger strikes. And if the increasing attention to physical and mental health crises among faculty throughout academic institutions is any indication, we must recognize that this labor continues to have a human cost. In 1989, Barbara Christian, the first Black woman to earn tenure at Berkeley, wrote:

> Many of us chose to be black feminist scholars because we believed ideas would help to effect social change and that the university, though imperfect, *was* a place where ideas are important. . . . We thought our presence in academia would be a galvanizing one. However, many of us were not prepared for the exclusive ways in which the categories of race, class, and gender are studied, the way the very definitions of these concepts imply that women of color do not exist. (Cited in Christian, 2009, p. 88)

The type of work many of us engage in, particularly in these fields, shines light on the problematic processes and racist and sexist systems that enable institutions like the contemporary academy to function. Although the academy's promise for change is powerful, there is a cost to engaging in various forms of radical honesty.

Subsequently, radical honesty, as a politics of truth, is a feminist transgression of the highest order—it demands that scholars of color acknowledge the failings of an academic system with which we remain engaged, recognize our vulnerabilities, and most importantly, share—with colleagues and students—our strategies for self-care and self-love. As we gain entrance to this privileged world and earn the right to access its substantial social and economic resources, we are required to be radically honest as we acknowledge the ways we are sometimes implicated in the oppressions we seek to destroy. This requires vigilance and self-awareness. It requires us to be authentic and emotional—to bring the person that lives outside the classroom to the person who is the professor, instead of drinking the Kool-Aid of emotional disconnection and neutralized "professionalism" often encouraged by university higher-ups. Radical honesty enables me to teach with anger, frustration, happiness, and joy, as I bring my full humanity to the classroom. As universities fetishize quantitative data on teaching outcomes, as classrooms grow cold and sterile in the context of increasingly corporatized academic spaces, and as university mission statements pronounce desires to be diverse but refuse to genuinely engage in the institutional changes and shifts that "real" diversity requires, radical honesty reminds us that professors are allowed to be human, and our emotional experiences are even more important in a time when our labor is becoming ever more disconnected from ourselves. It demands that we are honest—with ourselves, trusted colleagues, and our students—when we are experiencing and working through the shame that these disconnects can induce.

Radical honesty also demands a great deal from my students. It insists that they bring their best reflexive selves to the classroom. It requires vulnerability and a trusting relationship that is mutually constructed with their peers and me. There must be an inner hunger—a desire to figure out how the theories and debates we have in class influence their lives in the "real world" and how they can turn these knowledges—these multiple ways of knowing—into action. Furthermore, it asks that they work through the shame that sometimes plagues this critical time in their adult lives, as they learn about the world and decipher who they want to be.

Prominent researcher of shame and vulnerability, Brene Brown (2012), argued that if you put shame in a Petri dish, the only thing it needs to grow is silence. Radical honesty and a pedagogy of truth-telling in my writing and teaching remind me and my students that we are empowered to destroy the stronghold that racism and sexism in academic spaces attempt to have on us. I hope you will use it to do the same for you.

Notes

1.   I thank my colleague and friend Tami Navarro for suggesting the phrase "radical honesty," after years of listening to me discuss my strategies and methods for being honest with my students in the classroom.

2.   Although this chapter focuses on racialized and gendered assumptions, I hope that radical honesty will be a useful practice for interrogating sexualized, ability-related, religious, and classed assumptions that also influence how power operates in academic spaces.

3.   This student went on to graduate successfully from the institution and is making great strides toward progress in her emotional wellness. She, and her classmates, gave me permission to write about this powerful teaching moment, a moment I will never forget. They also read a draft of this chapter and provided detailed feedback, for which I am grateful. I hope I've made you proud, Class!

References

Brown, B. (2012, March). *Brene Brown: Listening to Shame* [Video file]. Retrieved from http://www.ted.com/talks/brene_brown_listening_to_shame?language=en

Christian, B. (2007). Camouflaging race and gender. In G. Bowles, M. G. Fabi, & A. Keizer (Eds.), *New black feminist criticism 1985–2000* (pp. 216–224). Champaign: University of Illinois Press. (Reprinted from *Representations,* Summer 1996, 55, pp. 120–128)

Christian, B. (2009). But who do you really belong to—black studies or women's studies? In S. M. James, F. S. Foster, & B. Guy-Sheftall (Eds.), *Still brave: The evolution of black women's studies* (pp. 86–91). New York: Feminist Press at City University of New York.

Du Bois, W. (1994). *Souls of black folk.* New York, NY: Dover. (Originally published in 1903)

Gutierrez y Muhs, G., Flores Niemann, Y., Gonzalez, C. G., & Harris, A. P. (Eds.). (2012). *Presumed incompetent: The intersections of race and class for women in academia.* Logan: Utah State University Press.

Harris-Perry, M. (2011). *Sister citizen: Shame, stereotypes, and black women in America.* New Haven, CT: Yale University Press.

White, D. G. (2008). *Telling histories: Black women historians in the ivory tower.* Chapel Hill: University of North Carolina Press.

5

USING THE BARNGA CARD GAME SIMULATION TO DEVELOP CROSS-CULTURAL THINKING AND EMPATHY

David S. Goldstein

Undergraduates often encounter materials about various cultures throughout a liberal studies curriculum, helping them understand *intellectually* the experiences and perspectives of individuals and groups different from themselves. Even more challenging, though, is providing them with *empathy* toward others, which is crucial to genuinely affect global society. I hope in this chapter to present the growing body of empirical evidence that demonstrates the pedagogical power of experiential learning, and of games and simulations in particular. In that context, I shall describe a popular but understudied classroom simulation game called Barnga, which leads students to deeper empathy for individuals with different cultural backgrounds, including those from other ethnic groups and from other nations. Moreover, the simulation game's ability to disorient all of the players in the classroom levels the playing field, negating the typical disadvantages experienced by many students of color, first-generation college students, and students from cultures other than mainstream American, thus exemplifying a form of inclusive pedagogy. This simple classroom exercise provides significant and lasting lessons for students to a degree that is difficult to match with other approaches.

Dewey and the Transformative Power of Experiential Education

Although scholars frequently cite education philosopher John Dewey (e.g., more than a thousand "hits" in both EBSCO's Academic Search Complete database and in ERIC, the education database) and despite a substantial emphasis on experiential education in K–12, many, if not most, higher education teachers continue to rely principally on static, passive modes of learning—having students read books and articles, listen to lectures, and so forth. A growing body of scholarship (e.g., Bergsteiner, Avery, & Neumann, 2010; Coker & Porter, 2015), however, has convincingly demonstrated that the principles propounded by Dewey (1938) in his seminal book *Experience and Education* do, indeed, lead to deep and transformative learning, as he claimed more than 70 years ago.

At the core of Dewey's (1938) theory lies his belief that individuals learn only when new experiences are connected to existing knowledge, thereby expanding what the individual knows and understands. Memorizing facts, therefore, does not constitute learning, because the facts, metaphorically speaking, float about the individual's mind without latching onto or altering his or her worldview. Genuine *learning* comes from *doing*. Dewey further observed that learning is *social:* "The principle that development of experience comes about through interaction means that education is essentially a social process" (p. 58). Therefore, rather than serve as a disseminator of knowledge, the teacher "loses the position of external boss or dictator but takes on that of leader of group activities" (p. 59). Dewey acknowledged that teachers must understand their students in order to provide educational group activities that are useful and appropriate for a particular group and, although less crucial in traditional, lecture-based courses, lead to far greater learning. When considering experiential learning activities, such as the Barnga simulation game, teachers must have a reasonably strong sense of their students in order to decide whether, how, and when to use such a simulation.

Building on Dewey's (1938) learner-centered orientation, proponents of inclusive pedagogy have advocated for a holistic conceptualization of students. Tuitt (2003), for example, noted that inclusive pedagogy practices "embrace the whole student in the learning process," recognizing that "students enter the classroom as personal, political, and intellectual beings" (p. 243). By foregrounding affective as well as cognitive dimensions of students' experiences, simulations like Barnga help students develop empathy, while increasing their sensitivity to diversity issues in the classroom and beyond.

Having students experience a real-world phenomenon (or, in this present case, a *simulation* of such a phenomenon) teaches them not just the present material, but also *how to learn*. Students who engage in experiential learning are more likely to become effective lifelong learners because of the critical thinking and reflection involved, which enables them to continually learn from new experiences. Especially when confronting issues of social justice through simulations, such reflective work exemplifies what Ladson-Billings (1995) called "critical consciousness," a key component of critical pedagogy claiming that "students must develop a broader sociopolitical consciousness that allows them to critique the cultural norms, values, mores, and institutions that produce and maintain social inequalities" (p. 162).

In his day, Dewey (1938) was imagining real-world immersion when he promoted experiential education—field trips, laboratory experiments, and other activities outside the classroom. Such excursions still certainly hold tremendous value, but are not always feasible or practical, and often are difficult to arrange, for financial, temporal, or fiscal reasons. Fortunately, we as contemporary educators worldwide can reproduce many of the benefits of experiences outside the classroom by simulating such experiences *in* the classroom, either instead of or in addition to field-based learning opportunities.

The Pedagogical Power of Games and Simulations

A growing body of empirical research (e.g., Feinstein, 2001; Keys & Biggs, 1990; Ruben, 1999; Wolfe & Crookall, 1998) has demonstrated the value of games in simulations across a broad variety of disciplines and educational settings. We know from cognitive science, for example, that humans—especially content-area novices as our students tend to be—hold tenaciously onto preconceptions and misconceptions that are difficult for teachers to dislodge (Bransford, Brown, & Cocking, 2000). Explaining to students why their thinking is flawed (e.g., in my courses on race, ethnicity, and immigration, students persist in believing that "race" has biological—not just socially constructed—meaning and significance) often has little effect. If students personally undergo a well-designed experience that affectively and cognitively undermines their preconceptions, however, they themselves can change their thinking. Such a paradigmatic shift is crucial for critical pedagogy because students must begin to relinquish mistaken preconceptions before internalizing a more socially just perspective. Genuine empathy and a more sophisticated and global worldview, in turn, enable students to navigate the diverse society and world they encounter.

Zawadzki, Shields, Danube, and Swim (2013), for instance, found that an experiential learning activity reduced undergraduate students' endorsement of sexist beliefs compared to a control group that received the same materials but without the experiential learning component:

WAGES [Workshop Activity for Gender Equity Simulations] participants (vs. both controls) reported less endorsement of sexist beliefs after completing the activity and/or at a follow-up 7–11 days. . . . Both studies demonstrated that these effects were attributable to WAGES providing more information, evoking less reactance, eliciting more empathy, and instilling more self-efficacy compared to the other conditions. (p. 75)

The simulation, then, led to better outcomes than an approach that did not involve a simulation.

Such dislodging of firmly held but problematic beliefs can disconcert students. When carefully designed, however, such experiences can be tremendously beneficial for student learning. In fact, pushing students out of their comfort zones—as long as teachers rely on emotionally circumscribed activities, such as vetted simulations and games that can keep students from plunging into a panic, which can hinder learning—is arguably the only way to lead students to new understanding. LePine, LePine, and Jackson (2004), for example, found that "stress associated with challenges in the learning environment had a positive relationship with learning performance and that stress associated with hindrances in the learning environment had a negative relationship with learning performance" (p. 883).

Classroom simulations, such as Barnga, which provide a more-or-less controlled experience for students, can be instrumental in that endeavor. The sense of discovery and the complex emotions around it, which characterize experiential learning, are crucial in both inclusive pedagogy (because no teacher can simply command students to feel compassion and empathy) and in critical pedagogy (because many social inequities and injustices, such as unearned privilege, tend by their very nature to be hidden). In my own experience using Barnga in a variety of courses with hundreds of students, I have witnessed widespread frustration, but it is nearly always accompanied by smiles, suggesting that students are not distressed beyond their ability to learn. The game seems to strike just the right level of anxiety. As Pugh (2014) put it,

An important condition of experiential learning is creating cognitive dissonance, where students experience discomfort when unrealized beliefs or attitudes conflict with new ideas and experiences. . . . Attending to this dissonance with the experiential learning cycle is necessary to transform that discomfort into learning. (p. 19)

Students' critical consciousness ultimately depends upon a disruption of their preconceptions and assumptions. Experiential simulations thereby help clear the intellectual and emotional path to the deeper understanding that characterizes critical pedagogy. Pugh further noted that simulations can be instrumental not only in overwriting misconceptions but also in fostering the values and ethics required for a particular realm of human endeavor, such as social justice and cultural competence in his field of social work.

Pugh's (2014) findings highlight a crucial aspect of how experiential learning can entail both inclusive pedagogy and critical pedagogy (which, of course, are not mutually exclusive). In Giroux's (1988) influential conception, critical pedagogy produces critical knowledge that

> would instruct students and teachers alike about their status as a group situated within a society with specific relations of domination and subordination [and would] help illuminate how such groups could develop a language and a discourse released from their own partially distorted cultural inheritance. (p. 8)

By eliminating the unearned privilege that accrues to students who are least alienated by academic English—most typically students who identify as White and middle class and for whom "standard" English is a familiar and native language—Barnga is inherently counterhegemonic and radically inclusive. It provides an opportunity for students to recognize what heretofore might have been an invisible subordination of, for example, native speakers of languages other than English, insofar as students who grew up speaking languages other than English fare just as well (or just as poorly) in Barnga as native speakers of English. By illuminating how perceived cultural outsiders are systemically treated, Barnga can begin modestly to deconstruct persistent "relations of domination and subordination" as Giroux (1988) advocated.

Similarly, Brynen (2014) described how classroom simulations can help teach complex ideas and processes in his field, international peacekeeping, which requires students to integrate theory and practice. Students in fields that depend upon deep self-awareness among practitioners, such as mental health counseling, can also benefit from experiential, play-based activities that foster cognitive and affective self-awareness (Bell, Limberg, Jacobson, & Super, 2014). Moreover, simulations can temper undergraduates' tendency to overestimate the impact they can have on international affairs. Schnurr, De Santo, and Green (2014) found that a role-play simulation increased students' appreciation of the complexity of international negotiation, which also undermined their oversimplified, idealistic assessment of their own negotiation skills:

> Many of the undergraduate students who gravitate toward the study of global environmental geography suffer from a well-meaning but idealistic

sense of their own abilities to change the world. As instructors, we feel it is our responsibility to nurture this idealism, but also to challenge it. The CBD [Convention on Biological Diversity] simulation forces students to confront the real-life realities of international negotiation: Such processes are often painstakingly slow, nuanced, and unpredictable. They fail more than they succeed. The dose of realism offered by the simulation might allow student idealism to be channeled more effectively. (p. 412)

Even *losing* at classroom games and simulations can thus be instructive if not transformative for students. In careers and in life, if we embrace reflection, we learn even from our mistakes and failures.

Simulations and games can help students master content knowledge as well. Dib and Adamo-Villani (2014), for example, found that playing a game about sustainability fostered civil engineering students' mastery of Leadership in Energy and Environmental Design (LEED) concepts and of sustainability concepts more broadly, particularly in their ability to *use* the knowledge procedurally, even though their "declarative knowledge" was no better than students in the control group, who did not play the game.

Unsurprisingly, computer-based games are becoming more prominent in higher education, especially in more developed nations. In a meta-analysis of 26 papers, Boyle and colleagues (2014) concluded:

The general thrust of the evidence [for the efficacy of computer-based games in student learning] was positive and there is reason to be optimistic about the potential of a games-based approach. The activities provided by games, animations and simulations provide active approaches to learning which are consistent with modern ideas about how best to teach research methods and statistics. (p. 9)

Other highly sophisticated, complex, and challenging skills cannot be practiced by students except through simulations. Stokell (2014), for example, discussed the difficulty of training general practice medical students in how to conduct effective and humane patient consultations: "Simulation is effective for learning practical skills, providing an opportunity to practice in an environment where mistakes are possible but no harm will come to the learners" (p. 167)—or to actual patients, one might add.

Other scholars are less sanguine about computer-based simulations and games. Referring positively to Barnga and another classroom simulation game, Starpower, both of which are in-person activities rather than computer based, Powers (2014) noted that most computer games are created with the goal of seducing individuals to continue playing rather than to learn. "By contrast," wrote Powers, "some excellent educational games . . . generate stimulating debriefings with the potential for significant personal insights for players" (pp. 14–15). The value of the surprise element inherent in games like Barnga makes them one-time experiences for students, but, fortunately, that single instance of playing such a game can generate significant learning.

Although the pedagogical purpose of classroom simulations and games is serious, the fact that most are fun to play should be appreciated. In fact, Lang (2014) pointed out that the element of fun is crucial to the effectiveness of games and simulations in fostering student learning:

> The games accomplish that [piquing students' interest] by establishing immediate goals that students can attain only by learning and applying course content. We often spend weeks throwing content at our students, and perhaps by the end of the semester we hope to have convinced them that what they have learned is relevant beyond the classroom. In a simulation game, by contrast, [they] are confronted immediately with the realization that what [they] are learning will help achieve a goal, one usually based on a real-world scenario. (p. B34)

The Barnga card game simulation capitalizes on all of these advantages. As a classroom-based exercise, it piques students' interest because it is fun and engaging, and, in line with inclusive pedagogy, it involves all students equally; it relies on but ultimately challenges students' preconceptions (what they think they already know); it fosters a new understanding of complex social phenomena such as intercultural clashes; it helps to nurture empathy and ethical attitudes and behavior; and it enables students to start improving intercultural understanding and communication without the potential for harm to themselves or others, reflecting the social justice principles of critical pedagogy.

Barnga: A Simulation Game on Cultural Clashes

Barnga, a classroom simulation that involves a simple card game, can initiate the critical analysis of structural discrimination as well as empathy for those who struggle with it. Designed by prolific simulation game designer Sivasailam "Thiagi" Thiagarajan, Barnga is available in a slim manual, written by Barbara Steinwachs and published by Intercultural Press for the International Society for Intercultural Education, Training and Research in 1990. (A special 25th anniversary edition was published in 2006.) The game can be played by nine or more individuals and typically takes 45 to 90 minutes of class time.

The simulation exercise itself is called Barnga, reportedly named after the West African town where Thiagarajan, working collaboratively with local colleagues, came face-to-face with a realization when his hosts suggested an illness remedy that seemed bizarre to him: "I had to understand and accept our cultural differences before we could function as a collaborative team" (as cited in Thiagarajan & Steinwachs, 1990, p. 5). He subsequently sought to create a game that simulated his own transformative, intercultural experience.

The Barnga simulation entails a simple card game called Five Tricks in which participants, seated in small groups around numbered tables, receive a modified deck of playing cards and a copy of the instructions for the game. The instructions are taken away after a few minutes, and the participants are instructed to refrain from any verbal or written communication. In mandated silence, the participants—students—in each group play the game for a few minutes, upon which the winners of each group move up a table and the losers move down a table. After several iterations, play stops. The participants seated at Table 1 at the end of play are declared the winners.

What students do not know until the game ends is that *the instructions given to each table differ slightly from one another,* leading to frustrating moments when the students—forbidden to speak or write—must navigate as best they can. In my Exploring American Culture: Race, Ethnicity, and Immigration course and in others in which I have used Barnga, I have watched students first shake their heads incredulously when they find their new tablemates to apparently be shockingly ignorant of the Five Tricks game's simple rules. As play proceeds, students become visibly more agitated, often gesticulating and sometimes rising to their feet. Meanwhile, students who remain at the same table gradually watch helplessly as newcomers impose new but inscrutable rules, some of which conflict with rules that other newcomers wish to foist upon the players.

The distress and bewilderment students experience then lead to the crucial debriefing session that immediately follows the game. During the debriefing, students reflecting upon their thoughts and feelings typically describe significant frustration with their inability to reconcile their perspective on the rules with those at other tables. They quickly make the connection, by analogy, to the often bewildering experience of navigating a different culture or subculture. Students begin to understand, for example, what it feels like to immigrate and how the greatest challenges are invisible, an experience that often gets corroborated by the international students in the class and those whose first language is not English (which, by the way, provides the opportunity for them to be seen by their peers in an asset-oriented rather than deficit-oriented perspective). This reflection exercise thus exemplifies the core principles of critical pedagogy in that it leads students to recognize—on not only a cognitive level but also an affective level—the otherwise easily ignored issues of social power, privilege, and inequity. Students cannot engage in social change, or even check their own unwitting participation in perpetuating such inequities, without the cognitive understanding of these issues and the empathy it takes to feel motivation.

Starting with my open-ended prompts—"What was that like? What was going on for you?"—students move quickly from how they feel to what they think. Invariably, students, on their own, express several simple but profound observations, tying the simulation to real-world social phenomena, with practically no intervention from me, such as the following (paraphrased):

- This is what it must feel like to come to the United States from another country, especially if one's native language is not English. Immigrants must have many challenges trying to understand the unspoken "rules" of American culture.
- I have more sympathy for people in the United States who seem afraid of immigrants and minority subcultures. I used to think they were just bigots; now I see that maybe they thought they knew the "rules," but the rules keep changing in unpredictable and unclear ways.
- It was really unfair that I started at Table 6 and had no chance of getting to the "winning" table. I felt resentment toward the people who had the unearned advantage of starting at a higher table than I did. That's kind of like real life.
- Some people cheated. I saw them whispering to each other when we were supposed to be silent. But because I was supposed to refrain from talking, too, I couldn't report them. It's like people in communities where they are afraid to call the police because their experience tells them that "authority" is not on their side.
- I have to admit I looked down at people at lower tables. I felt like they were there because they just didn't try as hard as I did to figure out the rules. I think that must be a common feeling among the "haves" in society.
- I felt like the rules at my starting table were the "right" ones. I know that every table felt the same way, but it was hard not to feel like our rules were "better" rather than just "different and equally valid." That made me think about how I feel like my values, which I incorporated from my family, my friends, my school, and my church, are somehow better than other people's values, but I think I have to overcome that attitude and try to appreciate other people's values. Those values come from *their* experiences and *their* "truths."
- I noticed that the men in the class seemed to get their way more often. They seemed more insistent that their way was the right way and came across as more aggressive.

No amount of reading or lectures could have elicited these observations from students, especially not in an hour. In student evaluations for this course and others in which I have used Barnga, respondents typically cited the Five Tricks game as the class activity that led to the greatest learning.

The importance of the debriefing session cannot be overstated. As Dewey (1938) stated, "No experience is educative that does not tend both to knowledge of more facts and entertaining of more ideas and to a better, a more orderly, arrangement of them" (p. 82). Brynen (2014) concurred, noting that "debriefing is an absolutely essential part of the simulation process. Indeed, considerable evidence suggests that it is during debrief that much of the actual learning takes place" (p. 535). What most impresses me, however, is that the Barnga simulation leads students to make those connections—a "better, a more orderly, arrangement" of ideas, in Dewey's words—with virtually no intervention on my part besides a careful facilitation of the debriefing session.

I do, however, help students recognize connections between their observations and other course materials with which they engage in subsequent class meetings, having found that I do have a crucial role in facilitating this post-simulation learning. Barzilai and Blau (2014) found that a simulation they used in a business course did not significantly improve students' performance on subsequent assessments, compared to a control group that did not participate in the simulation, concluding that "learners might not spontaneously create connections between the game concepts and disciplinary concepts" (p. 75). That work, however, is much more easily accomplished when students already have the cognitive and affective preparation for it, and I simply have found no more efficient and effective way of accomplishing that than the Barnga simulation exercise. The emotional response among students playing Barnga is particularly important because recognizing structural and institutional inequities is necessary but not sufficient to effect change; students must feel motivated to act. As Burbules and Berk (1999) noted, "Not only is the critical person adept at recognizing injustice but, for Critical Pedagogy, that person is also moved to change it" (pp. 50–51). They further stated:

> Critical Pedagogy would never find it sufficient to reform the habits of thought of thinkers, however effectively, without challenging and transforming the institutions, ideologies, and relations that engender distorted, oppressed thinking in the first place—not as an additional act beyond the pedagogical one, but as an inseparable part of it. (p. 52)

Because it takes place in a college classroom, Barnga is particularly effective in prompting students to project their feelings of injustice from the game to the institutional setting in which they experience those feelings—the university.

My experiences corroborate those described by Pittenger and Heimann (1998), who used Barnga in a business course:

> Before I launched into questions, I asked the participants to narrate their experiences. It was funny for the entire group to hear their classmates accuse each other of cheating, not learning the rules well, being too aggressive, not being aggressive enough, not being smart enough to figure out a simple card game and such. I used this discussion as a spring board to address the issues of the impact of cultural differences in building and managing effective interpersonal work relationships. I posed to them questions such as why or why you would not want to work with so and so, what happened to your feelings when someone behaved in an unexpected fashion from your point of reference, or how was your subsequent behavior impacted after experiencing someone's unexpected behavior? The issues of trust and betrayal were very predominant in this discussion which tied in nicely with the management of diversity—the topic I was covering in the class. The discussion can just as easily be tied in with cross-cultural communication and doing business in a global market. (p. 254)

Indeed, I would claim that the power of the Barnga simulation—especially the debriefing session afterward—stems from its ability to lead students to their own observations and conclusions. Most of us educators seem to be perpetually questing for ways to foster creative thinking and reflective practice for our students, believing wholeheartedly, for good reason, that these are lifelong learning skills that transfer to essentially any vocation or avocation that our students will undertake after college. Well-designed simulations like Barnga provide hands-on opportunities for students to build those intellectual skills as well as the motivation to do so.

The thinking that students do in the Barnga simulation, especially in the debriefing period, also pushes them up Bloom's Taxonomy (Figure 5.1) to what Bloom identified as higher (not "better," just more sophisticated) orders of thinking. As Benjamin Bloom's protégé Krathwohl (2002) explained:

> Bloom . . . believed [the Taxonomy] could serve as a
>
> * Common language about learning goals to facilitate communication across persons, subject matter, and grade levels;
> * Basis for determining for a particular course or curriculum the specific meaning of broad educational goals, such as those found in the currently prevalent national, state, and local standards;

Figure 5.1 Bloom's Taxonomy (revised).

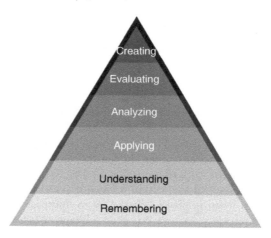

Note. Adapted from *The Assessment Cyberguide for Learning Goals and Outcomes* (2nd ed.), by T. Pusateri, J. Halonen, B. Hill, and M. McCarthy, 2009. Washington, DC: American Psychological Association.

- Means for determining the congruence of educational objectives, activities, and assessments in a unit, course, or curriculum; and
- Panorama of the range of educational possibilities against which the limited breadth and depth of any particular educational course or curriculum could be contrasted. (p. 212)

Increasingly, since Bloom and his colleagues first published the taxonomy of what he called the cognitive domain in 1956, teachers around the world have sought ways to provide their students with learning experiences at all levels of the taxonomy. Simulation games like Barnga constitute one effective tactic.

For instance, in the debriefing session, students typically move from foundational *knowledge* (remembering facts) to *understanding,* by analogies that they themselves create, some crucial concepts and their implications; next, to *applying* their content knowledge to other, real-world phenomena; then, to *analyzing* the implications of their observations in interpersonal, intercultural, and international relations and communication; and, finally, to *evaluating* their own and others' attitudes, preconceptions, and emotions.

Conclusion

Simulations and games can be effective in a practically unlimited range of courses, such as history, sociology, communication, journalism, health sciences, healing arts, political science, psychology, business, international relations, and social work. Students certainly can benefit from games and simulations like Barnga in cocurricular environments, such as residential life, clubs and organizations, athletics, and student government, but in a classroom setting, students are more likely to have the opportunity to link their experiences with the other materials with which they engage, in service to the course's learning goals and with the guidance of a content expert—the teacher. The beneficial results, however, in terms of student thinking and empathy, extend well beyond the classroom. Using simulations like Barnga can transform a classroom, and a campus as a whole, from a site of reinscribed, invisible privileges to one in which mutual understanding is valued and fostered. Even small steps toward such transformation of our classrooms and campuses, and the students studying therein, can pay greater dividends as students graduate and take their places as global citizens.

References

Barzilai, S., & Blau, I. (2014). Scaffolding game-based learning: Impact on learning achievements, perceived learning, and game experiences. *Computers & Education, 70,* 66–79.

Bell, H., Limberg, D., Jacobson, L., & Super, J. T. (2014). Enhancing self-awareness through creative experiential-learning play-based activities. *Journal of Creativity in Mental Health, 9,* 399–414. Retrieved from Academic Search Complete.

Bergsteiner, H., Avery, G. C., & Neumann, R. (2010). Kolb's experiential learning model: Critique from a modeling perspective. *Studies in Continuing Education, 32,* 29–46.

Boyle, E. A., MacArthur, E. W., Connolly, T. M., Hainey, T., Manea, M., Karki, A., & van Rosmalen, P. (2014). A narrative literature review of games, animations and simulations to teach research methods and statistics. *Computers & Education, 74,* 1–14.

Bransford, J. D., Brown, A. L., & Cocking, R. R. (2000). *How people learn: Brain, mind, experience, and school* (expanded ed.). Washington, DC: National Academies Press.

Brynen, R. (2014). Teaching about peace operations. *International Peacekeeping, 21,* 529–538.

Burbules, N. C., & Berk, R. (1999). Critical thinking and critical pedagogy: Relations, differences and limits. In T. S. Popkewitz & L. Fendler (Eds.), *Critical theories in education* (pp. 45–66). New York, NY: Routledge.

Coker, J. S., & Porter, D. J. (2015). Maximizing experiential learning for student success. *Change: The Magazine of Higher Learning, 47,* 66–72.

Dewey, J. (1938). *Experience and education.* New York, NY: Simon and Schuster.

Dib, H., & Adamo-Villani, N. (2014). Serious sustainability challenge game to promote teaching and learning of building sustainability. *Journal of Computing in Civil Engineering, 28*(5) (September–October), A4014007-1–A4014007-11.

Feinstein, A. H. (2001). An assessment of the effectiveness of simulation as an instructional system. *Journal of Hospitality and Tourism Research, 25*(4), 421–443.

Giroux, H. A. (1988). *Teachers as intellectuals: Toward a critical pedagogy of learning.* Westport, CT: Bergin & Garvey.

Keys, J. B., & Biggs, W. B. (1990). A review of business games. In J. W. Gentry (Ed.), *Guide to business gaming and experiential learning* (pp. 48–73). East Brunswick, NJ: Nichols/GP.

Krathwohl, D. R. (2002). A revision of Bloom's Taxonomy: An overview. *Theory Into Practice, 41* (Autumn), 212–218. Retrieved from EBSCO.

Ladson-Billings, G. (1995). But that's just good teaching! The case for culturally relevant pedagogy. *Theory Into Practice 34*(3), 159–165.

Lang, J. M. (2014, September 19). How students learn from games: A professor looks at the use of simulations in the classroom. *Chronicle of Higher Education, 61,* B34–B35.

LePine, J. A., LePine, M. A., & Jackson, C. L. (2004). Challenge and hindrance stress: Relationships with exhaustion, motivation to learn, and learning performance. *Journal of Applied Psychology, 89*(5), 883–891.

Pittenger, K. K., & Heimann, B. (1998). Barnga: A game on cultural clashes. *Developments in Business Simulation and Experiential Learning, 25,* 253–254.

Powers, R. B. (2014). How I became addicted to simulations and games. *Simulation & Gaming, 45,* 5–22.

Pugh, G. L. (2014). Revisiting the pink triangle exercise: An exploration of experiential learning in graduate social work education. *Journal of Teaching in Social Work, 34,* 17–28. Retrieved from EBSCO Academic Search Complete.

Pusateri, T., Halonen, J., Hill, B., & McCarthy, M. (2009). *The assessment cyberguide for learning goals and outcomes* (2nd ed.). Washington, DC: American Psychological Association.

Ruben, B. D. (1999). Simulations, games, and experience-based learning: The quest for a new paradigm for teaching and learning. *Simulation and Gaming, 30*(4), 498–505.

Schnurr, M. A., De Santo, E. M., & Green, A. D. (2014). What do students learn from a role-play simulation of an international negotiation? *Journal of Geography in Higher Education, 38,* 401–414.

Stokell, R. (2014). The use of a brief episode of experiential learning to develop the skills used by trainers in teaching consultation skills for GP specialty training (GPST). *Education for Primary Care, 25,* 166–167.

Thiagarajan, S., & Steinwachs, B. (1990). *Barnga: A simulation game on cultural clashes.* Yarmouth, ME: Intercultural Press.

Tuitt, F. (2003). Afterword: Realizing a more inclusive pedagogy. In A. Howell & F. A. Tuitt (Eds.), *Race and higher education: Rethinking pedagogy in diverse college classrooms* (pp. 243–268). Cambridge, MA: Harvard Educational Review.

Wolfe, J., & Crookall, D. (1998). Developing a scientific knowledge of simulation and gaming. *Simulation and Gaming, 29*(1), 7–19.

Zawadzki, M. J., Shields, S. A., Danube, C. L., & Swim, J. K. (2013). Reducing the endorsement of sexism using experiential learning: The Workshop Activity for Gender Equity Simulations (WAGES). *Psychology of Women Quarterly, 38,* 75–92.

6

CAMPUS RACIAL CLIMATE AND EXPERIENCES OF STUDENTS OF COLOR IN A MIDWESTERN COLLEGE

Kako Koshino

This study was initiated as an attempt to shed light on the problems that contributed to the high dropout rate of students of color in the Midwest—specifically, African American students. The study examined classroom practices, personal interactions, and the general climate of the college through the narratives of six African American students. The contexts of these practices, interactions, and college climates were also evaluated based on the students' experiences in the aspects of socialization, academic vigor, and motivation. The study also sought explanation for the low retention rate of students of color by considering the experiences of the study participants, the college culture, and the learning environment into which they were socialized.

The study drew on the theoretical frameworks of campus racial climate and culturally responsive teaching to illuminate the patterns of how the students were acclimated into college culture and infused into classroom norms and practices, where they started to have problems with respect to their socialization, motivation, and academics. In order to identify these problems, qualitative interviews were conducted with six African American students who attended the college for at least one year. This study was also conducted for the purpose of promoting awareness about the general pattern of students' experience. Hopefully, the findings from the study will help to encourage thoughtful and constructive dialogue around the experiences of African American students and students of color, provide focus on the role of the academic institution in developing inclusive and affirming campus culture, and clarify why awareness and responsiveness are needed to ensure the success of teaching and educational equity for students of color.

Previous Research on Campus Racial Climate

As the issue of race on college campuses drew more attention within the policy areas of higher education, it became paramount to develop a common framework to promote awareness about racial climate issues on campus. According to Hurtado, Milem, Clayton-Pedersen, and Allen (1998), historically, higher education leaders and institutions had not taken an active role in addressing existing issues and concerns about student interactions. As the importance of research on campus racial climate began to be recognized, however, its findings informed and enhanced policies and practices in education.

Previous studies on campus racial climate attested that discriminatory behavior, prejudice, and hostility against minority students have existed and are still a problem in U.S. colleges and universities today (Altbach & Lomotey, 1991; Farrell & Jones, 1988; Hurtado & Ruiz, 2012). Incidents of violence were reported and hostile environments existed where students of color were underrepresented in Midwestern predominantly White institutions (PWIs) (Farrell & Jones, 1988). According to Hurtado and Ruiz (2012), however, "nationally, many incidents of stereotyping or harassment go unreported. Only 13% of all students report racial incidents to a campus authority" (p. 2). The study also indicated that among other students of color, these discriminatory incidents were more likely to be reported by African American students in low-diversity institutions (a range of 0% to 20% representation of minority students). One out of two African American students also experienced some level of exclusion in schools with lower representation of minority students, whereas 67.2% and 66.7% of African American students reported incidents of verbal comments in low-diversity and moderately diverse colleges (a range of 21% to 35%), respectively. Additionally, offensive visual images were reported as a form of discrimination by 40% of African American students in low-diversity colleges and 41% in moderately diverse colleges.

Culturally Responsive Teaching

Culturally responsive teaching gained increasing momentum as U.S. schools diversified and educators became aware of the widening achievement gaps between majority and minority students. According to Gay (2010), culturally responsive teaching starts with the educators' recognition of the intimate relationship between culture and education, because "culture determines how we think, believe, and behave, and these, in turn, affect how we teach and learn" (p. 9). In her paraphrase of the work of Delgado-Gaitan and Trueba (1991), Gay described a culture as "a dynamic system of social values, cognitive codes, behavioral standards, worldviews, and beliefs used to give order and meaning to our own lives as well as the lives of others" (pp. 8–9). This means that educators must understand the context within which the students are educated and socialized, how information is presented and interpreted in the classroom, how different frames of reference are evaluated, and whether different values and needs are recognized and validated in every aspect of educational practices. Consequently, this means that achieving cultural competency requires educators' tireless efforts to understand the experiential world of students and to achieve "genuine commitment to educational equity, justice, and excellence for students of color" (Gay, 2010, p. 245).

Context and Method

The study was conducted at a Midwestern liberal arts college in a small town. The town had experienced a moderate increase in the Asian population, those claiming two or more races, and American Indians or Alaska natives alone, as well as a significant population increase in persons of Hispanic or Latino origin. The town's meatpacking industry drew immigrants and people of color, contributing to the increase of these groups in the community. The populations of Black or African American alone and White alone, however, decreased (Census Viewer, 2011–2012). Like the community, the college also became increasingly diversified because it recruited students from inner-city schools in the state's major cities.

According to the National Center for Education Statistics (2014b) the student population consisted of 66% White, 13% Black or African American, 11% Hispanic or Latino, 1% Asian, 1% American Indian or Alaska Native, 1% two or more races, 2% nonresident alien, and 5% race/ethnicity unknown. The percentage of full-time, first-time Black or African American students who began their studies in fall 2007 and received a bachelor's degree by fall 2013 was 44%, which is substantially lower than the rest of the groups.

Participants

The participants in the study consisted of a total of six African American students (three females and three males) who were enrolled in the college for at least one year at the time of the interviews. To collect narratives from a wide range of students about their experiences in classrooms and on campus, the participants were recruited according to the predetermined criteria set for this intentional purpose. The participating students were selected based on their academic standing, grades, number of years at the college, and their involvement in on-campus activities and student organizations. In this way, the participants were selected to address a wide range of backgrounds. The recruitment of these student participants was made possible by the assistance of a staff colleague who had access to the information on all enrolled students at the college. These students were also selected as participants because they had been in the college long enough to be immersed in and familiar with the college culture and would be able to provide insight into the college climate and classroom practices based on their experiences.

Procedures

The data collection started in January 2014 and ended in October 2014. Each interview lasted approximately one to two hours. Follow-up interviews were requested as needed, to which the participants responded well. Pseudonyms are used throughout this chapter in order to protect the identities of participants. The method of data collection consisted of semistructured interviews, observation, and reflective notes. The topics of the semistructured interviews ranged over the following areas of inquiry: why the participants chose to come to the college; how the participants imagined their college life before they arrived on campus; how the participants perceived classroom practice and interaction with professors and peers; how the participants perceived the motivating factors to remain and continue their studies at the college; how they perceived academic advising; and what expectations or requests the participants might have for the college. The standard coding process for qualitative research was used for the data analysis. First, the audiotaped interviews were transcribed. Then the researcher read the whole text to get a general sense of the interview. Next, the text was divided into segments, and codes were used to label each segment. Redundancy and overlap in the codes were reduced, and a small number of themes were generated as a result (Creswell, 2005, p. 238).

Researcher's Identity

The study was conducted by a female faculty member of Asian descent with an immigrant background, who became increasingly aware of and concerned about the students' pattern of disengagement and isolation, often followed by academic probation or dismissal from the college. The college's lack of support and appropriate intervention when the students were involved in culturally disaffirming and racially hostile situations appears in their observations and narratives. When the study was first initiated, the researcher was relatively new at the institution and unfamiliar with the college culture and had not been exposed to previous incidents or affairs that had significantly impacted the college. The lack of affiliation with these incidents made it easier for me, as the researcher, to assess the college climate, culture, and students' experiences without being tied to preexisting sentiment.

As I immersed myself into the college culture, I became familiar with the pattern of dropping out and discontinuing education by the students of color. I became increasingly concerned about this. I entered this research with awareness of my racial location as an Asian woman scholar in a PWI where faculty of color were severely underrepresented. As the research progressed, I actively reflected on how my race, ethnicity, and gender might impact interviews with the African American student participants. My continuous reflection allowed me to further deliberate on what it meant to conduct this research as a faculty woman of color while immersed in the experiential worlds of African American student participants and while conscious of the intersections and disjunctions of our raced experiences as an Asian woman and African American men and women. Irrespective of racial and experiential differences, there were common concerns and issues shared by being persons of color in the PWI, which served as a framework to understand general experiences of being members of underrepresented groups.

Findings

The following section describes the findings from the data gathered from the interviews conducted with each participant. Excerpts from the participants' narratives are highlighted.

Lack of Support, Expectations, and Faculty of Color

> Students who went to my high school went to historically Black colleges and universities. Coming here, I thought I was gonna get involved in a lot of events, do a lot of stuff just to have a vibrant life on campus and just meet more people from all racial backgrounds, but that didn't happen. I expected everyone would be more open to me. (Interview with Shaunee, October 16, 2014)

This excerpt is from an interview with Shaunee, an African American female student in her sophomore year. Most of the participants of this study had similar reasons for choosing the college and expectations for what the college could offer in terms of exposure to "diversity," because they were willing to immerse themselves in an environment where they would have contact with people from different cultural backgrounds. Like most of the other participants, Shaunee grew up in a racially homogeneous part of a populous urban area. Shaunee had certain expectations for how her college life would proceed, especially in regard to her interracial/cultural experiences. However, her hopes and expectations were met by the reality of an unwelcoming climate and uncollegiate responses. When Shaunee was in her freshman year, she would walk into her class and talk to her classmates, but the class did not respond to her well:

> I went to class every day and I said, "Hi, good morning everyone, how is everyone doing?" and no one would respond. . . . I gave up. Literally, every time I went to class [and said] good morning, how are you . . . silence, a big silence. We are all freshmen. We will be together if everyone stays for the next 4 years of our lives; shouldn't we be making it a little bit easier for everyone on campus? If you are not talking to me while I'm putting myself out there, it's worthless, you are wasting my energy and my positivity could go somewhere else and not here. (Interview with Shaunee, October 16, 2014)

These incidents in the classroom left her with a deep sense of disappointment and alienation. The reality of unresponsiveness and negative climate overshadowed what she might have perceived as realistic expectations with respect to peer interaction and the classroom climate.

Another student, Vantrice, had similar expectations to those of Shaunee, although she made her decision to go to the college against her mother's suggestion:

> My mom actually wanted me to go to an HBCU. I told her that I don't wanna go anywhere I am surrounded by nothing but myself, people just like me; I want to be involved with a mix of people because I feel like you grow more from that experience. So when I applied here, they told me there was an African American professor and I was thinking, cool, I got it! (Interview with Vantrice, February 24, 2014)

Once she arrived at the college, she learned that there was no African American professor in the math department. Her expectation of becoming friends with an African American professor was, therefore, shattered.

Concern regarding the underrepresentation of faculty of color was addressed by Thomas, a sophomore, as he contemplated the seriousness of the matter and how it might be affecting motivation for the academic success and emotional well-being of African American students:

Honestly, when you come in [to the classroom], you get a vibe, oh, there aren't many Black professors. . . . It's hard to explain really. To get more teachers [African Americans] would help. It definitely matters. You should and you better work hard regardless of the ethnicity of the professor, but if you wanna make learning for students easier, it just would help a lot. It has its sparks without having any negative effects. (Interview with Thomas, September 11, 2014)

Thomas and other African American students' concerns speak to the historical reality of underrepresentation of faculty of color at the college. According to the Integrated Postsecondary Education Data System for the National Center for Education Statistics (2014a), the college has consistently had a substantially low percentage of faculty of color over the past two decades. Between 1993 and 2011, the total number of faculty of color at the college varied between three and eight.

Underrepresentation of faculty of color in the U.S. academy has brought certain consequences. The findings from the study conducted by Turner, Myers, and Creswell (1999) revealed that a persistent trend of low percentages of tenure-track and tenured faculty of color was substantially affected by such factors as "the academic pipeline, market forces, and chilly climate problems" (p. 54). Although there is general agreement on the need for efforts to diversify faculty in higher education, any structural plan to effectively recruit, support, and retain faculty of color is rarely enforced in reality. Finding themselves the only person of color in the sea of whiteness, faculty of color are subject to "isolation and lack of mentoring" (Williams & Kirk, 2008, p. 23). As a result, the absence of effective recruitment, support, and retention causes early departure of faculty of color from academic institutions.

The patterned behavior of early departure of faculty of color contributed to the situation of racial disparity and cultural disconnection between the growing demographics of students of color and the overwhelming majority of White faculty. The minuscule number of faculty of color caused some serious cultural discontinuity and disconnection in the ways students of color were perceived and advised on campus and acculturated into faculty–student interactions and classroom practices.

Academic Advisement and Lack of Support

Sensible and appropriate academic advisement, coupled with cultural sensitivity and responsiveness, is crucial in order to ensure academic success and positive college experiences for students of color. Student success largely depends on whether or not students are appropriately advised and informed about the options available for planning their academic schedule. Affirming faculty–student relationships with the adviser are also important.

Abelina was not doing well in three of her classes in her freshman year, and she dropped these classes, which she later realized was not a sensible decision. Abelina reflected on her experience of working with her academic adviser:

> In my first year, when I was having some difficulty in classes and she [her former adviser] made this comment to me. She said, "You know, the difference between the college and high school is that if you don't like the class, you can drop it." Alright, within my first year, I dropped three classes. I didn't know the impact of these three drops had on me until I actually picked my major. (Interview with Abelina, January 24, 2014)

Abelina changed to a new academic adviser in her sophomore year. Her new adviser looked at her transcripts:

> He got my transcript and he was looking and said, "Okay, no D's and no F's, a lot of C's and lot of B's, but you have three withdraws." And I was like, "Oh, yeah." He was like, "You know, you have to make credits up, right?" He asked who was your adviser? I told him that it was Professor Smith. And he told me, "So she allowed you to drop three classes?" I had no idea of the impact of that on me in the future. If I had known that, I would not have let this happen and would not be in the position where I am today. . . . It hurt me, the fact that someone that I'm supposed to trust would give me this type of information. (Interview with Abelina, January 24, 2014)

When Abelina told her new academic adviser about the interaction that she had had with her previous adviser, she thought, "He saw it," but doubted he would try to engage in a dialogue with her about the nuanced exchange made between Abelina and her former adviser. Abelina continued:

> He was kind of baffled, but I can see him say that it was not her trying to be racist or prejudiced. But I do think that she carries that "I don't care" type of attitude, because I do believe that it was her job to say, "Abelina, I want you to know if you do drop this class, then the credit has to be fulfilled. So make sure you know you have to pick up another credit next semester." I am the first person in my family [to go] to college. I never knew the severity of any type of decisions that I will make and how it would affect me in the future. You don't know, and if you don't know, no one tells you, you are oblivious, and all of a sudden, you are slapped and you have to figure out the way to fix it now in such a limited time. (Interview with Abelina, January 24, 2014)

At the time of the interview, Abelina was trying to make up for the credits that she lost in her freshman year. According to her, her life thereafter was "not easy," and she was unsure if she could graduate within the time frame that her financial aid lasted. One day, she ran into her previous academic adviser at the financial aid office:

> When I was trying to work with a financial [aid] person, she was there. And when she saw me, she was kind of like in a shock because I hadn't seen her. It was kinda like, "Oh! Hi, how are you! Have you ever . . . did you . . . uh . . . did you figure out where you were gonna go?" and I'm like, "Yeah, I chose to be an English major." And she had this look on her face "Wow, I mean I can't believe you are still here." She had a very quiet way of dismissing me, as if she thought I was insignificant or I wasn't gonna come back anyway. (Interview with Abelina, January 24, 2014)

Overall, Abelina was disappointed and disheartened by the way her former adviser advised her. Her adviser's surprised look and reaction when she saw Abelina at the financial aid office seemed to suggest her low expectations and commitment level to cultivate affinity and develop a trustful relationship with Abelina.

Abelina's insight was also shared by Jadyn, who felt that professors seemed to have lower expectations for students of color: "I feel like some professors, not all professors, . . . expect students of color not to do as good as other students . . . probably African American students most because of the correlation to the high drop-out rates" (interview with Jadyn, November 11, 2014). According to Jadyn, many times he had awkward interactions with White professors, as if they were not sure exactly how they should talk or interact with him. These instances included when he approached professors after class to ask more about the detail of the assignment or whenever he attempted to talk to them casually outside the classroom. Jadyn grew up in a predominantly White neighborhood and went to schools that consisted of predominantly White students and teachers, and he always considered himself someone who was able to "connect to everyone across all races." His open-mindedness and willingness to expand his supportive network and cultivate affinity with his peers and professors from a wide range of racial and ethnic backgrounds, however, were met by unwillingness, awkwardness, and even a certain level of hostility subtly conveyed by White professors. Jadyn felt that they "tried to end the conversation as fast as possible, kind of like in one-word answers."

As exemplified from the experiences and the perceptions of Abelina and Jadyn, they sensed low expectations for students of color implicitly expressed by their professors. The students' thoughtful assertions offered an insider perspective of how students of color interpreted, made meaning of, and evaluated the sincerity and genuine intentions conveyed through their interactions with their professors. Lack of caring, cultural sensitivity, and support sensed from the professors resulted in students' loss of interest, vigor, and trust, which could have been promoted by a positive student–professor relationship.

Curriculum and Culturally Responsive Teaching

One problem for students of color that complicates their receiving education in a PWI is a curriculum that lacks cultural relevancy to their heritages, cultures, and experiential worlds. Given the racial disparities between teachers and students in U.S. schools, "there is a growing cultural and social distance between students and teachers that is creating an alarming schism in the instructional process" (Gay, 1993, p. 287).

Jessie talked about the systemic problem of Whiteness that "prepares some of us to be disaffected" because the Eurocentric values and perspectives embedded in the educational curriculum tended to prevent African American students and other students of color from access to meaningful learning opportunities:

> At a small college, a lot of students know each other and then, along with teachers, are predominantly White. I feel like that's just the norm for academic culture. It's like the academic culture is designed for White people to teach us. I think it's obvious even in curriculum. When I was younger, I learned about Christopher Columbus or I learned about American history. I was born in America and I am American, but I'm African American. I don't know anything about my people before the Atlantic slavery. (Interview with Jessie, October 17, 2014)

It was mainly his parents, the grade school he went to, and people with whom he interacted within his community where he learned about historically significant events relevant to African Americans, including the Rastafari movement and Harlem Renaissance. In this way, Jessie's home literacy practice helped him build his knowledge about what was culturally relevant and significant to him as an African American man. In school literacy practice, however, he noticed not only the lack of representation of prominent African Americans and persons of color in textbooks but also the way certain African Americans were presented and celebrated in U.S. mainstream education. As was the case in many U.S. schools, Black History Month was celebrated in February to honor and recognize the contributions made by African Americans, and "that's only when Black people matter," according to

Jessie. "It's like pacifying the people of color. Why does it not educate us all year round? Why not offer all year round?" (Interview with Jessie, October 17, 2014).

Jessie's concern about the lack of African American history may have resonated with the school district that he attended for his K–12 education. Beginning fall 2013, the school district decided to integrate Black history instruction into the curriculum year-round and system-wide, instead of celebrating Black History Month only in February. One of the crucial components that shapes culturally diverse curriculum, according to Gay (2010), is "to *regularly* provide students with more accurate cultural information about groups of color in order to fill knowledge voids and correct existing distortions" (p. 169). Subsequently, such cultural information "needs to be capable of facilitating many different kinds of learning—cognitive, affective, social, political, personal, and moral" (p. 169). This implies how crucial it is for educators to be able to understand the perspectives of students and seek ways to support and maximize students' potential and affirm their identities.

Thomas was both shocked and upset when his speech professor dismissed his classmate, an international student from the Middle East, when he gave a speech on "consciousness." The professor stopped the student in the middle of his speech to say it was going over the students' heads. She said, "It's too complex for them." Thomas further explained:

> It was gonna be a deep speech, but she stopped him, and I'm like, why did you stop him? Why did she do that? It makes you not even want to try. I mean, he would really like to share these ideas, but clearly you don't see them fit for everyone else. In his speech, he was going to do a good job. But many professors, teachers, and tutors shoot down ideas. . . . [If they do that,] how can we make the ideas realistic, make the ideas more beneficial to you or to others? They don't do that [try to develop new ideas and expand their worldviews], but they want us to be average. Professors don't shoot down an idea. . . . Don't do that. After the student finished his speech, she told the class, "He used a phrase 'politically incorrect.' Does everybody in class know what that means?" The international student was "booted" from the course by the professor immediately after the incident in class. (Interview with Thomas, September 11, 2014)

This incident made Thomas see how silencing was done. In this situation, the professor allowed different points of view to be invalidated. An incident like this also reflects the educator's lack of cultural competency and sensitivity—the crucial ability required when teaching in racially and ethnically diverse classrooms.

Toward a More Inclusive Learning Environment

The students experienced rejection, invalidation, and disconnection through their interactions with professors and peers, inside and outside the classroom, emerging from systemic faults. However, this study's data also indicated some of the positive and inclusive practices seen in faculty interaction with the students.

Shaunee talked about how some professors made her feel included and comfortable in the classroom. One instructor made everyone feel comfortable:

> I really appreciate this class because in my other classes, the teachers would come in and teach and leave. It's just silly things that he did. He was inclusive; he made sure that everyone had a chance to say something whether that meant for him to pick on someone or calling someone randomly. I liked that. He made us all feel validated. Even if someone said something wrong, he would say, "Uh, try to think about it in a different way" as opposed to say, "Oh no, that isn't right." (Interview with Shaunee, October 16, 2014)

Vantrice also shared how faculty mentoring might improve the campus climate for students of color when she discussed her new academic adviser: "She contacts me all the time regardless of my grades or what's going on, checks on me, and she became more of a friend. I can interact with her and talk about the school" (interview with Vantrice, February 24, 2014).

Gay (2010) asserted, "[It is crucial that] whether in formal classroom settings, advising situations, or informal contacts on and off campus, [educators ought] to be supportive and facilitative of students' intellectual, personal, social, ethnic, and cultural development" (p. 216).

Jessie also offered insights as to how the presence of African American professors on campus would positively impact African American students, increase overall cultural climate, and promote an inclusive learning environment on campus:

> I feel like just their [African American professors] presence here would really help African American students, because it's like when we come to school, most professors are White. When you see an African American professor, man, we also can do this as well, you know. It's like if you don't think it's possible, why would you even pursue that? It gives encouragement. (Interview with Jessie, October 17, 2014)

Overall, these students' insights imply what an inclusive learning environment would look like. Clearly, providing models for students of color by adding faculty and staff of color is of primary importance. However, increasing cultural sensitivity in White faculty and staff also helps support an inclusive environment with the potential for supportive mentoring relationships between students and faculty.

Conclusion

The problems addressed by the students, whether in adjustment to the college culture, motivation to go to class, development of genuine interest in what they were learning, or establishment of affinity and trustful relationships with professors and peers, implied a lack of crucial elements that shape the supportive system for students of color to feel affirmed and validated about their presence at the college. The ways that power operated within the PWI caused hierarchical divisions, access issues to information and resources, and gaps in knowledge and experience between the members of the majority society and those from historically oppressed communities. As seen in the response by Jessie, lack of culturally relevant instruction for students of color (i.e., the legacy inherited from their ancestral experiences and cultural meanings relevant to the community) raises an important question for the curriculum that lacks multiple perspectives.

As prospects change, it is recommended that colleges actively seek ways to connect to their students and engage in the reflective process of aligning culture, identity, and education by asking relevant questions: How does culture affect one's identity? How do you utilize students' cultural resources in your teaching? What are school and home literacy practices? How does teachers' awareness about students' culture affect students' motivation and their academic work?

The goals of this research were to raise awareness about and find links among experiences of students of color and the pattern of disengagement and isolation contributing to academic probation or dismissal and, consequently, early departure. By creating a space for educators to engage in a dialogue around more inclusive practices, this chapter attempts to engage readers in discussing the development of an academic environment where well-being and meaningful learning are ensured for students of color through equity-minded educational reforms.

References

Altbach, P. G., & Lomotey, K. (Eds.). (1991). *The racial crisis in American higher education.* Albany: State University of New York Press.

Census Viewer. (2011–2012). *Monmouth, Illinois population: Census 2010 and 2000 interactive map, demographics, statistics, quick facts* [Data set and map]. Retrieved from http://censusviewer.com/city/IL/Monmouth

Creswell, J. W. (2005). *Educational research: Planning, conducting, and evaluating quantitative and qualitative research.* Upper Saddle River, NJ: Pearson Education.

Delgado-Gaitan, C., & Trueba, H. (1991). *Crossing cultural borders: Education for immigrant families in America.* New York, NY: Falmer.

Farrell, W. C., Jr., & Jones, C. K. (1988). Recent racial incidents in higher education: A preliminary perspective. *Urban Review, 20*(3), 211–226.

Gay, G. (1993). Building cultural bridges: A bold proposal for teacher education. *Education and Urban Society, 25*(3), 285–299.

Gay, G. (2010). *Culturally responsive teaching: Theory, research, and practice.* New York, NY: Teachers College Press.

Hurtado, S., Milem, J. F., Clayton-Pedersen, A. R., & Allen, W. R. (1998). Enhancing campus climates for racial/ethnic diversity: Educational policy and practice. *Review of Higher Education, 21*(3), 279–302.

Hurtado, S., & Ruiz, A. (2012). *The climate for underrepresented groups and diversity on campus.* Los Angeles, CA: UCLA Higher Education Research Institute.

National Center for Education Statistics. (2014a). *IPEDS* [Data set]. Retrieved from http://nces.ed.gov/ipeds/datacenter

National Center for Education Statistics College Navigator. (2014b). *Monmouth College.* Retrieved from http://nces.ed.gov/collegenavigator/?q=Monmouth+College&s=IL&id=147341#enrolmt

Turner, C. S., Myers, S. L., Jr., & Creswell. J. W. (1999). Exploring underrepresentation: The case of faculty of color in the Midwest. *The Journal of Higher Education, 70*(1), 27–59.

Williams, S. E., & Kirk, A. (2008). Recruitment, retention, and promotion of minority faculty. *Department Chair, 19*(2), 23–25.

7

HUMANIZING PEDAGOGY FOR EXAMINATIONS OF RACE AND CULTURE IN TEACHER EDUCATION

Dorinda J. Carter Andrews and Bernadette M. Castillo

A s teacher educators, we know all too well the challenges of helping preservice teachers unlearn many of the firmly rooted biases, stereotypes, and assumptions they harbor that prohibit them from adequately meeting the academic, social, emotional, and psychological needs of students in schools. Many students enter our teacher education program with basic assumptions about teaching, learning, and schools that can ultimately prove harmful to students who are typically marginalized in educational settings. One commonly held assumption is that schools—and perhaps even students—are broken, and these future educators can be the fixers. Another assumption is that many poor students and students of color who are growing up in disenfranchised communities need someone to rescue them—to pull them out of the vestiges of where they call home; many of our preservice students believe they are those saviors. Perhaps one other commonly held belief that we encounter in our classrooms is the idea that teaching is primarily about imparting the subject-matter; preservice teachers believe they have expertise and their students are empty vessels waiting to be deposited into (Freire, 1970). Often our preservice students have given very little attention to the idea that nurturing the development of positive relationships with young people is essential to getting them to learn anything. They also have given little attention to understanding how their social identities (e.g., race, ethnicity, social class, gender, sexuality, and schooling background) inform their thoughts about teaching and learning and *who* they will be teaching.

As teacher educators, we have come to understand more deeply that we are in a continual process of engaging our preservice students in deconstructing the colonized mind-sets they bring to our learning spaces that lead them to harbor deficit orientations about their future students. These mind-sets are dehumanizing in that many of our preservice students bring oppressive and hegemonic learned ideals about culturally diverse students and schools to their teacher education classes, with few or no tools for engaging or embodying more liberating and emancipatory ideals and practices.

In the same way that Woodson (1933) posited that African Americans had been "mis-educated" about their cultural history through the education system, we believe the system has failed to adequately educate future teachers about race, culture, and power, rendering them *colorblind* (unwilling to acknowledge race and/or ethnicity as significant to teaching and learning and to student access and outcomes), *colormute* (unwilling/unable to engage in conversations about race and ethnicity in schools),[1] and *culturally incompetent*[2] in terms of their consciousness about the roles of power and privilege in teaching and learning. Thus, we engage our students in examining "the social, cultural, economic, political and historical knowledge that informs how societies and schools operate" (Brown, 2013, p. 319). In our teacher education classroom, we strive to model humanizing pedagogy for them, understanding that through this process, we all become more fully human (Freire, 1970); further, we want our students to embody and enact humanizing pedagogies and practices in their future classrooms.

Humanizing Pedagogy

A humanizing pedagogy is a process of *becoming* for teacher educators and their students. The work of Freire (1970), Bartolomé (1994), Fanon (2004), and others continues to inspire conceptual and empirical arguments regarding the need for all educators to develop and maintain mind-sets and practices that foster learning environments where the needs of the whole student are considered; power is shared by students and instructors; and students' background knowledge, culture, and life experiences are valued (del Carmen Salazar, 2013). The pedagogies and practices not only are liberating for instructors and students but also help students realize and enact more fully human identities. These humanizing pedagogies and practices foster inclusion in the classroom and can lead to transformative learning experiences that heighten students' critical consciousness and understanding of the negative systemic effects of bias and discrimination in the lives of historically marginalized people across the globe.

In her analysis of the literature, del Carmen Salazar (2013) identified key tenets of the process of humanization through a humanizing pedagogy. In this chapter, we aim to describe our teaching practices that operationalize two of the theoretical tenets she described: First, the journey for humanization is an individual and collective effort toward critical consciousness, and, second, critical reflection can lead to actions focused on challenging inequitable structures. We draw from del Carmen Salazar's discussion of the principles and practices of humanizing pedagogy to describe our attempts at humanizing the learning space for our students and fostering students' development of critical consciousness for their work as future educators. We argue that developing critical consciousness and challenging inequity in the educational system are central to preservice teachers' enacting culturally relevant and responsive pedagogies in classrooms (Gay, 2010; Ladson-Billings, 2009). Our use of humanizing pedagogy in teacher education is a project of humanization for the instructor *and* students. Here we discuss specific practices we use to enact humanizing pedagogy. Those practices include building trusting and caring relationships and developing students' critical consciousness. We posit that building trusting and caring relationships with our students is the first step toward promoting their heightened critical consciousness. Relationships are a key element to cultivating classroom environments where students can engage in critical dialogues that not only raise their awareness of societal and educational injustices but also give them the tools to challenge inequity in the educational system, thus advancing the pursuit of humanization. Next, we define *critical consciousness* as a concept and active state in challenging inequity in the educational system. We then provide an overview of the undergraduate teacher education course in which we strive to enact humanizing pedagogy and our reflections on our collective experiences in this journey.

Critical Consciousness and Challenging Inequity

Critical consciousness is "learning to perceive social, political, and economic contradictions, and to take action against the oppressive elements of reality" (Freire, 1970, p. 17). Scholars posit that critical consciousness is necessary for a humanizing pedagogy, because the process through which it is developed allows instructors and students to critically evaluate their own beliefs and engage in dialogue that challenges what cultural codes are considered normal in the larger society and become perpetuated in K–12 schools. For instance, a critically conscious K–12 educator might raise questions about how current policies and procedures unintentionally serve as gatekeeping mechanisms for allowing access to advanced placement and college preparatory courses. A critically conscious K–12 educator might also raise questions in data dialogue meetings that strongly suggest colleagues consider disaggregation of discipline referral and suspension data by subgroups (e.g., race/ethnicity, gender, and social class) in order to have a more accurate reading of what interventions are needed and how they need to be implemented to address discipline gaps. By critiquing societal and educational inequity, privilege, power, and oppression—and one's own social status—our teacher education students develop new lenses through which to understand how to improve education for historically marginalized youth. We know that preservice teachers should critically examine how policies and practices dehumanize students, parents, and communities. They must also challenge the role of educational institutions in perpetuating oppression as well as their own participation in such processes.

Employing a Humanizing Pedagogy: Deconstructing Our Teaching

Human Diversity, Power, and Opportunity in Social Institutions is a required course for all undergraduate students in the teacher education program. The class focuses on the effects of social inequalities on education within a U.S. context. Students examine how socially constructed categories, such as race, gender, sexual orientation, and social class, privilege some individuals and groups and marginalize others in the broad context of education. We ask students to consider several overarching questions, including the following:

1. In what ways do schools create, perpetuate, and exacerbate social inequality?
2. How do systems of privilege impact individuals' and groups' opportunities for social and economic mobility?
3. Why is the acquisition of "school knowledge" easier for some students and more difficult for others?

A focus on the relationships among culture, difference, and power is foundational to understanding the course competencies. The key themes that guide the course include: (a) identity and positionality; (b) opportunity and systems of power and privilege; (c) social, political, and historical contexts; and (d) structural and organizational issues in schooling. Students consider their own positionality with respect to their multiple identities and how those identities shape their views and assumptions about education in the United States. In an effort to connect theory with practice, students engage in a semester-long service-learning inquiry in a local public school or community-based organization. Placements are typically in urban communities but can sometimes be in suburban communities.

The design of the course is meant to provide a space for future teachers to develop a strong foundation of knowledge about social inequality as well as build their capacity to critically analyze their assumptions about schooling based on aspects of their own identities and those of future students. The materials, field experience, and assignments for the course are grounded in analyzing power relations that exist within systems of schooling in the United States. The nature of the course encourages difficult conversations, and we ask students to learn to sit with discomfort in some of the discussions. We assure our students that our classrooms are safe spaces *and* courageous spaces. In order to facilitate a readiness to engage in difficult conversations, it is necessary to structure the course in a way that simultaneously fosters community and risk-taking. We accomplish this goal through classroom exercises and assignments. Although there is a team of instructors, we design our individual courses from agreed-upon content, and we are able to utilize a bank of assignments designed specifically for the course. Each instructor approaches the content, assignments, and classroom practices in a unique way, providing the freedom to tweak assignments and enact individual classroom practices.

Although the teaching of the course remains an independent endeavor, there is a mechanism for support. The instructors of the course meet regularly throughout the semester to discuss teaching strategy, content, and relevant connection to current events and issues that arise during the semester. This structure allows instructors to examine their own experiences in light of others'; instructors often bring teaching dilemmas to the group where they can receive constructive feedback. Often, instructors encounter the same types of predicaments. This chapter is an extension of the conversation between two instructors, as we simultaneously examine our personal experiences to better understand the ways we utilize and promote humanizing pedagogies within our teaching practices as part of a broader striving toward humanization. What follows is a discussion of how humanizing pedagogy informs our teaching and its impact on student learning and praxis. The next two sections provide insight into our individual choices and dilemmas as instructors working toward the same goal.

As we guide our students through classroom exercises and content, we must consider our own backgrounds as instructors along with those of our students. If we wish to recognize our students as intellectual, emotional, and spiritual individuals who possess particular experiences, then we must reflect upon our own as we situate ourselves as instructors within the classroom. As women of color, we encounter other considerations when engaging with our predominantly White students. Following, we provide our personal backgrounds as a way to shed light on our unique circumstances and challenges, as well as a brief narrative about our experiences enacting humanizing pedagogy in the teacher education classroom.

Dorinda

I am an African American female educated in the southern part of the United States during the time of voluntary busing as part of school desegregation efforts. I grew up in a racially desegregated suburban community, and I attended predominantly White schools for middle and high school. My experiences navigating these White spaces as a high-performing student of color had their own share of privileges and challenges. Thus, I am well aware of how my race and gender shaped my schooling experiences and my understandings of racism and sexism. My K–12 teaching experiences span math classrooms in urban and suburban public schools. I have taught in predominantly Black suburban communities, predominantly White suburban communities, and inner-city charter schools. In all of these spaces, I worked hard to ensure that low-income and Black and Brown youth had access to the same opportunities as my economically advantaged and White students. I bring to the teacher education classroom my experiences in the daily struggles as a teacher trying to enact a culturally responsive and humanizing pedagogy in a high-stakes and often racially hostile educational climate.

I also bring to the teacher education classroom the understanding that I, too, was socialized to believe that if I just worked hard and always did my best in school, I would succeed. The myth of meritocracy is so ingrained in the fabric of U.S. society that even though I knew racism, sexism, and White privilege could be potential barriers to my upward mobility, I sometimes attributed my successes to my work ethic (not considering my strong support network) and the failure of my peers to their inability to work hard enough or play by the rules. As an adolescent, I was too naïve to understand that no matter how hard some students worked, they would be systematically disadvantaged in school based on their social positioning. I also did not fully realize that there were certain social and cultural codes that one needed to acquire to "do school" in a way that led to a White-constructed success. Although I had acquired those codes early on, many of my same-race peers had not. This epiphany in my early 20s provided me greater insight into how hard I have to work today to deconstruct the meritocracy myth with my preservice teachers.

For the last 10 years, I have taught an urban-focused section of Human Diversity, Power, and Opportunity in Social Insitutions. This means that freshman and sophomore students who are interested in teaching in urban schools are enrolled in my section of the course. In the early years, my classes were almost equally populated with African American students and White students. Over time (due to changes in teacher education enrollment patterns and access to scholarship funding for certain students), my student population has become predominantly White. In fall 2006, the student class composition was 13 African Americans, 1 Latina, 1 biracial, and 7 Whites. In fall 2014, there were 15 students in my class: 3 African Americans, 2 Latinas, 1 Asian American, and 9 Whites. Although many of my students of color over the years had been educated in K–12 urban, public settings, they had very limited experiences with analyzing their social identities and considering how they had been privileged or disadvantaged in school. I was quick to assume that only my White students would come to the learning space with low critical consciousness about their social identities. At the same time that my Black students' narratives needed to be heard in the learning space to deconstruct single stories that had been constructed about their identity group, they had to examine the deficit mind-sets that they also embodied about culturally diverse youth as well as enhance their understandings of systems of dominance and oppression.

Practices
Because building trusting and caring relationships is a central practice of a humanizing pedagogy, I utilize several strategies early in the course to establish these relationships. Although students are searching for safety in the classroom, I want them to understand that my construction of a safe learning space is one that is inherently risky and uncomfortable (Lynn, 1999). It is a courageous space in that the pedagogy I enact tackles racial power and other systems of oppression. In the first four class sessions, I use several community-building exercises to help students begin thinking about how our cultural differences make us unique as a learning community and also to begin their thinking about the similarities and differences in our life and schooling experiences.

A first-day exercise called "K-W-L-H" allows students to consider what they think they already know (K) about human diversity, power, and opportunity in schools and what (W) they want to learn about these topics. At the end of the semester, I have them reflect on what they learned (L) about these topics in schools and how (H) they will use what they have learned to enact positive change moving forward. Students engage in a pair-and-share with a partner about their K and W response, and then we have a large-group discussion about what we already know as a community and what we hope to learn. This activity is significant to students' creating a big picture view of the array of knowledge that already exists in our learning community about race, culture, and difference and where there is commonality in shared goals for what individuals want to learn and considerations for learning outcomes that one might not have thought about. It is important to develop trust with my students. They must understand that I affirm the knowledge they bring to the learning space about societal and school inequities, and I see them as possessing cultural assets. I also have students think about the importance of participating in the activity. I see part of my role enacting humanizing pedagogy as being transparent with my students about the fact that I strive to model the types of practices that I hope they utilize in their future classrooms. Every activity is purposed to question students' understandings of normality and privilege, promote marginalized voices and experiences, engage in critical self-reflection, counter our inclinations to engage in "othering" individuals and groups, and consider how we can be transformative participants in the struggle for educational equity.

An activity for the second day of class focuses on students' examination of social identity markers and the salience to their overall self-perception. The Diversity Toss (Nieto, 2004) requires students to engage in a simulated process of giving up three social identities (race, gender, religion, name, or other important feature of their identity) and having a fourth identity taken away from them, leaving them with only one identity marker. We engage in a debrief conversation over what identities students found easy to give up and others that students did not want to give up. We also discuss how it felt to have an identity taken by a classmate without their permission. I then have students consider how the activity relates to the real-world experiences of students in K–12 classrooms and how institutional structures take identity away (Nieto, 2004).

Through the dialogues and discussions that occur, these activities help students begin to practice risk-taking in the courageous learning space by considering how they have been simultaneously privileged and disadvantaged, how others might view the significance of a social identity differently from them, and the application of these understandings to systemic privilege and oppression of students in schools.

Assignments

As a way to continue my students' engagement with readings and class discussions that build critical consciousness and require risk-taking in the learning space, I use writing assignments that further their examination of culture, difference, and power in society and schools. Because the class is primarily writing based, my assignments pose critical questions to students that help them connect theory from the readings and lectures, insights from risk dialogues in class, and practice from their field placements. The first major writing assignment, a cultural autobiography, requires students to compose a miniautobiography in which they reflect on the ways two social identity markers (e.g., race, ethnicity, language, gender, social class, or sexuality) have informed their school experiences and development of self and how school has shaped the development of the two aspects of their identity. This assignment is split into two parts. In Part 1, students write the paper during the first 3 weeks of class and then are asked to complete the assignment again in week 11. In Part 2 of the assignment, students are asked to explain if they have decided to write about different identity markers than those in Part 1 and, if so, what informed the shift in their thinking. In many cases, the White students will write about race in Part 2, where they shied away from doing so in Part 1. More commonly, White students will write about gender, social class, and cognitive ability as markers of privilege and disadvantage in Part 1. Many students attribute their change in perspectives on what identity marker to write about to the readings, videos, and class discussions about White privilege, racism, and multiple forms of privilege and oppression. Engaging in risk-taking in the course and hearing the narratives of their colleagues of color often help them realize the significance of breaking the silence around race talk in order to work toward more fully human identities and see their future students as more fully human. The cultural autobiography writing assignment in two parts allows students to examine how their social identity shapes their mind-sets about culturally diverse students and what aspects of their ideas and practices need to be transformed. This writing assignment, along with several others in the course, helps students develop their critical consciousness about educational inequity and work toward becoming the type of educators who will transform systems and policies for positive development of all youth.

One additional way that I enact a humanizing pedagogy in the teacher education classroom is through engaging students in praxis (Freire, 1970). In order to help students deconstruct their misconstrued notions of high-need schools and communities and students of color, it is important for them to establish meaningful relationships with K–12 students in high-need schools. Thus, in my class, students have a 10-week field placement in an urban school, working with individuals or small groups of students in a classroom setting or community-based organization. This allows my students to connect what they are learning in the teacher education classroom to the everyday benefits and challenges of teaching and learning in K–12 schools. It is my responsibility as the instructor to create opportunities for them to reflect in oral and written form about how they make meaning about their experiences in these schools. A danger in placing students in K–12 schools where teaching might not be exemplary, student behavior might not always be positive, and educational resources are scarce is that they walk away with their negative stereotypes and assumptions reinforced about culturally diverse youth. It is not the case that all placements are negatively reinforcing, yet part of my project of humanization is to help my students see the youth as winners and their communities as sites of richness and understand how institutional and systemic structures oppress and thwart students' opportunities for quality educational experiences. The dialogical space in my classes is one where I have to be continually examining what types of questions to explore with students and how to help them apply theoretical and empirical knowledge to practical schooling situations in ways that develop their critical consciousness for enacting change as professionals. Journaling weekly, engaging in individual interviews, conducting classroom observations, and working one-on-one with students help to complicate what my students often make simple and humanize culturally diverse students for them (Carter Andrews, 2009).

Humanization of the teacher education classroom learning space requires engaging students in critical dialogues that problematize reality (del Carmen Salazar, 2013). Community-building activities, self-reflective writing assignments, and engaging in praxis help me use the reality, history, and perspectives of my students as integral parts of their learning process to more critically understand the realities, histories, and perspectives of culturally diverse youth. My students must develop a knowledge base of teaching that is rooted in critical multicultural perspectives and that holds the goal of societal transformation; my modeling of humanizing pedagogy and practices hopefully moves them toward these goals. This process is not without its own dilemmas. I find myself caught between the goals of not wanting to indoctrinate students and wanting to indoctrinate them. In my attempts to be culturally inclusive in my classroom by striving to give voice to all students, there are ideological perspectives that I must exclude. Sometimes when my students verbalize their comments in discussions or write them in papers, the ideas represent deficit orientations about individuals and groups. Certain remarks further dehumanize K–12 students and their families. It is necessary that I challenge preservice teachers' assumptions in ways that do not alienate them, yet push them to consider alternative perspectives they may not have previously considered.

Bernadette

My path to teaching an undergraduate course is filled with experience as a public school educator for more than 15 years. I have pragmatic experience as an English teacher where I instructed middle and high school students. I possess firsthand knowledge of the everyday struggles of a teacher, yet my practical awareness did not help me understand the systemic issues that led to many of the struggles in my classroom.

My decision to leave my teaching career and return to graduate school was a conscious effort to learn about the systemic structures in place that continue to oppress my students. I felt my years of experience in public education as a classroom teacher and administrator validated my attempts to discuss these issues with my students. I could rely on knowledge of the course material as well as my classroom experiences to propel me forward in teaching this course. However, there were aspects of my own identity that I also had to consider.

My ethnicity as a Latina from the Southwest is an important aspect of my identity, especially in a Midwest state where Latinos comprise less than 5% of the population (United States Census Bureau, 2013). When I stand in front of my classroom at the university, I am fully aware of my racial and ethnic identity, gender, and position of power as the instructor. My students and I all come to the course with a set of experiences and knowledge about educational practices in the United States. Yet my students rely heavily on their personal experiences as a way to generalize the broad systems of education. Often my students enter the course with meritocratic ideals of education; many had positive experiences and feel those same experiences are available to most students in schools. The practice of schooling is not politically neutral, nor is the act of teaching (Bartolomé, 1994). As their instructor, I must enact pedagogies and introduce course materials that help to expand their view of education and assist them to begin developing a critical consciousness about the system of education.

Although each semester I taught the course yielded different combinations of students, the overall majority of students in each section identified as White and female. My most recent course section serves as an example of the composition of students. Out of 21 students, there were 2 international students from Asian countries, 1 identified as African American, and 1 identified as biracial; the remaining 17 students identified as White. There were 3 males in the course, all of whom identified as White. Although these numbers fluctuate slightly throughout each semester, they are representative of my typical class.

Practices

My first step toward enacting a humanizing pedagogy is to provide experiences that create a sense of community within the classroom. This task is accomplished by consciously constructing team-building exercises that encourage students to share aspects of their lives with each other. We spend the first few classes engaging in icebreakers, where students share details about where they grew up, family background, and school experiences. I also participate in these exercises, because I want to establish myself as a part of the community where students can see me as a facilitator and active participant.

Another method I enact is to establish base groups; students are assigned to groups of three to four students. These groups form the base of discussions over content and topics in the course. Although it is important that students have an opportunity to contemplate the materials with others in the course, they begin to form trust in their groups, which can help them feel more confident about sharing their ideas with the larger group. When I form the groups, there are several factors I take into consideration before I assign students. I consider year in the program, cultural background, race, and gender. I usually establish these groups after the first 2 weeks of class because it allows me at least a short time to get to know the students. The base groups serve two purposes. First, they facilitate voice from all students. Often, students will share comments, personal stories, and reactions to text that they may be uncomfortable sharing with the entire group. Second, the groups encourage community practices. Group members are asked to encourage all voices and support their peers in sharing ideas with the entire group. Building trust is an essential component on the path toward critical consciousness. In order for students to explore their own ideas and thoughts more fully, they must be willing to engage with others who will extend and challenge their beliefs.

Assignments

The first major writing assignment of the course is a cultural autobiography where students must analyze aspects of their identity in relation to their past educational experience. Specifically, students are directed to consider the following:

> In this assignment, you will compose a miniautobiography in which you reflect on your own identity and the ways in which social identity markers (e.g., social class, race, ethnicity, language, ability, gender, and sexual orientation) informed your schooling experiences and development of self (i.e., how you think about yourself in the world). It is impossible for you to write a complete story about your identity as a whole; therefore, you should **choose two aspects** of your identity to discuss.

There are three main purposes for this assignment:

1. Prompt students to critically view their educational experiences
2. Focus on aspects of specific identities and explore advantages and disadvantages in regard to schooling experiences
3. Integrate course concepts and theories connected to the readings

Another role of the assignment is to help students expand on their personal notions of education. Although the focus is on personal experience, students are required to make connections—specifically, to privilege and disadvantage. For many students, this is the first time they have had to critically analyze their experiences instead of making broad generalizations. One of my students reflected on her privileges:

> Before, I never gave much thought to my social identities, and did not view them as important aspects of my life. Now I realize that they are essential to my "puzzle" because they have shaped the opportunities and privileges I have been granted.

It is also an important exercise because students begin to realize that their personal experience is not indicative of every person's experience. One student reflected on the opportunities afforded to students:

> Having the opportunity to participate in extracurricular activities created an enriched learning environment for me, and enabled me to learn to balance a schedule, stay organized, work in teams, and it allowed me to stay in shape and make friends. Not all students are granted those opportunities, solely due to their socioeconomic standing. Children from lower-income families tended to struggle more in my school than children from middle class families, because they had fewer resources and less support at home. The educational community that was my public school system was set up with specific resources that were geared toward students of similar circumstance to mine, since the majority of students within that community fit into the middle class group. Since I didn't have to experience too many overwhelming struggles at home, and I fit the middle class mold, I felt catered to in school, and didn't have very many worries. However, some students had the burden of having little money, and had to worry about issues like free or reduced price lunches, and those sorts of issues can really distract a student from their studies.

Both examples show how students begin to complicate their understandings about their personal experiences in education. Students draw from their lived experiences to make connections to broader issues within the system of education. However, this is only the first step toward developing critical consciousness, and we must continue to challenge students' preconceived notions about education. The student in the second quote makes some important inferences about opportunities that are available for certain students, but not others. However, she makes some broad generalizations that students who are from lower-income families have less support at home. It is important that we question this idea of support and what that looks like for different families. We must find ways for students to further problematize ideas they have about the system of education and the opportunities it affords to students. This is a difficult task, and I must continue to challenge my own ideas and assumptions about my students.

This work is not without its tensions and dilemmas. As the instructor of the course, I must constantly step back and evaluate my pedagogies. Bartolomé (1994) warned us of the danger of "blind adoption" of classroom strategies without critical reflection. I implement a strategy of incorporating base groups into my teaching, but it is a practice I must evaluate each time I approach the course with a new set of students. In my most recent instruction of the course, I had to face the realization that this may not be the best strategy for all of my students. After class one day, one of my students stayed to talk with me. She proceeded to ask me if she could change to a different base group. I was surprised because this was the first time a student had made this request. She was visibly distressed as she confided in me that she did not feel comfortable in her group and could not express herself to her classmates. I immediately tried to recall the group's interactions. What did I miss? I had to make a decision about whether or not I would grant her request. After much deliberation with my colleagues over logistics, strategies, and implications, I decided to keep the student in her group. I felt it was important to address the situation with the classroom community, and I asked them to devise strategies to make all members comfortable to share their perspectives. But honestly, I utilized the base groups much less than I had in the past after her request. After monitoring her group more closely and noting little change in the interaction, I decided to change the configuration of the groups overall. I had to come to the realization that a strategy I heavily relied on was not conducive to the learning environment in this class. In this instance, trust had not been established, and students were not sharing their ideas. Without this trust, students were not making strides toward critical consciousness that could help them to approach challenging the systemic inequities in education.

We ask students to consider other perspectives, and although I do not want to indoctrinate my students, I struggle because there is a part of me that wants them to accept my beliefs as their own. However, I understand that indoctrination is not humanizing pedagogy nor does it facilitate the critical awareness I want to invoke in my classroom. The most important goal for my students is to learn to be critical thinkers on issues surrounding education and begin to form a critical consciousness as future educators. It is a skill I want them to continue to sharpen so they can challenge the inequitable systems that their students will face. By building trusting and caring relationships in my classroom, I hope to move closer to this goal.

Tensions/Dilemmas in Enacting Humanizing Pedagogy

In our respective narratives describing our attempts to enact humanizing pedagogy in teacher education classrooms, we have each provided some insight into the challenges embedded in this work. Even as two women of color who consider ourselves social justice educators and individuals who strive daily to enact antibiased and empowering pedagogies and practices, we acknowledge that this work is difficult. There are two additional ways we see tensions arise in humanizing the learning space and developing critical consciousness in ourselves and preservice teachers.

Not Recentering Whiteness or the White Voice

In order to build trusting and caring relationships with our students as a way to further their willingness to take learning risks in the classroom we must disrupt dominant group members' sense of safety. Because the project of humanization involves simultaneously highlighting the voices of those who have been historically oppressed *and* humanizing sociocultural knowledge, we are constantly monitoring the outcome of recentering Whiteness and/or the White voice. For example, in getting our students to examine racial inequity in schools, we engage in discussions and activities about White privilege and White supremacy. We engage the topics with the assumption that our White students are most in need of examining their race privilege at an individual level and White supremacy at institutional, structural, and cultural levels. We must be very careful not to recenter their perspectives in an educational space where the voices of students of color are already distorted and often muted. Yet we know that as individuals who benefit from the oppressive racial power structure and perpetuate its features (unknowingly and knowingly) in how we cover course material on race and racism, Whiteness, and White supremacy requires our not positioning our students of color as sacrificial lambs. Too often, students of color are burdened with educating White preservice teachers about various forms of oppression and what the concepts mean for their work as future educators. When we fall privy to this trap, we run the risk of allowing the courageous space to become a violent or volatile space.

Harboring Assumptions About Our Students

We must continue to question our own assumptions about our students. Although the majority of the students tend to be White and middle class, each student has unique experiences that provide valuable insight about the educational issues we are attempting to consider. Generalizing their experiences or making assumptions about their identities and knowledge of privilege and power leads to the dehumanizing practices that we are trying to combat. In the same way that we want our students to develop critical consciousness, we must remain vigilant in addressing our own biases that may affect our ability to practice humanizing pedagogies.

Concluding Thoughts

We began this chapter with the hope of providing some insight into how we humanize the teacher education learning space by drawing upon the reality, history, and perspectives of students as an integral part of educational practice (Bartolomé, 1994). Central to our project of humanization is enhancing students' critical consciousness and ability and willingness to challenge inequality through enacting two central practices: developing trusting and caring relationships and engaging preservice teachers in course content, dialogue, and field experiences that foster their development as social justice educators. We know that a humanizing pedagogy results from the individual and collective process of developing critical consciousness through dialogue (Freire, 1970), and risk discourse is central to this process. Humanizing pedagogy in teacher education keeps us in a continual journey toward liberation—the liberation of ourselves, of our preservice teachers, and subsequently of their students. Although we did not coteach this course, the collective intellectual engagement of a team of teacher educators working through the process of enacting humanizing pedagogy in the classroom allowed us, along with our colleagues, to share in the learning and journey toward humanization. The beautiful struggle continues, and we gladly partake in it.

Notes

1. In her book *Colormute: Race Talk Dilemmas in an American High School,* Mica Pollock (2004) eloquently described the problems inherent in teachers' inability or unwillingness to refer to students in racial terms or engage in conversations about educational inequities in a high school using race language. She defined this practice as being *colormute.*

2. The National Center for Cultural Competence at Georgetown University's Center for Child and Human Development website (nccc.georgetown.edu) identified five essential elements that contribute to an institution's ability to become more culturally competent. We apply these same elements at the individual/personal level, arguing that at a basic level, culturally competent teachers (a) value diversity, (b) have the capacity for cultural self-assessment, (c) are conscious of the dynamics inherent when cultures interact, (d) acquire and institutionalize cultural knowledge, and (e) adapt their pedagogy and practice to reflect an understanding of cultural diversity.

References

Bartolomé, L. (1994). Beyond the methods fetish: Toward a humanizing pedagogy. *Harvard Educational Review, 64*, 173–194.

Brown, K. D. (2013). Trouble on my mind: Toward a framework of humanizing critical sociocultural knowledge for teaching and teacher education. *Race Ethnicity and Education, 16*(3), 316–338.

Carter Andrews, D. J. (2009). "The hardest thing to turn from": Using service-learning to prepare urban educators. *Equity & Excellence in Education, 42*(3), 272–293.

del Carmen Salazar, M. C. (2013). A humanizing pedagogy: Reinventing the principles and practice of education as a journey toward liberation. *Review of Research in Education, 37*, 121–148.

Fanon, F. (2004). *The wretched of the earth* (R. Philcox, Trans.). New York, NY: Grove Press. (Originally published 1963, in French)

Freire, P. (1970). *Pedagogy of the oppressed.* New York, NY: Seabury Press.

Gay, G. (2010). *Culturally responsive teaching: Theory, research, and practice* (2nd ed.). New York, NY: Teachers College Press.

Ladson-Billings, G. (2009). *The dreamkeepers: Successful teachers of African American children* (2nd ed.). San Francisco, CA: Jossey-Bass.

Lynn, M. (1999). Toward a critical race pedagogy: A research note. *Urban Education, 33*(5), 606–626.

Nieto, S. (2004). *Affirming diversity: The sociopolitical context of multicultural education—Instructor's manual* (4th ed.). Boston, MA: Allyn & Bacon.

Pollock, M. (2004). *Colormute: Race talk dilemmas in an American high school.* Princeton, NJ: Princeton University Press.

United States Census Bureau. (2013). *State and County Quickfacts.* Retrieved from http://quickfacts.census.gov/qfd/states/26000.html

Woodson, C. G. (1933). *The mis-education of the Negro.* Sauk Village, IL: African American Images.

PART THREE

MEASURING THE IMPACT
OF OUR WORK

8

DEHUMANIZING AND HUMANIZING PEDAGOGIES

Lessons From U.S. Latin@ and Undocumented Youth Through the P–16 Pipeline

Lisa M. Martinez, Maria del Carmen Salazar, and Debora M. Ortega

*P*edagogy is ultimately about the process of teaching and is linked to the development of the human community as we enact those lessons taught to us by those whom we encounter. Most often this term is associated with educational institutions (i.e., schools) as opposed to organic forms of education (i.e., families and communities). Critical pedagogy in schools meets its first hurdle in the initial assumption that teaching and learning can take place only in educational institutions. Yet a second hurdle is the belief that educational institutions are culturally, politically, and racially neutral. When combined, the dehumanizing process begins to take root. Consequently, although the focus of this chapter is not on the family, it is important to name the family as the foundation for any work about Latin@s[1] and education. To do otherwise is to diminish the family's value, support, and contribution to the sometimes arduous trek through the educational pipeline. Although out-of-school factors are paramount to student success, this chapter begins with a focus on research describing the in-school P–16 experiences of Latin@ students and concludes with findings that inform Latin@ students' challenges and opportunities in higher education.

This chapter infuses the voices of Latin@ youth to highlight their experiences in an educational system that can simultaneously validate and invalidate all that makes them fully human and capable of developing their full potential. To understand the successes and struggles of Latin@ students is to understand the dynamics and operationalization of social power and the confluence of interests involved in the journey of Latin@ students toward higher education. Ultimately, Latin@ students in this study describe their own experiences of fighting to retain and protect their humanism as they interface with educational institutions. Before sharing insights from qualitative research with Latin@ participants in our study, we first turn to the framework that guides our work.

Theoretical Framework

Critical pedagogy guides the theoretical framework and analysis of our approach to analyzing the experiences of Latin@ youth through the P–16 pipeline. Critical pedagogy is focused on educational theories and practices that interrogate issues of power, culture, and privilege (Darder, Baltodano, & Torres, 2003; Leistyna, Woodrum, & Sherblom, 1996). Paulo Freire is considered to be "the most influential educational philosopher in the development of critical pedagogical thought and practice" (Darder et al., 2003, p. 5).

Freire defined *pedagogy* as "a practice for freedom" (as cited in Lake & Kress, 2013, p. 257). According to Freire (1980), all forms of pedagogy represent a particular way of understanding society and a specific commitment to the future. The great critical pedagogue Giroux (1988) eloquently captured Freire's conceptualization of critical pedagogy as the

> terrain where power and politics are given a fundamental expression, where the production of meaning, desire, language, and values engage and respond to the deeper beliefs about what it means to be human, to dream, and to name and struggle for a particular future and form of social life. (p. 110)

Giroux (1988) synthesized Freire's approach to critical pedagogy as expressing the language of critique, domination, and despair—juxtaposed with the language of struggle, possibility, and hope. Throughout his scholarship, Freire (1970, 1980) used the concepts of dehumanization and humanization to represent the binary of despair and hope in education.

Dehumanization

Whereas Freire's work originated in the poverty-ridden spaces of Brazil in the 1960s, his scholarship extended to the dehumanization of communities of color in U.S. society (Lake & Kress, 2013). Freire described dehumanization in the United States as based on White supremacy that reinforces deficit orientations and racist structures, thus resulting in "aggression against nature and against humanity" (Macedo & Bartolome, 1999, p. 90). Throughout the history of the United States, Latin@ students have experienced aggression against their humanity. For generations, they have been cajoled, or forced, to divest themselves of the linguistic, cultural, and familial resources they need to succeed in their journey through the P–16 educational pipeline. Such resources are inclusive of Yosso's (2005) conceptualization of *community cultural wealth*, or "an array of knowledge, skills, abilities and contacts possessed and utilized by Communities of Color to survive and resist macro and micro-forms of oppression" (p. 77). As a result, Latin@ students have been dehumanized, and thus stripped of cultural resources needed to survive and thrive in the educational system and in U.S. society (González, Moll, & Amantí, 2005; del Carmen Salazar, 2008; Nieto, 2010; Pizarro, 1998; Sadowski, 2003; Valenzuela, 1999).

The dehumanization of Latin@ students along the educational pipeline is often fueled by deficit notions of the resources of communities of color. Such notions have fueled intolerance, discrimination, and assimilation throughout the history of U.S. public education. Moreover, educators have compelled and at times coerced Latin@ students into Whiteness (del Carmen Salazar & Fránquiz, 2008; Sanchez, 1995). As a result, these students are expected to "act, speak, and behave as much as possible like the White middle class" (Warikoo & Carter, 2009, p. 374). Ladson-Billings (1995) suggested that successful students of color experience academic success "at the expense of their cultural and psychological well-being" (p. 475). These students may demonstrate a "raceless persona" (Fordham, cited in Warikoo & Carter, 2009, p. 379) to navigate the educational system, thus sacrificing an essential part of their humanity. Educational scholars have long documented the struggles of Latin@ students to resist assimilation and maintain their cultural roots, to merge their *hybrid* selves (Fránquiz & del Carmen Salazar, 2004; Reyes, 2007; Villenas, 2007).

Humanization

It is evident that Latin@ students are faced with a barrage of dehumanizing experiences along the educational pipeline. Freire (1970) lamented the state of dehumanization in education and asserted that "the only effective instrument in the process of re-humanization is humanizing pedagogy" (p. 55). A humanizing pedagogy is crucial for both teacher and student success and critical for the academic and social resiliency of students (Fránquiz & del Carmen Salazar, 2004; Reyes, 2007). Freire's conceptualization of *humanizing pedagogy* is a counterpractice to dehumanization in education. It is important to understand Freirian conceptualizations of the constructs of humanization, pedagogy, and humanizing pedagogy.

Humanization is the process of becoming more fully human as social, historical, thinking, communicating, transformative, creative persons who participate in and with the world (Freire, 1972, 1984). To become more fully human, men and women must become conscious of their presence in the world as a way to individually and collectively re-envisage their social world (Dale & Hyslop-Margison, 2010; Freire & Betto, 1985; Schapiro, 2001). Humanization is the ontological vocation of human beings and, as such, is the practice of freedom in which the oppressed are liberated through consciousness of their subjugated positions and a desire for self-determination (Freire, 1970, 1994). Humanization cannot be imposed on or imparted to the oppressed but rather can occur only by engaging the oppressed in their liberation. As such, Freire (1970) proposed that the process of humanization fosters transformation and authentic liberation of the oppressed; thus, "to transform the world is to humanize it" (Freire, 1985, p. 70).

Whereas Freire's (1970) conceptualization of humanization is key to understanding his educational philosophy (Dale & Hyslop-Margison, 2010), his ideological stance related to the underlying notions of pedagogy is vital to the enactment of humanization. Freire's use of the term *pedagogy* is a "complex philosophy, politics, and practice of education . . . that demands of educators a clear ethical and political commitment to transforming oppressive social conditions (as cited in Roberts, 2000, pp. 13–14). According to Freirean ideals, all pedagogy is political and requires radical reconstruction of teaching and learning (Giroux, 1988); moreover, pedagogy must be meaningful and connected to social change by engaging students with the world so they can transform it (Giroux, 2010). As such, meaningful social change can be triggered by curricular resources that are tied to the needs of marginalized students and locally generated by teachers and communities in order to interrupt patterns of exclusion (Giroux, 2010).

Freire's pedagogical assertions flow from ethical and political stances that challenge inequity and promote humanization (Dale & Hyslop-Margison, 2010). Freirean scholars have interpreted his pedagogical vision as a way of living in the world rather than a bundle of technical pedagogical practices. Freire repeatedly emphasized that his pedagogy is not transferable across contexts but, rather, should be adapted to the unique context of teaching and learning (Roberts, 2000; Weiler, 1991). Dale and Hyslop-Margison (2010) asserted, "Although there are not precise technical methods emerging from Freire's pedagogy, its potential application is limited only by our creativity and imagination" (p. 74). In fact, Freirean pedagogy necessitates that educators reinvent his philosophy and pedagogy across contexts (Rodriguez & Smith, 2011). Above all, Freire encouraged educators to listen to their students and build on their knowledge and experiences in order to engage in contextualized, dynamic, and personalized educational approaches that further the goals of humanization and social transformation.

Throughout his many literary works, Freire grappled with the meaning of human existence and the purpose of pedagogy; as a result, he envisaged a *humanizing pedagogy*. In *Pedagogy of the Oppressed*, Freire (1970) described humanizing pedagogy as a revolutionary approach to instruction that "ceases to be an instrument by which teachers can manipulate students, but rather expresses the consciousness of the students themselves" (p. 51). Teachers who enact humanizing pedagogy engage in a quest for "mutual humanization" (Freire, 1970, p. 56) with their students, a process fostered through problem-posing education where students are coinvestigators in dialogue with their teachers. This dialogic approach to education should be pursued with the goal of developing *"conscientizacao"* (Freire, 1970, p. 26), or critical consciousness, which is "learning to perceive social, political, and economic contradictions, and to take action against the oppressive elements of reality" (Freire, 1970, p. 17). There are limitless possibilities for Freire's pedagogical philosophy, and Freire urged his followers to reinvent his ideas in the context of their local struggles.

Building on Freire's philosophy, del Carmen Salazar (2013) identified five key principles of a humanizing pedagogy:

1. The full development of the person is essential for humanization.
2. To deny someone else's humanization is also to deny one's own.
3. The journey for humanization is an individual and collective endeavor toward critical consciousness.
4. Critical reflection and action can transform structures that impede our own and others' humanness, thus facilitating liberation for all.
5. Educators are responsible for promoting a more fully human world through their pedagogical principles and practices.

We draw on these principles in our discussion of Latin@ and undocumented youths' experiences through the P–16 pipeline and discuss how they might inform critical pedagogies in institutions of higher education.

In the sections that follow, we use data from in-depth interviews to highlight the experiences of participants in our study. Following a discussion of our methods and findings, we address how Latin@s' experiences in P–16 can inform our understanding of their trajectories into and through institutions of higher education and, specifically, the role critical pedagogies play in this process. We also shed light on the resources Latin@ students bring with them to institutions of higher education and how they build on these to successfully navigate through the pipeline. Lastly, we incorporate del Carmen Salazar's (2013) five principles of humanizing pedagogy in the discussion of our findings. This includes a discussion of the lessons learned from Latin@

and undocumented youth to facilitate the enactment of humanizing pedagogy in higher education, including the implications for creating inclusive
higher education learning environments.

Methods

The questions guiding this paper are twofold: (a) What are the dehumanizing and humanizing pedagogies experienced by Latin@ and undocumented
youth along the P–16 pipeline? (b) How can these experiences inform critical
pedagogies in institutions of higher education? Data for this paper are from
in-depth, semistructured interviews with 60 Latin@ and immigrant youth,
ages 16 to 26. Using a life history approach (Goodson, 2001; Goodson &
Sikes, 2001), we captured Latin@ youths' experiences at five important life
stages: elementary school, middle school, high school, college, and postcol-
lege. In addition to demographic questions, we asked respondents a series
of questions related to their experiences in P–12. For participants who were
attending, had attended, or graduated from institutions of higher education,
we asked about their experiences in college as well. Questions highlighted
the role of parental support in academic achievement; support from school
administrators, including teachers, counselors, coaches, principals, and other
mentors; support in the form of college-readiness, tutoring, and academic
programs; and the influence of peers in their schooling experiences. For those
who were in college or had graduated from college, we also asked about
the challenges they encountered in the P–16 pipeline, including those they
encountered upon entering college. This approach allowed us to identify the
"turning points" that set respondents on their trajectories. And because a
majority of our respondents attended underresourced schools, came from
lower socioeconomic backgrounds, and were mostly first-generation college
students, we situated their experiences within larger structural inequalities
facing Latin@s and other youth of color. All interviews were transcribed ver-
batim, coded, and analyzed for emerging themes using Atlas.ti.

Of our 60 study participants, 18 were undocumented and came to the
United States prior to the age of 10, making them part of the growing 1.5
immigrant generation. Thirty-two respondents were second generation (children born in the United States to immigrant parents), but were living in
mixed-status families where at least one family member was undocumented
(Fix & Zimmerman, 1999). Ten respondents reported being third generation or more, meaning they and their parents were born in the United States.
We interviewed 23 males and 37 females. Respondents' average age was just
over 20 years old. Almost all respondents (57 of 60) were living, working,
or attending schools in a western state at the time of the interviews. Two

respondents were living out of state while attending college. Interviews were conducted in English and in person, with the exception of the out-of-state interviews, which were conducted via Skype. Data collection spanned June 2012 through August 2013.

Findings

Building on the Freirean (1970) critical notions of dehumanization and humanizing pedagogy, we use interview data to illustrate how school experiences through the P–16 pipeline validate and invalidate Latin@s' humanism and, consequently, affect their academic trajectories. First, we highlight the dehumanizing experiences of Latin@ and undocumented youth. Second, we present narratives of the humanizing experiences of Latin@ and undocumented youth in our study to elucidate how critical early interventions, support, and emphasis on the whole student result in positive academic outcomes. By providing examples of both, we demonstrate the ways in which youths' educational trajectories can be marked by hope or despair.

When asked about the challenges they encountered through the P–16 pipeline, participants shared a range of dehumanizing experiences, including feelings of isolation, negative peer influences, teachers' low expectations, and the lack of resources and other support programs for college-bound students. Even the college prep programs, meant to support high-achieving students, served to segregate and alienate them from other students of color or required them to shed cultural and familial ties.

Isolation

Feelings of isolation were common among all respondents but were especially palpable among undocumented youth who discussed the challenges of learning in a new land (Suarez-Orozco, Suarez-Orozco, & Todorova, 2010). The circumstances surrounding their families' migration, settling in a new environment, and entering schools not knowing English caused difficult schooling experiences for many. Gabby, 21, was a senior majoring in biology at a private university. When we met for the interview, she began by recounting her family's experience migrating to the United States from Mexico shortly after the September 11th terrorist attacks. Fearing that the borders would stay closed permanently, Gabby's father, who had already been in the United States, called her and her mom saying, "You need to leave now. Grab your stuff and just come over here." On such short notice, the family was unable to fully prepare for the move and, even though they eventually made it across, the process of acclimating to a new life was difficult for Gabby that first year in the United States. She struggled to learn English and recalled never really talking to any of her classmates or having any friends because she could not understand them. However, with support from a teacher and her older brothers, she was fully fluent in English within a year.

At school, Gabby quickly revealed herself to be a stellar student. By the time she reached middle school, she was in the international baccalaureate (IB) program at a school she described as half White and half Latin@. Although language barriers were no longer an issue, she encountered other challenges on the IB track:

> I never had that many friends anyway, but the one friend I did have, I would hang out with her. But I hardly ever saw her in class because I was in IB. So there was a group of 20 or 30 of us [in IB] and everyone was White except me and two of my friends. I never really interacted with the Latino population except at [student organization]. . . . I remember being in regular classes once, because freshman year, I was still part of regular and IB [classes] and I always hated it. I felt like no one was putting any effort in, that it was so easy. I could just write in my name, turn it in, and get an "A."

Gabby's experience her first year of high school in both regular and IB courses gave her a point of comparison between instruction in "regular" classes and what she was learning in IB classes. She said, "I felt like no one was putting any effort in" and that students were not being challenged. Low expectations of students in regular classes was not the only issue Gabby confronted; given that she was one of only three students of color in the IB classes, she experienced some backlash from friends who felt she was too busy participating in school activities or doing community service, which was required of IB students. Gabby recounted that friends would ask her, "Why are you doing this and that and running around? What are you doing all this for? We never see you." Gabby offered that she liked being involved and liked volunteering. Academically, IB courses kept her interested and motivated beyond simply getting an "easy A." But this came at a cost because, as Gabby shared, "I actually got called whitewashed pretty much all throughout high school." As Gabby's experiences show, feelings of isolation stemmed from her status as an immigrant and, later, being placed on the IB track that set her apart from her Latin@ peers.

Negative Peer Influence

Thomas, 20, was majoring in a business-related field at a private university. He described himself as a shy and quiet child, the second youngest of five children. He was brought up in a household where he and his siblings felt sheltered from the outside world because all they knew was family, school, and church. His parents were very strict but also encouraging. As he explained:

> My parents told us we had to do good in school and I listened to [them] at that time. My dad always told me that if I did good in school, then we would have a better life. So like I said, when I was younger, I didn't really understand that completely, but I understood real quick after high school.

Although Thomas was a good student and placed in an advanced math class in the grade above him in elementary school, his school lacked the kinds of programs to support academically motivated students. Thomas felt not only that his school "didn't really provide much opportunity to challenge students at that time," but also that they had failed at preparing him for college. In middle school, things were different. Thomas became more sociable and came out of his shell, but he never felt challenged at school, and at home, his family was dealing with the aftermath of his parents' divorce. From that point on, he was raised by his mother, who struggled financially, and yet he still managed to avoid the pull of negative peer influences. This changed in high school when his mother was facing foreclosure on their home, and, in need of money, Thomas began selling drugs to help support the family. He began hanging out with "the wrong kind of people" and lost interest in school. Eventually, during his senior year of high school, Thomas distanced himself from the negative influences and began to focus on graduating and going to college, though he acknowledged that he had little support from teachers, counselors, or anyone else at school. His diligence paid off in that he was accepted into and graduated from a four-year university and later earned a master's degree in a highly sought-after field. When asked to look back on the challenges he encountered while in school, he said,

> The main challenges I have encountered are associating with the wrong people and being one of a very few minorities in my field of study and now, work. I am no longer facing the challenge of negative associations [but] I am reminded daily as I walk through the office that I am one of few minorities in this position.

Thomas's close-knit family provided an environment where education was valued and buffered him from negative experiences early on in his schooling experiences. However, the lack of support from school administrators, coupled with growing negative influences, temporarily derailed his academic success. Thomas found his way back on the college track, but the challenges of being one of the few people of color in his field brought a new crop of issues that affected his experiences.

Low Expectations and Lack of Preparation

At the time of the interview, Luis, 20, was a junior majoring in engineering at a public university. Given his major, he was one of very few students of color, a situation that was similar to his experience growing up, having gone to private school since sixth grade. The middle of six children, his parents were migrant workers who spent periods of time in the United States and Mexico. Although he was born in the United States, it was more than a decade before his mother received residency and his father earned his citizenship. Luis's mom was determined that he learn English and that he and his brothers do well in school. By third grade, Luis was fully fluent and began to excel at school, which he attributed to his mom's support. With his parents' encouragement, Luis applied for and received a scholarship to attend private middle and high schools. He flourished at both schools and further developed a love of math and science, programs that his private schools had more resources to support, a departure from the public schools he would have attended otherwise. His eventual dream was to become an astronaut or, at the very least, work for NASA, which explained his choice of major and college. Once he entered college, Luis found the transition to be more difficult than he imagined, and although he continued to enjoy school and science in particular, he struggled in his courses because, as he stated,

> School has always been easy for me, so I never knew what it was like to go to a hard school and actually have to try. So I don't really know how to study effectively and so I'm barely learning how to really try and struggle with school.

During his first few semesters of college, Luis struggled, earning lower grades than he was accustomed to, which prompted him to seek out a tutor. He felt like he was making some progress but was behind in a few courses and was in danger of not graduating on time. When asked to reflect on the factors that contributed to his academic success, Luis said, "Interested teachers that were willing to diversify their teaching style have been very effective for me. The pressure from my parents to always have my homework done, attend class, etc. has also kept me on track." By his own account, Luis had a mostly positive school experience, especially given the support he received from his parents. Still, when asked to reflect on the challenges he encountered, he remarked,

> Teachers who are uninterested in what they are teaching or are just not effective teachers. The material a few classes had to teach, set by either the school or school district, I feel, limited the capabilities of a few teachers to teach relevant material, and I think that held me back, especially for college.

Luis had the tools needed to succeed in school—motivation, supportive parents, clear educational and career goals—but once in college, he struggled to perform at the level to which he was accustomed.

Respondents' experiences through the P–16 pipeline were not all negative, and in fact, many recounted positive, affirming, and humanizing experiences. These included supportive teachers, counselors, and administrators who not only set high expectations but also took the time to get to know students. Others had humanizing experiences when teachers incorporated students' histories, cultures, and values as part of their pedagogy.

Emphasizing Cultural Values

Teresa, 21, an undocumented immigrant, was a part-time student attending a private 4-year university at the time of the interview. She described the many educational challenges she encountered due to her status, including language barriers when she first entered school, but she had nonetheless achieved considerable academic success thereafter. Teresa described having supportive parents and teachers throughout her schooling; however, it was her high school principal, in particular, who had a significant impact on her life. Her principal not only supported her but approached his students as though they were members of a family. Teresa commented,

> He was nice to all of us, and he always said our high school was like a family, and he always made it seem that way. That we were close and that we were kind of like a family and we all had each other's back. He shows he cares about everybody. I never got in trouble or anything like that, so I was never in his office, but yet I knew who he was. Like some other people at their high schools, they don't really know who their principal is. Like they know who their principal is but they don't really *know* their principal. He was always very involved with us, and now he's very involved in the community.

Later in the interview, Teresa mentioned how meaningful her principal's support had been to her, especially when it became more widely known that she was undocumented and would have difficulty receiving financial support to attend college. Despite their immigration status, Teresa's principal encouraged all his students—who were predominantly Latin@—to aim for college. Teresa said,

> He just really cares for us to get a higher education and he's always pushed us to that ever since we were in high school, ever since we were in ninth grade. We knew that his goal was to get us to college and to get all of us graduated and to get all of us to college. And he achieved that. All of us graduated.

Teresa's principal created a school environment where academic success was expected but not seen as antithetical to her culture or values. Indeed, having a supportive principal who treated his students like family gave Teresa the sense that academic success was valued but did not have to come at the price of rejecting her community. Moreover, by using a communal approach, Teresa's principal was building on cultural values, which in turn created a greater sense of accountability because they saw themselves not as accountable to a school administrator but to a family member. By helping to define success in ways that resonated with students' cultural values, he created an environment where students could work toward the individual and collective goal of getting into college.

Setting High Expectations

Pancho, 20, a sophomore at a private 4-year university, was the older of two children being raised by a single parent. He was identified as academically motivated at an early age; had experienced academic success throughout K–12; and earned a reputation for being a smart, hard-working student among his college-age peers. Pancho noted that several teachers in K–12 helped him along the way and credited them for encouraging him to go to college. One of those teachers was Mr. Buddy, the advanced placement teacher at Pancho's high school. Mr. Buddy encouraged his students to approach high school as though they were in college and operated on the assumption that all his students were college bound. Pancho elaborated,

> He would treat us like college students. He had an honor code where he wouldn't supervise us as much and he would expect us to be honest about what we did. All the kids in that class had a higher caliber, and I think also because of being in that class, they felt that they were of a higher caliber student. I think that was a big change for me instead of just taking normal classes. Language arts had never been my strong subject, but he really had high expectations of us. And even if we were the math kid or the science kid, he said anybody can be good at language arts; it's just how you work at it. So I think he was a really important teacher in my high school years.

Mr. Buddy was an integral part of Pancho's experience in high school because he wanted students to do well and approach their schooling as though they were already in college. He also encouraged students to recognize abilities they did not see in themselves. Mr. Buddy also treated students as young adults and relied on an honor code as opposed to strict rules and sanctions to encourage good behavior. Although Pancho had benefited from supportive teachers throughout his schooling, it was Mr. Buddy who proved to be integral to his educational trajectory because he was the first teacher who tried to connect what they were learning to serve students well in college. Pancho shared, "He's really interested in how his class affects our experience in college because he purposefully tries to set us up with the language arts skills and the writing skills to do well in college." By emphasizing skills that would be important in college, Mr. Buddy was utilizing humanizing principles and practices to encourage his students to be successful and coupled those skills with the underlying expectation that his students were going to college. Much like Teresa's principal, Mr. Buddy expected his students to go to college, which informed his pedagogy but also instilled in students the skills he knew they would need *in* college. For him, then, the goal was not only about getting them into college but also helping them succeed once there. His humanizing approach was also fruitful in that students worked to meet his high expectations.

Identifying and Inspiring High-Achieving Students

Lupe, 20, was a student at a public university majoring in a social science field. She shared how she had mixed experiences throughout her schooling but recalled how, in elementary school, a fifth-grade teacher who recognized Lupe's promise had encouraged her to develop her writing skills:

> She was one of those really tough teachers that not a lot of people liked because she was very strict and she had a rigorous coursework. But she was the one that inspired me to start writing and really develop my poetry, which is something that up until this day keeps me sane and really empowers me.

For Lupe, having a teacher who encouraged her creativity made a significant difference in her schooling experiences because she was a student at an underresourced school that had little financial support for the arts. Lupe's teachers recognized her academic promise and encouraged her to apply for a competitive scholarship that would enable her to attend a prestigious private secondary school. She would eventually receive the scholarship, which radically altered the dynamics of her school experiences. Where she had once attended a predominantly Latin@, predominantly lower-income school, Lupe found herself at a private secondary school where she was one of only two Latin@s and one of the few students who came from a working-class and immigrant family. Feeling out of place at her new school while also feeling increasing pressure from extended family members who felt she was "selling out," Lupe became involved with a gang in high school. She described in detail the unlikely juxtaposition of being a private school student by day and gang member by night, which she equated with "living a double life." Eventually, the death of a family member compelled her to get out of the gang, which she was able to do through a program for gang-involved youth. One of the program participants taught Lupe about her Mexican heritage and history, which was her way out of gang life. She said,

> The way that I was approached was through my history, which was something that going to [public school] I was surrounded by Latinos, but I never learned my history. I learned George Washington. I learned the colonization even though they called it the founding of America. . . . I learned all that but I never learned what role as *Mexicas* [Aztecs] or as Latinos, what we brought to it . . . so the way that I was approached, just gave me a whole different perspective about humanity and something that I didn't know. And by giving me a little lesson in the history of my people, it was such a changing thing.

As Lupe's comments suggest, the opportunity to learn about her history—as opposed to the traditional curriculum taught at her school—was an eye-opening experience. It not only helped pull her out of gang life, but also served as an awakening of sorts, which enabled her to channel these insights into social activism at her university.

The previous examples shed light on the ways in which school experiences can have humanizing effects in what are often dehumanizing contexts. Teresa, Pancho, and Lupe were beneficiaries of principals, teachers, and mentors who recognized the value and significance of investing in students, the result being they were more motivated to do well in school.

Discussion

del Carmen Salazar's (2013) five key principles to a humanizing pedagogy offer a theoretical foundation that can guide faculty in addressing the needs of historically underrepresented and marginalized students, not the least of whom are undocumented Latin@s. The principles, like any application of Freire's concepts, are not a standard menu of items but rather require the educator to engage the student with flexibility rooted in these principles. Consequently, the following is an example of the first principle.

The students in our study experienced education as an acculturative process in which they were forced to develop hybrid identities or become shapeshifters who learned to split their identities dichotomously between White school life and Latin@ home life. The educational process then became the vehicle for dehumanization via the content and process of education that was

Anglo-centric and, by extension, that defined *success* in terms of the dominant culture. At the same time, Latin@ youths' families and cultural identification were thought of as deficits that should be erased from the student's experience, despite the claim that education is culturally neutral.

Simultaneously, students in our study reported experiences of humanization that occurred as they learned about their identities and cultural histories through interactions with key educators. In this way, they understood their own subjugation and social position not as individual to themselves, but as part of a larger political and historical legacy. In some cases, the cultural aspects, such as collectivism, were used to engage and support students as they worked toward the ultimate goal of college education.

The first principle, believing that the full development of the person is essential for humanization, requires an understanding of the Latin@ student context, even as it is an indictment of an educational system. Students repeatedly described their engagement with the education system as isolating. They learned to negotiate this isolation as a coping strategy for educational success. Faculty and school administrators, especially those associated with student life activities, must be able to engage students with an understanding of their isolation experience. Students themselves will likely not have the words or have developed a deep understanding of their own isolation as they step onto college campuses. In these cases, higher education faculty and staff must be able to partner with students and be open to naming the dehumanizing experiences through the P–16 pipeline. In this way, faculty and staff should understand how isolation takes place and how it is supported by same and different racial and ethnic peers, while acknowledging students' responsibility to family concerns and engaging culturally isolated students in campus life by utilizing key cultural processes, such as collectivism instead of competition. This type of engagement on college campuses can be the vehicle to support students' development from subjugated to liberated.

Each of the five principles of humanizing pedagogies requires understanding the result of the dehumanizing process of education for Latin@ students along the P–16 pipeline. Institutions of higher education then need to move from doing more of the same in a one-size-fits-all manner to engaging marginalized students by understanding them as cultural beings whose success is rooted, not hindered, by their families and communities.

Conclusion

Respondents' experiences challenge us to revisit the funding of poorly resourced schools and to use collectivism in the classroom as tools to support students in acquiring education. Latin@ students begin every school day with a book bag filled with experiences affected by opportunity gaps, cultural assets, and laws and policies that are counter to the individualistic worldview of U.S. society. These factors, coupled with the support of their families, their connection to their communities, and their engagement with educators, serve to support or thwart their development as they are transported through the educational pipeline. Freire (1970) provided a framework to think about the education of historically marginalized students in a context that provides challenging materials to meet the needs of each student; to recognize their parents and siblings as part of the educational family propelling them forward to success; and to hold a vision of college success as they design, develop, and deliver curriculum to students whose generational experience of education is that of oppression and suppression. Overall, the participants in our study described the humanizing pedagogy in their lives as stemming from curricular, programmatic, and relational elements. High-level curriculum set high expectations that pushed the participants to rise to rigorous standards; this included gifted education, honors, and advanced placement courses. College preparation programs engaged the participants in high-level learning, developed skills for college and career readiness, demystified the college-going experience, and fostered a relentless belief in their own abilities. Last, the participants were most impacted by their relationships. Their parents, siblings, extended family members, coaches, counselors, teachers, and mentors immersed them in a protective cocoon that allowed them to flourish. Ultimately, Freire offered this word of warning: To turn a blind eye to the dehumanizing structural inequity of an educational system that continues to devalue historically marginalized people results in the surrendering of the full human potential of the oppressed and the oppressor.

Note

1. We have used the gender-neutral terms *Latin@* and *Latin@s* throughout the chapter.

References

Dale, J., & Hyslop-Margison, E. J. (2010). Pedagogy of humanism. *Explorations of Educational Purpose, 12*, 71–104.
Darder, A., Baltodano, M., & Torres, R. D. (2003). *The critical pedagogy reader.* New York, NY: Taylor & Francis.

del Carmen Salazar, M. (2008). English or nothing: The impact of rigid language policies on the inclusion of humanizing practices in a high school ESL program. *Equity & Excellence in Education, 41*, 341–356.

del Carmen Salazar, M. (2013). A humanizing pedagogy: Reinventing the principles and practices of education as a journey toward liberation. *Review of Research in Education, 37*(1), 121–148.

del Carmen Salazar, M., & Fránquiz, M. (2008). The transformation of Ms. Corazon: Creating humanizing spaces for Mexican immigrant students in secondary ESL classrooms. *Journal of Multicultural Perspectives, 10*, 185–191.

Fix, M., & Zimmerman, W. (1999). *All under one roof: Mixed status families in an era of reform*. Washington, DC: Urban Institute. Retrieved from http://www.urban .org/UploadedPDF/409100.pdf

Fránquiz, M., & del Carmen Salazar, M. (2004). The transformative potential of humanizing pedagogy: Addressing the diverse needs of Chicano/Mexicano students. *The High School Journal, 87*, 36–53.

Freire, P. (1970). *Pedagogy of the oppressed*. New York, NY: Continuum.

Freire, P. (1972). *Pedagogy of the oppressed*. Harmondsworth, UK: Penguin.

Freire, P. (1980). *Pedagogy of the oppressed*. New York, NY: Continuum.

Freire, P. (1984). *Pedagogy of the oppressed*. New York, NY: Continuum.

Freire, P. (1985). *The politics of education: Culture, power, and liberation*. Westport, CT: Greenwood Publishing.

Freire, P. (1994). *Pedagogy of hope: Reliving pedagogy of the oppressed*. New York, NY: Continuum.

Freire, P., & Betto, F. (1985). *Essa escola chamada vida—Depoimentos ao reporter Ricardo Kotscho*. Sao Paulo, Brazil: Atica.

Giroux, H. A. (1988). *Teachers as intellectuals: Toward a critical pedagogy of learning*. Westport, CT: Bergin & Garvey.

Giroux, H. A. (2010, November 23). *Lessons to be learned from Paulo Freire as education is being taken over by the mega rich*. Retrieved from http://archive.truthout .org/lessons-be-learned-from-paulo-freire-education-is-being-taken-over-mega-rich65363

Goodson, I. (2001). The story of life history: Origins of the life history method in sociology. *Identity: An International Journal of Research and Theory, 1*, 129–142.

Goodson, I., & Sikes, P. (2001). *Life history in educational settings: Learning from lives*. Buckingham, UK: Open University Press.

González, N., Moll, L., & Amantí, C. (2005). *Funds of knowledge: Theorizing practices in households, communities, and classrooms*. Mahwah, NJ: Lawrence Erlbaum.

Ladson-Billings, G. (1995). Toward a theory of culturally relevant pedagogy. *American Educational Research Journal, 32*, 465–491.

Lake, R., & Kress, T. (2013). *Paulo Freire's intellectual roots: Toward historicity in praxis*. New York, NY: Bloomsbury.

Leistyna, P., Woodrum, A., & Sherblom, S. A. (1996). *Breaking free: The transformative power of critical pedagogy*. Cambridge, MA: Harvard Educational Review.

Macedo, D., & Bartolome, L. (1999). *Dancing with bigotry: Beyond the politics of tolerance.* New York, NY: St. Martin's Press.

Nieto, S. (2010). *The light in their eyes: Creating multicultural learning communities* (10th anniversary ed.). New York, NY: Teachers College Press.

Pizarro, M. (1998). "Chicano power!" Epistemology and methodology for social justice and empowerment in Chicana/o communities. *International Journal of Qualitative Studies in Education, 11,* 57–80.

Reyes, R. (2007). Marginalized students in secondary school settings: The pedagogical and theoretical implications of addressing the needs of student subpopulations. *Journal of Border Educational Research, 6,* 3–5.

Roberts, P. (2000). *Education, literacy, and humanization: Exploring the work of Paulo Freire.* Westport, CT: Bergin & Garvey.

Rodriguez, A., & Smith, M. D. (2011). Reimagining Freirean pedagogy: Sendero for teacher education. *Journal for Critical Education Policy Studies, 9,* 91–103.

Sadowski, M. (2003). *Adolescents at school: Perspectives on youth, identity, and education.* Cambridge, MA: Harvard Education Publishing Group.

Sanchez, G. J. (1995). Reading Reginald Denny: The politics of whiteness in the late twentieth century. *American Quarterly, 47*(3), 388–394.

Schapiro, S. (2001). *A Freirean approach to anti-sexist education with men: Toward a pedagogy of the "oppressor."* Retrieved from http://www.fielding.edu/research/ar_papers/Schapiro.pdf

Suarez-Orozco, C., Suarez-Orozco, M., & Todorova, I. (2010). *Learning a new land: Immigrant students in American society.* Cambridge, MA: Belknap Press.

Valenzuela, A. (1999). *Subtractive schooling: U.S.-Mexican youth and the politics of caring.* Albany: State University of New York Press.

Villenas, S. A. (2007). Diaspora and the anthropology of Latino education: Challenges, affinities, and intersections. *Anthropology & Education Quarterly, 38*(4), 419–425.

Warikoo, N., & Carter, P. (2009). Cultural explanations for racial and ethnic stratification in academic achievement: A call for a new and improved theory. *Review of Educational Research, 79*(1), 366–394.

Weiler, K. (1991). Freire and a feminist pedagogy of difference. *Harvard Educational Review, 61*(4), 449–474.

Yosso, T. (2005). Whose culture has capital? A critical race theory discussion of community cultural wealth. *Race, Ethnicity and Education, 81,* 69–91.

9

DE-RACIALIZING
JAPANESENESS

A Collaborative Approach to Shifting Interpretation and Representation of "Culture" at a University in Japan

Ioannis Gaitanidis and Satoko Shao-Kobayashi

In the past decade, a series of reforms aimed at making Japanese universities more competitive on a global scale have pushed for the creation of a variety of courses that prepare students to study, volunteer, or find work abroad. Many of these courses focus on the Japanese students' ability to comprehend, debate on, and present about Japanese culture and society to a broad audience, using the English language.

Yet in the process of conducting these courses, instructors are bound to face a question that has preoccupied research on racial homogeneity and minorities in Japan since at least the early 1990s: Who are the "Japanese" we are talking about? As most academic work on this question has shown, the word *Japanese* conflates notions of race, ethnicity, language, citizenship, and culture (Yamashiro, 2013), and university students frequently mix all of these associations when they are asked to talk about a specific aspect of Japanese culture.

This chapter focuses on the process and product of instructor–student interactions in the framework of a collaborative learning course called Global Project Work: Presenting About Japan in English, which the authors cotaught under the liberal arts curriculum of a Japanese university. More specifically, we show how, inspired by Bakhtin's (1984) polyphony and dialogism, we set up and engaged with students, encouraging them to break down the aforementioned conflation of race and culture into its constitutive components.

The "Global" Wave in Japanese Higher Education Policies

In a *Japan Times* special feature dated September 2, 2013, Hakubun Shimomura, then Japanese minister of education, culture, sports, science and technology (MEXT), lamented on the lack of internationalization of Japanese universities on the basis of two statistics: "Compared to the OECD average of foreign students accounting for 7.1 percent of the total university enrollment, in Japan, the percentage is as low as 3.1 percent" (p. B1).[1] "Moreover," Shimomura continued, "since fiscal 2004, the number of Japanese students going abroad to study has been decreasing. . . . In fiscal 2010 falling to 70 percent of the peak number of 58,000" (p. B1). These declining trends in both Japanese interest in studying abroad and foreign interest in experiencing Japanese higher education have forced the Japanese government to devise a series of projects that, starting in 2009, have seen the budget accorded to encouraging outward and inward mobility in Japanese higher education climb from 2 billion yen in 2008 to 12.7 billion yen in 2014 (Semba, 2014). The latest[2] of the MEXT-sponsored projects, called Project for Promotion of Global Human Resource Development, was launched in 2012 with a budget of 2.2 billion yen and for a period of 5 years.

On the successful reception of MEXT's latest grant, our university, Chiba University, launched, among other activities, a new category of courses called Japanese Studies. This category of courses became part of a new liberal arts curriculum offered by Chiba University's Center for International Research and Education (CIRE), an institution that had formerly hosted Japanese language and culture courses for international students and some training courses for students on a Japanese language instructor's career track. Since their launch, the aim of Japanese Studies classes has been to not just provide students with foundational knowledge about Japanese culture and society but also to offer an environment that allows students to reconsider their image of Japan by reflecting on their own experiences and cultures, and to acquire new perspectives and a deeper awareness of a variety of global phenomena.

In effect, Japanese Studies courses at CIRE have been an attempt to integrate the pedagogical method of collaborative learning into an area studies approach that would be devoid of essentialist interpretations of Japan. In a nutshell, CIRE's new curriculum tries to push students to overcome the stereotypical models that usually adorn guidebooks and other Japan-related promotional material produced for tourist purposes, constantly encouraging them to reflect on their assumptions about their own culture.

Theoretical Framework

Race, Racialization, and Higher Education in Japan

The aforementioned need for internationalization in Japanese higher education is also a matter of survival in an academic world increasingly obsessed with national and international rankings. Indeed, with a numerical majority of private institutions, few of which feature in international rankings, Japan needs to get its university students more mobile in order to increase its international profile (Eades & Cooper, 2013). Yet the more Japanese students come in contact with non-Japanese nationals, the more the term *Japanese* becomes racialized. In fact, officially there are no races in Japan. "[T]here are no provisions in Japanese law for racially classifying Japanese individuals as African, Ainu, Caucasian, Chinese, Happa, Hawaiian. . . . Japanese are just Japanese—a raceless nationality" (Wetherall, 2008, p. 266). This situation creates a particular image of "homogeneity" that joins wider social imagery of Japaneseness, as portrayed in a range of official, media, and popular outlets today. Consumers of Japanese animation and video games, for example, often tend to look for characteristics that are allegedly "typical" of Japanese culture. However,

> it is one thing to observe that Japanese animation and video games are influencing children's play and behavior in many parts of the world and . . . it is quite another to say that this cultural influence and this perception of coolness are closely associated with a tangible, realistic appreciation of "Japanese" lifestyles or ideas. (Iwabuchi, 2002, p. 456)

This conceptual "jump" between appreciation of the product and appreciation of its country of origin is a fundamental issue in the classes that aim to develop in Japanese students the ability to talk about Japanese society and culture to a non-Japanese audience.

In a polemical study of Japanese higher education, McVeigh (2002) employed the example of English language teaching to argue that the general lack of communication in Japanese university classes and the emphasis put on passing written examinations contribute to reinforcing this homogenization of knowledge and, by extension, to ironically demonstrating the "Japaneseness"

(p. 123) of the Japanese university students. Although McVeigh's observations should not be generalized, it is not difficult to imagine that a situation of near-zero interaction between students and instructor during a class on contemporary Japanese culture may produce a very unified, monocultural understanding of the subject if students are not encouraged to at least voice their opinions and become aware that not everyone shares the same views.

Polyphony and Dialogism in Collaborative Learning in Higher Education in Japan

Possibly alarmed by the detrimental effects of such an instructor-based approach to learning, a report announced by the Central Education Council of MEXT on August 28, 2013, clearly emphasized the need for an "active, collaborative and creative knowledge-based learning model" (p. 7). As previously discussed, the central concern of collaborative learning courses that purport to support students' ability to "present about Japan" is the breaking down of a general tendency to racialize Japaneseness. In our case, we sought a way for students to actively and collaboratively engage in finding their own ways of reaching the aforementioned goal. Before we delve into a more detailed description of our methods, it is first necessary to understand some of the key ideas related to collaborative learning.[3]

One of the frequently utilized approaches in the study of collaborative learning revolves around *polyphony* (or multiple voices) and *dialogism,* both of which originate in the works of early twentieth-century Russian scholar Mikhail Bakhtin (see Koschmann, 1999; Wegerif, 2007). Bakhtin (1981) asserted the polyphonic and dialogic nature of language and discourse as follows:

> [Language] is populated—overpopulated—with the intentions of others. . . . The word in language is half someone else's . . . the word does not exist in a neutral and impersonal language . . . but rather it exists in other people's mouths, in other people's contexts, serving other people's intentions. (p. 294)

Bakhtin (1981) theorized how language is multivoiced and interconnected, and meaning is dialogically created. Building on this idea, some scholars have examined how knowledge is dialogically built between an instructor and students or among students engaged in collaborative learning. In discussing polyphony in computer-supported collaborative learning, Trausan-Matu, Stahl, and Sarmiento (2006) analyzed online collaborative learning in grades 6 through 11 by illustrating how texts produced in student chat rooms interanimated and co-constructed meaning as students collaboratively solved math problems. Indeed, knowledge is collaboratively built within dialogues among people (Wells, 1999).

Together with this idea of knowledge building in the design of collaborative learning, *dialogic space* is often cited in scholastic work. Dialogic space is "the space of possibilities that opens up when two or more incommensurate perspectives are held together in the creative tension of a dialogue" (Wegerif & Yang, 2011, p. 312). Wegerif and Yang (2011) explained that the cognitive distance between people creates this dialogic space and that considering an "infinite other" instead of the direct addressee in a dialogue would help people search continuously for alternative views. Stenton (2010) proposed a program vision in which "dialogism enables students to experience learning as a process of changing understanding where success is driven by engagement, creativity and willingness to add their voice to the discussion" (p. 19).

In order to de-racialize Japaneseness, students are required to rethink and rebuild their knowledge continuously. Hence, an engaging and creative learning environment in which polyphony and dialogism are orchestrated effectively needs to be carefully planned, designed, and implemented.

Global Project Work: A Case Study

To illustrate the problems involved (and the solutions suggested) in the recent efforts to globalize Japanese higher education, we have selected one of our courses, Global Project Work (GPW) (Presenting About Japan in English) as a case study. In the following sections, we provide an overview of the course; we explain our pedagogical framework using the concepts of polyphony and dialogism; and we give some preliminary information on Group A, our focus group, composed of students who enrolled in our class in the spring semester of 2014.

GPW: Overview of the Course

The foundational elements of GPW emulated MEXT's project objectives— namely, (a) present about "Japan" in English, (b) learn in a collaborative and active manner, (c) gain new/alternative perspectives, and (d) acquire presentation skills adapted to a multicultural global audience. Furthermore, the authors considered it an educational opportunity for students to critically and reflexively rethink and rebuild their stereotypical images of "Japan."

Every semester, the number of participants in GPW fluctuates,[4] and their backgrounds vary in ages, majors, and English language skills, with the majority recognizing themselves as ethnically Japanese. The main and only goal of GPW is for students to collaborate on making a 15-minute presentation about contemporary Japan in English for a global audience. Because GPW is not an English language class, much of the pedagogical emphasis is placed on the content of the presentation.[5] Therefore, we give lectures in English and students create presentation slides and scripts in English, but for the sake of efficient communication, students usually have discussions in Japanese. Each group of students chooses a topic it finds interesting, usually among a variety of areas (society, economy, politics, science, and technology), and after agreeing on the message to convey, the students create their presentation, practice it, and publicly present their final project in front of faculty and other domestic and international students. Throughout the semester, students are given several opportunities to practice their presentations and to familiarize themselves with public speaking. In the spring 2014 class, four groups of students had five practice presentations, one midpresentation, and one rehearsal before their final public presentation.

Eight "Voices": Pedagogical Framework and Approaches

We designed GPW's curriculum inspired by Bakhtin's (1984) concepts of polyphony and dialogism. Within the cycle of a 15-week course, we embedded multiple occasions for a student to experience polyphony and to create dialogic space implicitly and explicitly. Figure 9.1 illustrates the "voices" that make up GPW's dialogic space, as explained:

a. *Lectures.* As instructors, we gave lectures on basic presentation theory and skills and also lectured about how to give critique and not criticism, considering that peer feedback ("voices" d and g) formed an important part of the course design.

b. *Readings.* Aside from the lectures, we provided an academic reading, which offered a specialist's disciplinary and often critical perspective on each group's topic.

c. *Public speech critique homework.* Along with readings, students were assigned to watch two public speeches online and write a page-long critique. We suggested famous historical speeches, such as Martin Luther King Jr's, as well as contemporary speeches, such as the TED (Technology, Entertainment, Design) series.

d. *Out-group peer feedback.* After every practice session, the presenters had the chance to receive feedback from their classmates. In fact, it was expected that watching and critiquing the other groups' practice presentations would allow them to reflect, rethink, and rebuild their own.

Figure 9.1 Dialogic relations of a student.

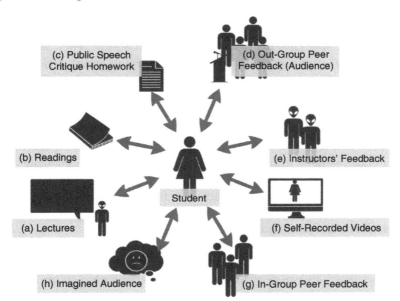

e. *Instructors' feedback.* We, as instructors, functioned as a source of knowledge that encouraged students to take initiatives and search for serious academic evidence to support their arguments. We remained aware that our ideologies informed our questions, but we tried to limit the impact that these ideologies may have had by avoiding telling students what exactly they should do about their topic.

f. *Self-recorded videos.* All seven practice presentations were video-recorded by students on their smartphones. This was intended as a way for students to review themselves from a third-person viewpoint, at least virtually, and, as a result, add a third dimension to the feedback received from instructors as well as out-group peers. "When we were presenting, I thought the presentation was going well, but when I watched ourselves on the video, I thought otherwise" (Ayumi, Group A follow-up interview, November 24, 2014).

g. *In-group peer feedback.* We also regularly set time for each group to have discussions following our lectures, during which they had the opportunity to informally receive feedback from instructors and classmates and give feedback to other groups.

h. *Imagined audience.* By using the conceptual device of the "imagined audience," we repeatedly reminded students of alternative possibilities, so that they would continue to search for the best way to convey the content to an audience of possibly very different cultural backgrounds and presumptions.

Figure 9.2 illustrates the typical cycle of a GPW class. First, each group gives and self-records a practice presentation, based on group research and a reading given by the instructors (b). They then receive critiques from their classmates (d, g) and instructors (e). Then the instructors give the lecture of the week (a, h). Depending on the week's focus, each group engages in in-group peer feedback (g) and works on the refinement of the presentation using the video (f) along with the comments from peers and the instructors. Students also work on improving their individual sections, occasionally learning from the public speech critique assignment (c). Throughout the semester, we repeat this cycle in a spiral manner, with midpresentations and rehearsals in between and final public presentations in week 14. Then the last week is dedicated to a self-reflection session and a group evaluation.

As shown in Figure 9.3, the interaction among the eight voices forming GPW's dialogic space affects every student. By working collaboratively, each group negotiates its voices and creates a presentation, which is an amalgam of the voices of each group member, adapted and transformed into one single group voice. In this way, our polyphonic approach is designed not only to encourage students to acquire a reflexive, critical, and multiangular perspective on their own ideas but also for them to embody collaboratively "a philosophy of interaction personal lifestyle where individuals are responsible for their actions, including learning, and respect the abilities and contributions of their peers" (Panitz, 1997, para. 4). We intend this pedagogical framework to stimulate the creation of dialogic space among and within students and to work toward a more reflective acquirement of knowledge, devoid of racialized images of Japan.

In this chapter, we focus on the work of Group A, which took part in GPW in spring 2014. This group consisted of four members (all names are pseudonyms): Yōsuke, a male sophomore student in education; Takashi, a male junior student in science; Mai, a female junior student in literature; and Ayumi, a female junior student in literature. All four members shared an interest in food, particularly *washoku* (Japanese cuisine). Since the start of GPW, we have video-recorded student presentations and classroom activities, collected student works, and interviewed the participants in follow-up sessions. Our analysis of Group A's progress toward the final presentation on *washoku* employs the following material: video recordings of the four consecutive draft versions of the group's presentation (weeks 5, 8, 10, and 13); the instructors' and Group A's memos of student–instructor/student–student feedback sessions; each member's reflection in writing; and two follow-up interviews with Group A members. Findings show how we engaged with

Figure 9.2 A typical cycle of a class.

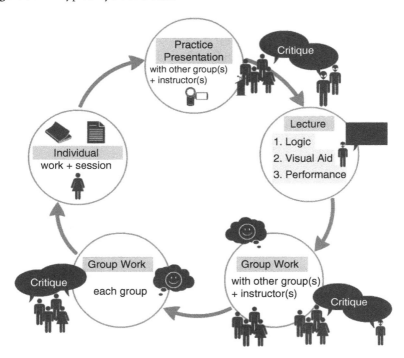

Figure 9.3 Dialogic relation of a group.

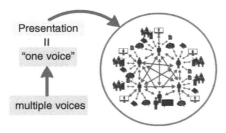

Group A students and encouraged them to break down their initial idea about "Japan"—*washoku* to be exact—into its constitutive components, then rebuild these constituents into the shape of a group presentation with a single message. To achieve this objective, we use the course framework introduced previously and point throughout the analysis to each of the eight voices that contributed to Group A's progress. We conclude with a discussion of the possibilities that our method offers for students to embody collaboration through a polyphonically and dialogically structured course.

Racialized *Washoku:* Group A's First Presentation

Group A's first presentation bore the title "*Washoku*: Japanese-Style Food."
After brief introductions, the group showed a percentage on screen, asking
the audience what they think it referred to. The number, 32.8%, was, we
were told, the rate of obesity in Mexico, which is the "fattest country in the
world. . . . Mexico is followed by the United States, where one third of the
population is obese," the students continued, warning us, on the next slide,
that developed nations are prone to ingesting excessive amounts of energy. So
the answer, the students suggested, was eating healthy. And that was where
washoku was introduced:

> [Ayumi]: *Washoku* was paid attention to overseas as healthy food [slide:
> pictures of sushi, tempura, and a classic Japanese traditional menu of fish,
> rice, and miso soup]. . . . The amount of Japanese restaurants keep growing
> in other countries year by year [slide: "number of overseas Japanese restau-
> rants '55,000'"]. . . . But those restaurants are not necessarily managed by
> Japanese. There are strange *washoku*.
> [Takashi]: One of the most famous ones is California roll, which uses avo-
> cado and crab with mayonnaise. . . . In Japan, it is also popular, but are we
> able to call this *washoku*?

A series of further pictorial examples of "strange" *washoku* followed: sushi
with strawberries and sushi-shaped doughnuts. And some "strange *washoku*"
from Japan were introduced too, such as ramen (noodle soup), curry-rice,
and *omurice*.[6] "Are these dishes that are made in Japan with foreign ingredients *washoku*?" we are asked again.

To find an answer to this question, Mai, the next presenter, relied on
the recent news about *washoku*'s addition to the United Nations Educational, Scientific and Cultural Organization's (UNESCO) list of intangible
cultural heritage, quoting UNESCO's website as saying that *washoku* represents the Japanese spirit and its respect for nature. Referring to another
definition provided by the Japanese Ministry of Agriculture, Forestry and
Fisheries (MAFF), the fourth student, Yōsuke, again used photos to illustrate the characteristics that allegedly make up what *washoku* is today. Then
he concluded:

> [Yōsuke]: Japanese people enjoy food with their five senses, and they have
> an important food culture. We say . . . "*itadakimasu*" and "*gochisōsama*"—
> Japanese unique culture. It is a greeting to appreciate those who prepare the
> meal. Such a unique culture has spread around the world. Do you appreci-
> ate food and nature like the Japanese?

Group A's presentation reflects many of the issues discussed in the introductory section of this chapter and expresses the pervasive tendency in scholarly, policy, and media sources of considering Japanese culture as "uniquely unique: fundamentally and qualitatively different" (Sugimoto, 2014, p. 192) from any other society. The uniqueness of Japan relies on the argument that the country is racially and ethnically uniform and, by extension, that all cultural products of Japanese society are "imbued" with a monoethnic Japanese spirit, as the UNESCO website argues. Such racialization of food is neither rare nor specific to Japan. As Chen (2012) noted, food has always been a "powerful metaphor and tool of those seeking to define and redefine the national character of the nation" (p. 429).

In Group A's presentation, *washoku* is endowed with Japanese racial attributes in three consecutive stages. First, *washoku* is constructed as "the Japanese cuisine" through statistical data that claims to show the popularity of *washoku* among non-Japanese nationals, such as tourists or residents of countries other than Japan. Second, *washoku* dishes using ingredients that have entered the Japanese food market more recently than in other parts of the world, such as avocado, are deemed strange. And third, *washoku* itself is presented as a symbol for the harmonious, close-to-nature Japanese society because of the "freshness" and seasonality of its ingredients and its association with communal and festive rites. *Washoku* is also presented as a metaphor for the well-known orientalist view that associates Japan, and East Asia in general, with communitarianism, exoticism, and an almost "mysterious" connection to a primitive nature in which people, we are told, *still* use all of their five senses.

Toward De-Racializing *Washoku*: Second, Third, and Final Drafts

Based on the format of the course described in the previous section, Group A students found themselves in possession of a number of opportunities (dialogic voices a to h described earlier) to voice their thoughts, receive feedback, and reconsider their arguments individually within their group, within the class, and with us, the instructors.

Toward Draft Two of the Presentation

Group A's first presentation was criticized for failing to convince us of the trustworthiness of the sources employed to back up their arguments. Much of the statistical evidence combined quantitative analysis with subjective uses of the word *washoku*. If, for example, *washoku* is indeed healthy, is "strange" *washoku* healthy too? And if *washoku* is what is made in restaurants offering

Japanese cuisine, how is the word different from the general term *nihon-ryori,* which literally translates as "Japanese cuisine"? Furthermore, a major issue noted and pointed out in our feedback (e) was the use of the word *strange.*

> [Ioannis]: I don't know what you mean by *strange.* . . . I don't think people know what you compare *strange* to. . . . Do you compare it to your ideal image of *washoku?* . . . Imagine you tell this to people who eat California rolls every day.

By formulating our questions while referring to an imagined audience (h), we encouraged students to think about their idea of what is "strange" about those *washoku* dishes. If being "strange" for sushi is related to the idea that on foreign soil, consumers and cooks prefer foreign ingredients, then how do students explain that "foreign-ized" sushi are also popular in Japan?

To help Group A grapple with our comments, a brief class lecture (a) about logic in presentation was given. Moreover, a short academic article (b) (see Bestor, 2011), taken out of an introductory volume on Japanese society and culture, was sent out to students. The article was chosen for its argument that "most if not all contemporary Japanese do not closely observe these culinary traditions in actual daily food choices, and honor them more abstractly *as sources of heritage and identification*" (Bestor, 2011, pp. 279–280). In addition, the students were assigned a public speech critique (c) as homework to submit the week after.

Description of Second Draft of the Presentation

The second midsemester presentation by Group A had undergone some improvements. Yōsuke opened the talk with a very dramatic sentence written in white letters against a black background: "Four people will die." This, we were told, was the number of Americans that will have died by the end of the presentation because of unbalanced diet–related diseases. And Yōsuke continued:

> [Yōsuke]: [Shows a YouTube video of Jamie Oliver on reforming school lunches in the United Kingdom and the United States] In Japan, we have a subject, *seikatsu-ka* (life environment studies) . . . but in some countries, they don't have that. They don't care about what they eat, calories or nutrition. . . . In Japan, we say, "*itadakimasu*" and "*gochisōsama*" . . . we feel that these words exist because we grow and we study about food.

Following Yōsuke, Ayumi launched into a statistics-based explanation of the amount of food waste observed in Japan, noting, for example, that

Japanese waste was as much as the equivalent of nine million bowls of rice per day. For that, Ayumi blamed the lack of intergenerational learning. Next, Mai added more information on the origins of the *washoku* boom abroad:

> [Mai]: Especially sushi got attention as low-calorie and low-fat food. [Shows photos of California roll and other dishes that Group A had called "strange" the last time]. . . . But can we call these *washoku*, or Japanese food? First, what is the difference between Japanese food and *washoku?* [Explains the dictionary definitions.] The message of *washoku* is to respect and appreciate nature and food. Is this message understood all over the world? Do not Japanese people forget the spirit [of *washoku*]?

The answer to those questions was presumably provided by Takashi, who argued next that *washoku* is neither about eating healthy nor about the quality of the ingredients, but about sharing an idea: to do something about Japan's food waste and to spread around the world the "essence of *washoku*," which is the "appreciation for food."

Toward Draft Three of the Presentation

During the feedback session with another group, the student audience (d) first commented on the length of the presentation, and particularly on the substantial use of statistical data, which had resulted in blurring the message of the presentation.

> [Sayo]: *What is the connection between* washoku *and world peace? You complain about food waste in Japan, but then you talk about the spirit of* washoku, *. . . which is supposed to show appreciation for food.*
> [Sohei]: *Isn't this contradictory?*[7]

Group A seemed to have followed our advice and provided clear and relevant data for their arguments, but they miscalculated the amount of data needed to prove their point. They had taken in what they read or watched on the Internet at face value, and they had split the presentation in to four parts, which developed in independent directions. Satoko's comments (e) noted in Group A's memo included the following:

> No logical connection between each section. There's overwhelming appearance of "numbers," which is not well-connected to and does not support your main idea. Think of the entire flow and message. The video is taken out of context. The comparison between a case in the United States and Japan is not valid without solid and appropriate data and resources.

In order to tackle these comments, during the following week, Group A asked the instructors (e) for a feedback session outside of the classroom. During that session, we encouraged students to use the whiteboard to brainstorm with our help on the complexity of views reflected in their presentations. This intensive session, which according to the follow-up interviews, took the form of an in-group peer feedback (g) session after we (the instructors) had left the room, eventually inspired a triangular depiction of the three actors involved in defining *washoku* in the contemporary world (see "Description of Third Draft of the Presentation").

In follow-up interviews with Group A students, we discovered more about the way the dialogical space created by GPW had impacted the second draft of their presentation. First, influenced by a lecture (a) emphasizing the importance of using (and specifying) solid data that would lead to a meaningful and informed message, Ayumi said, *"I thought, 'Oh okay, then we can just cover up with statistics, and it'd look legit'"* (Interview, November 24, 2014). Second, in conjunction with Ayumi's suggestion, Takashi, who had just completed the speech critique assignment (c) on Jamie Oliver's TED talk "Teach Every Child About Food"[8] suggested, *"Jamie's message for food education was so strong and I thought we can use this to emphasize how Japan has food education and thus the healthiness of washoku"* (Interview, November 24, 2014). In a sense, Takashi was proposing to increase the degree to which *washoku* was racialized, by claiming that the specific qualities of *washoku* were shared by all Japanese because they were part of their educational background, contrary to what he imagined the situation in the West depicted by Jamie Oliver was.

Description of Third Draft of the Presentation

The order of appearance had again changed from last time. Takashi first announced that their talk was about the "true meaning of *washoku*."

> [Yōsuke]: [Explains a survey by a private cooking school which shows that their students' top image of *washoku* is sushi and *sukiyaki*.] However, *sukiyaki*, for example, has only a 130-year history, dating back to the late nineteenth century when the Japanese, influenced by Western tastes, started eating beef. Can we say that this is Japanese traditional food? And what about the fact that *sukiyaki* contains a lot of sugar, and is further dipped into raw egg before we eat it? Is this really healthy food? Is *sukiyaki* *washoku*?

Mai followed with a simplified version of her previous talk. She noted that our image of *washoku* is based on the idea that Japanese restaurants use seasonal ingredients and specific preparation techniques to cook dishes. "On the other hand, let us look at unique Japanese food, meaning food that does not fit our image of *washoku*." Mai explained the origin stories of *omurice* and spaghetti *napolitan* (a pasta dish characterized by its tomato ketchup–based sauce), which were created by Japanese chefs in the twentieth century. She then added examples of Japanese adaptations of imported cuisines, such as Japanese curry-rice or ramen (the Japanese noodle soup), which she compared with adaptations found abroad, such as the California roll. Mai's part ended on an interesting comment: "All 'unique' Japanese food seemed to have been based on adaptations, whether these may be adaptation to specific circumstances in Japan, or adaptations to the tastes of the non-Japanese, local consumers. 'So, what is *washoku*?'"

Complicating the argument further, and drawing us to an interesting finale, Ayumi first seemed to be using UNESCO's definition of *washoku* (see "Racialized *Washoku*: Group A's First Presentation") as an answer to Mai's question; but referring back to Yōsuke's part, she noted that Japanese food culture changes through time. Ayumi explained the change in food self-sufficiency rate and rice consumption in Japan and added how the government tried to protect particular types of *washoku*. Ayumi explained, "Originally *washoku* is a culture including various elements. . . . *Washoku* is a changeable culture. Though *washoku* was registered as Intangible Cultural Heritage, the government is trying to give it a tangible characteristic." In the end, Takashi summarized the arguments of the presentation and ended on an insightful note. "We tried to find the definition of *washoku*, but we could not. This is because we think that *washoku* is what you think it is."

Toward Final Draft of the Presentation

There were evident improvements in Group A's presentation: The flow of the story made more sense, and this is what the rest of the students noted during the feedback session (d). As conveners, our comments (e) also became much more precise. Ioannis, for example, noted two points. First, although clearly defined by Mai, the use of the word *unique* could be misleading because the idea overlaps with what *washoku* is also claimed to be, namely, "unique Japanese cuisine." Second, Ayumi's part inspired rightful criticism of Japanese official policies, but it lacked the perspective of other actors involved in defining or, rather, imagining *washoku:* the restaurant owners and the consumers themselves.

It was clear that Group A had already taken a significant turn in the way in which they were thinking about *washoku*. According to comments made during the follow-up interview, the self-recorded video (f) of their presentations had made a major impact. Ayumi, for example, remembered, "When I watched that black screen with the sentence 'four people will die,' I thought that we had gone too far." Takashi added, "We had a long discussion after we received feedback on the second presentation, and we came up with the conclusion that we simply could not define *washoku*; so that became our message."

At the same time, Ayumi, who was searching for more critical material on the use of *washoku* as a kind of Japanese "soft political power," found newspaper articles that criticized the Japanese government's attempts to extend its authority on deciding who could make *washoku* outside of Japanese soil. Yōsuke, on his side, had a look back to the reading (b) handed out to the group after the first presentation and stumbled across the following reference:

> In the 1870s, there was a boom in consumption of beef, emulating European tastes for red meat (officially, long forbidden by Buddhist proscriptions), in the form of a traditional kind of dish simmered with soy sauce: a dish now internationally known as sukiyaki. (Bestor, 2011, p. 281)

De-Racialized Washoku: Final Presentation

Group A's final presentation integrated most of our comments, and although students still lacked essential presentation skills (e.g., Ayumi, ended up reading from her script), the flow of the narration had been substantially improved.

> [Takashi]: *Washoku*. It's a familiar word, isn't it? But almost all of us cannot explain it well. So today, in this presentation, we will talk about the essence of *washoku*.
> [Yōsuke]: [Explains an analysis of the public surveys of Japanese people's image of *washoku*, noting that these were "stereotypes," then illustrates *sukiyaki*'s origin and unhealthiness.] We can say that some images of *washoku*, such as "traditional" and "healthy," do not apply to all dishes. So, our question is, what is really *washoku?*

Mai repeated her talk from the previous draft of the presentation, with some significant changes: She had replaced the appellation *unique* with *original,* and she critically quoted the MAFF as saying that "Japanese restaurants abroad are the showrooms of Japanese foods and the starting point for allowing foreigners to understand Japanese food." Finally, Ayumi's section had not changed in content but had been enriched with more graphic features that were meant to better convey her message. Takashi, finally, grouped each of the other members' talks into a logical format: Yōsuke talked about consumers, Mai provided the view of the owners of Japanese restaurants, and Ayumi discussed the Japanese government's perspective. The conclusion of Group A's presentation had not been altered, but the rationale behind it had now become much clearer: *Washoku* was an amalgam of different voices, each claiming its own authority on defining *washoku*.

Discussion and Implications

Looking back at the reflection papers written by GPW students, some students noted the pressure of having to constantly revise the logic of their arguments from different points of views. This repetitive exercise had, as planned, impacted their perspective on Japanese culture, connecting thus the spiral, polyphonic structure of the course to the content element of GPW. The following is an excerpt of Yōsuke's follow-up interview, conducted in Japanese by a colleague, in which Yōsuke observed that, by participating in this course, he learned how to think about Japanese culture:

> *The class was quite different from my initial expectation. . . . I had to imagine what the audience may be like. . . . We had to think carefully about how to convey our message in a clear and logical manner. . . . We kept asking ourselves, "What is Japanese culture?" In the end, we presented about* washoku, *which we defined as an aggregate of what people imagine* washoku *to be. . . . I think that we can say the same for Japanese culture. That Japanese culture is an aggregate of what people think or imagine Japanese culture to be. . . . [A]t the beginning we were trying to define* washoku, *but we could not. So, we realized, ok, if what* washoku *means depends on people, then* washoku *is just an aggregate of people's perceptions. And the same stands for Japanese culture and other concepts alike.* (Follow-up interview, July 30, 2014)

Yōsuke's use of the expression "we realized" points to two important effects of our course. First, his and other students' frequent use of *we* means that, to some extent, they embodied collaborativity by normalizing the existence of multiple voices in their group and transforming them into one single voice. Second, our original objective of having students acquire a reflexive, critical, and multiangular perspective on Japanese culture, without explicitly teaching about it, seems to have been accomplished, considering that Group A students eventually acknowledged that "Japanese culture is an aggregate of people's perceptions."

Indeed, the polyphonic and dialogic course structure involving eight "others" embedded in a spiral curriculum created an infinite dialogic space, which, as Figure 9.4 illustrates, engaged and encouraged the students on each step of the way to unpack their initial idea, about not only *washoku* but also "Japanese culture," into its constitutive components. They subsequently

Figure 9.4 Polyphonic impact on each draft.

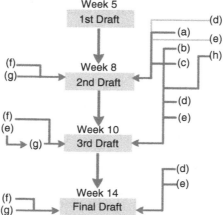

rebuilt these constituents into the shape of a group presentation with a single message: "It's all in our head," which sounds not merely logical but also ethical for the global audience to which it is supposed to be addressed. Not all voices, however, were heard. Feedback to the first draft, for example, seemed to not have been taken into account in the second draft (lines departing from d and e are thus marked in light grey color).

A characteristic tendency of the cross-national movement of beliefs and practices consists of the accompanying conceptual collapse of "biology" and "culture" in the manner that these ideas and practices are categorized, described, and "explained" to a global audience. This is exactly what the initial racialization of *washoku* by Group A consisted of: a conceptual "jump" connecting the assumed homogenous "biology" of the Japanese producers with their "cultural" product. By the end of the exercise, however, Group A came to consider Japan as a country sharing a lot of similarities with the rest of the world in the way traditions and modernities change, intermingle, and evolve, regardless of geographical and national boundaries.

Education on minority issues or multiculturalism, which aims at deconstructing these issues, finds itself frequently separated from "regular" classes, where the racial dominance and homogeneity of both content and audience are assumed. As the Japanese case here has demonstrated, however, it is preferable that the promotion of an equitable and inclusive educational and social environment for marginalized individuals in an increasingly globalized world starts with those who are part of an alleged "mainstream" and who are originally "deaf" to the various "voices" involved in our cultural expressions.

We hope that our case study, GPW, provided a model on how to begin tackling this challenging task.

Notes

1. For comparison, according to a recent report (Mervis, 2014), foreign students currently compose 8.1% of total U.S. enrollment.

2. A newer project (Top Global University Project) has recently started as a continuation to the one we describe in this section. It has a budget of 7.7 billion yen to be spent over a 10-year period. See MEXT's September 2014 press release available at www.mext.go.jp/b_menu/houdou/26/09/__icsFiles/afieldfile/2014/10/07/1352218_02.pdf

3. We are aware of the ambiguities of definition of *collaborative learning* (Dillenbourg, 1999, p. 1), but in this paper, we shall be using the term to simply indicate a group of students working together to achieve a common educational goal.

4. We had over 50 students with 4 instructors in spring 2013, 25 students with 3 instructors in fall 2013, and 2 of us cotaught 14 students in spring 2014 and 13 students in fall 2014.

5. We tend, however, to correct some of the most serious language errors of the final drafts of each group's presentation, in order to make sure their argument is conveyed correctly to the audience.

6. A dish of fried rice wrapped in an omelet.

7. Transcripts translated from Japanese into English are italicized.

8. See www.ted.com/talks/jamie_oliver

References

Bakhtin, M. (1981). *The dialogic imagination: Four essays* (M. Holquist, Ed., with C. Emerson & M. Holquist, Trans.) Austin: University of Texas Press.

Bakhtin, M. (1984). *Problems of Dostoevsky's poetics* (Vol. 8). Minneapolis: University of Minnesota Press.

Bestor, T. C. (2011). Cuisine and identity in contemporary Japan. In V. Bestor, T. C. Bestor, & A. Yamagata (Eds.), *Routledge handbook of Japanese culture and society* (pp. 273–285). London, UK: Routledge.

Central Education Council. (2013, Aug 28). *Report regarding the nurturing by universities of the ability to continue lifelong learning and independent thinking, for an era that is difficult to predict.* Retrieved from http://www.mext.go.jp/component/b_menu/shingi/toushin/__icsFiles/afieldfile/2012/10/04/1325048_1.pdf

Chen, Y. (2012). Food, race, and ethnicity. In J. M. Pilcher (Ed.), *The Oxford handbook of food history* (pp. 428–443). Oxford, UK: Oxford University Press.

Dillenbourg, P. (1999). Introduction: What do you mean by "collaborative learning"? In P. Dillenbourg (Ed.), *Collaborative learning: Cognitive and computational approaches* (pp. 1–19). Oxford, UK: Pergamon/Elsevier Science.

Eades, J. S., & Cooper, M. (2013). Training researchers in the Asia-Pacific: A regional response to global leadership in research. In A. Altmann & B. Ebersberger (Eds.), *Universities in change managing higher education institutions in the age of globalization* (pp. 201–216). London, UK: Springer.

Iwabuchi, K. (2002). "Soft" nationalism and narcissism: Japanese popular culture goes global. *Asian Studies Review, 26*(4), 447–469.

Koschmann, T. (1999). Toward a dialogic theory of learning: Bakhtin's contribution to understanding learning in settings of collaboration (Article no. 38). In C. Hoadley & J. Roschelle (Eds.), *Proceedings of the computer support for collaborative learning 1999 conference.* Stanford, CA: Laurence Erlbaum Associates.

McVeigh, B. J. (2002). *Japanese higher education as myth.* Armonk, NY: M. E. Sharpe.

Mervis, J. (2014, November). Data check: Why do Chinese and Indian students come to U.S. universities? *Science Magazine.* Retrieved from http://news.sci encemag.org/education/2014/11/data-check-why-do-chinese-and-indian-stu dents-come-u-s-universities

Panitz T. (1997). Collaborative versus cooperative learning: A comparison of the two concepts which will help us understand the underlying nature of interactive learning. *Cooperative Learning and College Teaching, 8*(2). Retrieved from http:// home.capecod.net/~tpanitz/tedsarticles/coopdefinition.htm

Semba, H. (2014, March). *Globalization of higher education in Japan.* [PowerPoint slides] Presentation at the Globalisation of Higher Education from the perspective of EU-Japan Collaboration Symposium, EESC, Brussels, Belgium. Retrieved from http://www.eu-japan.eu/sites/eu-japan.eu/files/1_1-Semba.pdf

Shimomura, H. (2013, September 2). Making Japanese higher education more international. In *The Japan Times: Global 30 Universities.* Retrieved from http:// info.japantimes.co.jp/ads/pdf/20130902_global_30_universities.pdf

Stenton, A. (2010). How could a dialogic approach to teaching transform students' learning? A discussion with reference to medical education. *Higher Education Research Network Journal, 4,* 15–21. Retrieved from http://www.kcl.ac.uk/study/ learningteaching/kli/research/hern/hern-j4/Alison-Stenton-hernjvol4.pdf

Sugimoto, Y. (2014). Japanese society: Inside out and outside in. *International Sociology, 29*(3), 191–208.

Trausan-Matu, S., Stahl, G., & Sarmiento, J. (2006). Polyphonic support for collaborative learning. In Y. A. Dimitriadis, I. Zigurs, & E. Gómez-Sánchez (Eds.), *Groupware: Design, implementation, and use* (LNCS 4154) (pp. 132–139). Heidelberg, Germany: Springer.

Wegerif, R. (2007). *Dialogic education and technology: Expanding the space of learning* (Vol. 7). New York, NY: Springer.

Wegerif, R., & Yang, Y. (2011). Technology and dialogic space: Lessons from history and from the "Argunaut" and "Metafora" projects. In H. Spada, G. Stahl, N. Miyake, & N. Law (Eds.), *Connecting computer-supported collaborative learning to policy and practice, CSCL2011 conference proceedings* (Vol. 1: Long Papers) (pp. 312–318). Hong Kong, China: International Society of the Learning Sciences. Retrieved from http://isls.org/cscl2011/doc/CSCL2011ProceedingsVol1.pdf

Wells, G. (1999). Dialogic inquiry in education: Building on the legacy of Vygotsky. In C. D. Lee & P. Smagorinsky (Eds.), *Vygotskian perspectives on literacy research* (pp. 51–85). New York, NY: Cambridge University Press. Retrieved from http://people.ucsc.edu/~gwells/Files/Papers_Folder/Building%20on%20Vygotsky.pdf

Wetherall, W. (2008). The racialization of Japan. In D. B. Willis & S. Murphy-Shigematsu (Eds.), *Transcultural Japan: At the borderlands of race, gender and identity* (pp. 264–281). London, UK: Routledge.

Yamashiro, J. H. (2013). The social construction of race and minorities in Japan. *Sociology Compass, 7*(2), 147–161.

10

UNSUNG HEROES

Impact of Diverse Administrators on the Creation of
Transformative, Affirming, and Equitable Learning
Environments

Stella L. Smith

I n her seminal work *Teaching to Transgress: Education as the Practice of Free-dom*, hooks (1994) spoke of the engaged pedagogy necessary to inspire and transform students in classroom learning environments. Aspects of implementing an engaged pedagogical stance include the following: (a) a grasp of the lives of students in both detail and outline, enabling a considera-tion of their experiences as central to the learning process; (b) the creation of transformational relationships; (c) a commitment to addressing one's per-sonal process of self-actualization and identity formation; (d) the deepening of knowledge creation and specific knowledge; (e) an emphasis on critical curriculum construction, critical reflection, and professional development; and (f) a mutual development process of students and educators (Glass & Wong, 2003; hooks, 1994). Although many aspects of engaged pedagogy focus on what happens in the classroom, in this chapter, I purport that, like faculty, African American female administrators in particular provide transformational experiences for students by approaching their work from an engaged pedagogical perspective. Through the data presented, I suggest that the African American female administrators in this study participated in engaged pedagogy by interacting and inspiring students as well as challeng-ing systems that stifle the creation of engaged learning and teaching environ-ments. Thus, they created transformative, affirmative, and equitable learning environments, even though they were not considered faculty in the academy.

This research is a secondary analysis of data collected through a phenom-enological study of 12 African American females in senior-level positions at predominantly White institutions (PWIs) in higher education to investigate how they infuse engaged pedagogy in their work. This work enhances the current literature related to the importance and connection of administrators to the formation of the learning environment at the institution. The chapter begins with the theoretical grounding of the research, including the experiences of African American women administrators in higher education, engaged pedagogy in higher education, and Black feminist theory. The chapter continues with narratives of the study participants regarding their purpose and impact on higher education and how they created transformative, affirmative, and equitable learning environments, even though they were not teaching in the classroom. The chapter concludes with the researcher's thoughts regarding how administrator perspectives relate to creating engaged pedagogical experiences for students outside the classroom.

Literature Review

Experiences of African American Women in Higher Education

Education is considered the great equalizer through which anyone has an opportunity to be successful (Hurtado, 2007; Lloyd-Jones, 2009). However, researchers have found that African American female professionals working in higher education experience an insider versus outsider phenomenon (Aronson & Swanson, 1991; Collins, 1986; Lorde & Clarke, 2007), the experience of being physically allowed to enter a place but not being recognized in the space. Moreover, Black women experience isolation, discrimination due to racism and sexism, and a lack of support in career development as compared to their male and White colleagues (Alfred, 2001; Allen, Jacobson, & Lomotey, 1995; Carroll, 1982; Collins, 2000; DuCille, 1994; Etter-Lewis, 1991; Fleming, 1984; Jackson, 2004b; James & Farmer, 1993; Johnson-Bailey & Cervero, 1996; Loder, 2005; Lorde & Clarke, 2007; Moses, 1989; Mosley, 1980; Myers, 2007; Wilson, 1989). In spite of these experiences, African American females continue to pursue administrative roles in academia.

A report from the American Council on Education (2005) indicated that there has been an increase in the number of African Americans in senior-level executive positions at PWIs. According to the National Center for Education Statistics (2010), in fall 2009, there were 230,579 higher education executive, administrative, and managerial professionals, of which 13,394 (5.8%) were African American women. This percentage was slightly higher than in the fall of 1999 when there were 159,888 higher education executive, administrative, and managerial professionals, of which 7,807 (4.9%)

were Black (National Center for Education Statistics, 2001). However, this number was low, given that in 2009, African American females represented 6.8% of the U.S. population and 8.8% of the fall undergraduate enrollment (National Center for Education Statistics, 2010; U.S. Census Bureau, 2010). In addition, African American scholars found that many of these new positions had less status, influence, power, and authority than existing positions (Bonner, 2001; Brown, 1997; Jackson, 2004a). They also found that these professionals were in positions tangential to the governance of the institutions—specifically academic support, student services, and diversity initiatives (American Council on Education, 2005; Brown, 1997).

Given the changes in the demographics of students who are attending institutions of higher education, the need for a diverse faculty and administration is dire. Diversity is necessary in academia because it enriches the educational experience for all students matriculating at the institution and fosters an exchange of ideas between people with varied life experiences (Turner, 2008). Student exposure to diverse people fosters acceptance of experiences and cultures that students might not have encountered prior to attending the institution (Allen, Epps, Guillory, Suh, & Bonous-Hammarth, 2000; Fleming, 1984; Gardiner, Enomoto, & Grogan, 2000; Patitu & Hinton, 2003). Although these diverse professionals do not teach in academia, they still serve as role models and advocates for underrepresented students as well as provide additional perspectives for their majority colleagues on issues related to diversity and higher education governance (Brown, 1997; Crews, 2007; Patitu & Hinton, 2003; Stroud, 2009).

Engaged Pedagogy

hooks (1994) defined *engaged pedagogy* as teachers' "active commitment to the process of self-actualization that promotes their own well-being to teach in a manner that empowers students" (p. 15). hooks purported that educators should approach their teaching using engaged pedagogy and that there should be a connection between the lived experiences of teachers and their interaction with students in the classroom. hooks (1994) stated, "Critical consciousness is rooted in the assumption that knowledge and critical thought done in the classroom should inform our habit of being and ways of living outside the classroom" (p. 194). Moreover, she asserted that we should "enter the classroom 'whole' and not as a 'disembodied spirit'" (p. 193). hooks argued that in order to actually create transformation in students, professors need to connect their teaching to their personal lived experiences and dismantle the false separation of the personal and the academic.

For administrators, applying an engaged pedagogical perspective to their work means going beyond the routine of their day-to-day transactional interactions with students to connect through shared lived experiences and develop mutually beneficial relationships. It provides a space for administrators to connect with students in a personal way as they assist them with the aspects of their college experience that occur outside the classroom. The opportunity to connect and support students on a personal level allows for the development of a relationship that is nourishing and rewarding for both the student and the administrator. However, using an engaged pedagogy can also be problematic for administrators because their colleagues might not understand the "non-traditional" student–administrator relationship.

Black Feminist Theory

Black feminist theory is used to investigate the presence of engaged pedagogy in the narratives of the African American women administrators because there is a similarity in presence of the tenets of Black feminist theory and an engaged pedagogy epistemological perspective. Collins (1989) declared that African American women's standpoint is unique due to their political and economic status, causing their experience of the world to differ from those who are not Black and not female. Collins stated, "A subordinate group not only experienced a different reality than a group that rules, but a subordinate group may interpret that reality differently than the dominate group" (p. 748). In higher education, a Eurocentric masculine knowledge-validation process is prominent. This process for creating knowledge and understanding includes two parts. First, knowledge is valued by a community of experts within the same standpoint of the community. Second, the community of experts must maintain their *credibility* as defined by the larger groups. Their knowledge-validation process suppresses the knowledge and ways of knowing for subordinate groups because it values and reinforces the beliefs of those in power.

Black feminist theory has the following tenets: (a) concrete experience as a criterion of meaning, (b) the use of dialogue in assessing knowledge claims, (c) the ethic of caring, and (d) the ethic of personal accountability (Collins, 1989). Moreover, a Black feminist perspective supports the desire to create engaged pedagogical learning environments. Black feminist theory supports the validation and creation of shared knowledge that is necessary to establish inclusive teaching and learning environments to foster open communication as well as create meaningful relationships and constructivist learning. Further, by taking personal responsibility for the teaching and learning of students and infusing an ethic of care into how they interact with students, a Black feminist epistemology is synergistic with the creation of inclusive teaching and learning environments. Black feminist theory provides insight into how African American women's unique perspectives affect how they see their roles in higher education, both as administrators and as role models for students.

Moreover, in praxis, Black feminist theory can be used as a lens to understand how Black female administrators develop the courage and fortitude to resist the traditional Eurocentric perspective of the role of the administrator–student relationship and develop engaged pedagogical relationships with students. Black feminist theory, coupled with engaged pedagogy, provides a salient mechanism for understanding the unique ways of knowing for African American administrators who engage in meaningful, mutually beneficial relationships with students. Aspects of the approach these Black female administrators use to develop relationships with students include emotional commitment to their growth and development, an ethic of caring, an ethic of being responsible, and an ethic of personal accountability. Because this perspective is counter to the Eurocentric tradition of administration, there is risk in operating from a Black feminist theory and engaged pedagogy perspective because it can be misunderstood by the Black female administrators' colleagues.

Methodology and Data

The original qualitative study used a phenomenological perspective to address the research questions (Guido, Chávez, & Lincoln, 2010; Perl & Noldon, 2000) and was framed using the theoretical concepts of Black feminist theory, biculturalism, and intersectionality (Barrett, Cervero, & Johnson-Bailey, 2003; Collins, 2000; Du Bois, 2007). The research design was a multicase oral history through guided interviews. The selection criteria for study participants included females who identified as (a) African American or Black, who were (b) currently or formerly employed in a dean, provost, vice presidential, or presidential track position in (c) administrative affairs, academic affairs, or student affairs at a PWI in the United States. Purposive sampling and snowballing techniques were used to obtain a sample size of 12 participants.

For this paper, I utilized a secondary analysis of the substantive interview data to investigate the engaged pedagogy that African American female administrators employ to create transformative learning spaces for students, given their role at higher education institutions. A secondary analysis technique was used to analyze interview transcripts through the lens of Black feminist theory to identify examples of engaged pedagogy in the experiences of African American female administrators. Secondary analysis is appropriate because previously collected data were used to look at a new research question. Strengths of using secondary analysis include the accessibility and availability of the data as well as reliability of the data. Limitations of using secondary data analysis include the possibility that it might not answer the new research question because the data were not collected for that specific purpose. Also, if the research was originally conducted by another researcher, there could be questions about the reliability of the data-collection process. In this research, these limitations are minimized because the same researcher conducted both studies (Long-Sutehall, Sque, & Addington-Hall, 2010). Furthermore, the broad aims of the original study—to understand the lived experiences of African American female administrators at a PWI—remain consistent. This chapter focuses on one aspect of the study participants' experience: how they navigate the PWI to create inclusive and engaged pedagogical environments. Thus, this study is actually an extension of the previous study, investigating a theme from the original study.

Findings

Using the theoretical framework of Black feminist theory to identify engaged pedagogy perspectives, participant interviews were analyzed and emergent themes identified. A synopsis of these findings is presented in this section of the chapter.

Engaged Pedagogy Perspectives

When asked about their experiences and approach to higher education, study participants had positive responses focused on the need and importance of their work. Moreover, they felt the work they did at the higher education institution served a greater purpose than themselves. They persisted because they believed they were in the best position to advocate for their particular expertise as well as diversity and inclusion efforts at their institution. This attitude was reflected in the remarks of Addison Michael, a study participant in a provost-track position in academic affairs at South One Public, about her senior-level executive role in higher education: "Higher education is about changing lives. It changes lives for young people. My job is the entry-level version of that. You have the opportunity to really change the trajectory for families." Addison Michael's quote exemplifies the importance and purpose the study participants placed on the position they held and the role they filled at the PWI. Moreover, the quote demonstrates a clear intent behind the work Addison Michael performed. She recognized that she had the opportunity to impact the lives of students, and she approached her position from that engaged pedagogy perspective.

The study participants mentioned that the way they were able to impact the lives of students, faculty, administrators, and staff at their respective institutions was a tangible example of how their presence in higher education was making a difference and increasing accessibility to educational opportunities for underrepresented populations. Isabella Jacob, a study participant in a dean-track position in academic affairs at Midwest College, shared the following regarding her experiences:

> I helped a lot of students to get through just in making sure they [were] aware of what they need to do so they [could] graduate and move into the position that they [were] really coming here for. Sometimes it was creating an atmosphere of hope, [which] motivated a lot of people.

Isabella Jacob's comment demonstrates the ethic of caring and uplift that many of the participants brought to the institution. Through mentoring, sponsoring, serving as a role model, and proactive advising, she created an environment that encouraged and supported authentic relationships with her students and, thus, encouraged and supported the students to be successful at the institution. Isabella Jacob went on to share that she often had conversations with students that gave them hope:

> Most of the students that I worked [with] were all working and had children, and many had issues with probation, child protection, and mothers and fathers of their children, and they needed someone to believe in them. They just needed to see hope on your face. One student said she would come to my office just to see me because there were so many people that did not believe.

Her influence was vital to successful matriculation of many of the students she worked with, and she has continued to mentor many of them even though she has left the institution. Because her interactions with students were different from the norm in the traditional culture of higher education, they became a beacon of hope for students at the institution. Moreover, she made herself available to the students to create a deeper connection by understanding them not only academically but also personally and spiritually. Because of this deeper, holistic relationship with students, she was an essential part of their academic experience, even though she was not in the classroom.

Emma Noah, a study participant in a vice presidential track position in administrative affairs at South One Public, also shared positive sentiments regarding her impact at the institution when she stated, "In due time [we] will see the fruits of our labor pay off and we are going to rise. We are going to elevate [the institution]." She used her position to advocate for structural systems that support inclusive learning and teaching environments. Although somewhat removed from direct student contact, the work she did supported an engaged pedagogical perspective. She admitted that institutional change was slow, but overall, the study participants were committed to advocating for that change at their institutions.

Regardless of the existing environment at a PWI, all of the participants were determined to make that environment positive. They understood that their "ways of knowing" how to manage the PWI environment stemmed from their personal experiences (based on historical, material, and epistemological conditions) as marginalized persons whose systems of knowledge were counter to and undervalued by the Eurocentric norm. However, they felt a spiritual calling to be at the higher education institution, and this was greater than a desire for a title or a salary. Their goal was to empower and change the institution for those students who would come after them. Participant Emma Noah described her connection to the PWI when she said, "We were drawn to try to help, motivate, empower, [and] mentor. Hopefully [we] have a seat at the table to allow people to hear what you have to say." Her comment reflects a theme throughout the interviews that African American women knew they were outliers in higher education, but rather than shrinking away from that, they used that difference to their advantage.

Ava Jack, a study participant in a vice presidential track position in administrative affairs at West College, also shared her approach to working in the higher education environment:

> I do know that you have to have a strong sort of a backbone. You have to like yourself. You have to be aware of yourself and how you come off as a leader. I think I am a work in progress. If I learn something new, I might change my mind. I believe in being open and accessible and being true to myself.

Ava Jack's comment demonstrated that her success in higher education was less about the institution and more about her professional code and her lived experiences. Her statement exemplifies the tenets of Black feminist theory in that her lived experiences informed how she grew and succeeded at the PWI. Moreover, her continual self-reflection exemplifies the self-actualization and personal development aspect of engaged pedagogy.

Olivia Ethan, a study participant in a vice presidential track position in student affairs at South One Public, expressed her sense regarding the responsibility she accepted as a visible leader at a PWI:

> I know that there were other people out there watching and wondering about African American women and people of color who have been

successful, what they have considered to be successful. And to know that I am one of those people was definitely something that I value. I know that there were people looking, and I want to set the best example for women who might be pursuing things like that.

Olivia Ethan's quote exemplifies a Black feminist perspective of the ethic of caring, mentoring others, and leading by example. She was cognizant of the work she was doing, and she was accountable to others who viewed her as a role model. This credence supported her success at the PWI.

Emily Aiden, a study participant in a vice presidential track position in academic affairs at South Two Public, shared the following regarding the need for a professional persona:

A part of my job here was to hear the woes and moments of disappointment that happen to Black faculty, staff, and PhD students. [And I tell them] when you walk back on this campus, you step like you were Daniel in the lion's den. Because it was not just for me, it was for all the students that were looking at you; it was for those that thought they cut you down and for all those that were not here and coming. So I need you to walk tall and walk strong, and you can't let anything bother you.

Emily Aiden's quote exemplifies the additional scrutiny placed on African American women and the perception of the environment at the PWI. The biblical reference of African American women (and men) as "Daniel in the lion's den" provides a visual of the African American against the PWI and highlights the continual struggle to integrate diverse peoples and perspectives into the PWI.

The Challenges of Engaged Pedagogy for Diverse Administrators

Taking an engaged pedagogical stance created several challenges for study participants. Based on this research, the juxtaposition of Afrocentric and Eurocentric perspectives manifested in negative perceptions, increased racism and sexism, and lack of work–life balance. For example, all the interview participants mentioned that their experiences in higher education were affected by the social construction of the character traits of being a woman and being African American. Stereotypes, such as African American women being aggressive, angry, loud, overly assertive, and incompetent, were mentioned in the interviews as affecting how they were perceived and how colleagues interacted with them at their institutions. This also affected them as they worked to create an engaged pedagogical experience for students. Colleagues sometimes misinterpreted engaged pedagogical support for students because they did not understand the approach. Participant Olivia Ethan further elaborated on this theme:

> I do not feel oppressed as an African American or as a female. I do not come to work every day having those thoughts. But I definitely do realize that when I am outside of the area in which I work that there were not [African American females there]. I can be sitting in a room where I am the only African American or I am the only female, so then when I go into the room, I definitely notice that. I am not sure that I am feeling oppressed by that, but feelings do come into play or thoughts do come into play as an African American woman, [like] how am I going to negotiate this? You have some historical thoughts coming with you. [I am thinking] I am in here with the dominant culture. How do they perceive me and my ability to be able to do what I am here to do?

Olivia Ethan recognized that she was very visible in certain situations and that she was not just representing her unit but also the societal and historical perception of African American women. In addition, in more gendered spaces, she was also challenged by patriarchy and societal gender roles. However, her quote demonstrates that even though she was aware of her perception, she was not crippled by it.

Further, study participant Emma Noah expressed her frustration with having to continuously fight the perception of being an African American female:

> You come in [and] you were African American [and] you were female and there was already some preconceived [thoughts about you]. You feel like you were working from a deficit. I feel like I came in and am working from a deficit. All of [my] forthrightness was now a negative, not a positive.

The previous quote expresses the constant struggle the African American women participants, in senior-level positions, faced—to continually demonstrate that they had the skills, knowledge, and credentials to serve in those positions. Moreover, regardless of the length of time they were in their senior-level positions, they had a continual struggle due to the dynamic nature of higher education. Study participant Sophia Mason summed this up by stating, "I never forget that I am a Black woman, but I don't think that it has prevented me from achieving the things that I wanted to achieve." Sophia Mason's comment exemplifies the resiliency of the study participants.

Participant Emma Noah mentioned the work expectation that racism and sexism places on African American females when she said, "They see me and they see that I am African American. You have to be better without question." She went on to say that in spite of this expectation, she was successful:

> I am not going to fail. I am not going to fail. I am just not going to let you take it from me. I am going to be successful. You are going to thrive. We are not going to waver, quiver, or whatever. I just was not going to. You can put whatever obstacle in front of me and I am going to grow, I am going to develop, I am going to learn. There was so much to do, and this was too important. I am going to take it, and I am going to do it.

Emma Noah's quote exemplifies the spirit of all the interview participants. They recognized that "isms" existed, but they worked to create a record of success, integrity, and credibility to counteract the effects of the ism's at the PWI. These oppressions were not first and foremost in their minds but, rather, they were a backdrop to their experiences.

All participants mentioned the imbalance that can occur in their higher education positions and how one should be willing to work through that imbalance to be successful. Included in this theme was work and role overload, so that even within the separate spheres of their professional and personal lives, there was disequilibrium.

Lily Carter, a study participant in a vice presidential track position in student affairs at South One Public, stated, "I don't believe in or support the notion of balance; I believe you choose at one time or another to accept the disequilibrium." Her statement exemplifies the sentiments of the interview participants that work–life balance was not an achievable goal. Sometimes one focused on work, and other times one focused on life. Participant Addison Michael concurred and explained how work-and-life imbalance manifested in her life:

> My life is my work. My work is my life. My work is my work. My life is my life. I know earlier I said that I know when to turn it off and I do, but I love what I do and what I do was part of who I am.

Addison Michael's sentiment exemplifies the passion that the interview participants had for higher education and the work they did. In some ways, they were so connected to the work that they chose not to balance their work and life.

In summary, the Black female administrators in this study understood how, through their roles at the institutions, they had the opportunity to impact the lives of students. Therefore, they approached their positions from that engaged pedagogy perspective. The study participants mentioned that the way they were able to impact the lives of students, faculty, administrators, and staff at their respective institutions was a tangible example of how their presence in higher education was making a difference and supporting increased accessibility to educational opportunities for underrepresented populations. Through mentoring, sponsoring, serving as a role model, and proactive advising, they created an environment that encouraged and supported authentic relationships with their students, thus helping the students to be successful at their institutions.

Their goal was to empower and change the institution for those students who would come after them. However, taking an engaged pedagogical stance created several challenges for study participants. Based on this research, the juxtaposition of Afrocentric and Eurocentric perspectives manifested in negative perceptions, increased racism and sexism, and lack of work–life balance. Furthermore, their colleagues sometimes misinterpreted engaged pedagogical support for students because they did not understand the approach.

Discussion and Implications

For hooks (1994), an engaged pedagogy perspective

> comes easiest to those of us who teach who also believe that there is an aspect of our vocation that is sacred; who believe that our work is not merely to share information but to share the intellectual and spiritual growth of our students. To teach in a manner that respects and cares for the souls of our students is essential if we are to provide the necessary conditions where learning can most deeply and intimately begin. (p. 13)

In the academy, the experiences of administrators are often overlooked when considering the academic experiences of students. This assumes that student learning only occurs in the classroom and that professionals and opportunities outside the classroom have no impact on how students experience their learning environment.

Although not a traditional application of engaged pedagogy, this research suggests that these Black female administrators used aspects of engaged pedagogy as an approach to their work in higher education. These administrators serve as employers, role models, advocates, and mentors for students in higher education. Their influence provides opportunities for students and thus transforms their experiences outside the classroom. The interview data confirm that these administrators intentionally shared their lived experiences and personal passions with their students and colleagues as well as supported critical thinking and the development of self-consciousness in students. Study participants' emotional commitment and responsibility to the work was synergistic with engaged pedagogy. They were committed to understanding and connecting holistically with students to assist them in having a positive experience at the institutions. Furthermore, they were driven with a sense of purpose and uplift and knew that education was the way to effect uplift for everyone, including African Americans and under-represented populations.

This research supports the idea that African American female administrators also contribute to the transformative, affirming, and equitable learning environment from outside the classroom. Aspects of implementing an engaged pedagogical stance that were apparent in this research include grasping the lives of students in both detail and outline, thus being able to consider their experiences as central to the learning process; creating transformational relationships; addressing one's personal process of self-actualization and identity formation; and manifesting critical reflection and professional development (Glass & Wong, 2003, hooks, 1994). This research also suggests that diverse administrators with different ways of knowing, based on their lived experiences and Afrocentric perspectives, could infuse national and international efforts by supporting diverse ways of knowing and accepting, and appreciation of the role that staff, administrators, and faculty have in supporting students.

This research highlights the need to consider the pedagogical experiences of administrators as possible alternatives for expanding education. Too often the experiences of administrators are not evaluated when developing learning models for students because they are not considered to have direct connections with students. Administrators in student affairs and diversity offices often employ unique and innovative methods for working with students that take into account the holistic student rather than just his or her classroom experiences. Administrators in business affairs, considered to be knowledgeable about how to interact with students, might also have strategies to create meaningful relationships with students, despite not being traditional. The interviews in this research study suggest that although these women are administrators, they frame their work around an ultimate purpose to support the students at their institutions. Understanding how these administrators interact with students in meaningful and engaged relationships can provide suggestions for faculty who want to develop a more engaged pedagogy but are unsure of how to connect with students. With the challenges in higher education today, we cannot overlook the benefits of including all higher education professionals in the conversation about creating a dynamic and engaged experience for students.

References

Alfred, M. V. (2001). Expanding theories of career development: Adding the voices of African American women in the White academy. *Adult Education Quarterly, 51*(2), 108–127.

Allen, K., Jacobson, S., & Lomotey, K. (1995). African American women in educational administration: The importance of mentors and sponsors. *Journal of Negro Education, 64*(4), 409–422.

Allen, W. R., Epps, E. G., Guillory, E. A., Suh, S. A., & Bonous-Hammarth, M. (2000). The Black academic: Faculty status among African Americans in U.S. higher education. *Journal of Negro Education, 69*(1/2), 112–127.

American Council on Education. (2005). *20 years of minorities in higher education and the ACE annual status report.* Washington, DC: Author.

Aronson, A. L., & Swanson, D. L. (1991). Graduate women on the brink: Writing as "outsiders within." *Women's Studies Quarterly, 19*(3/4), 156–173.

Barrett, I. C., Cervero, R. M., & Johnson-Bailey, J. (2003). Biculturalism—Outsiders within: The career development experiences of Black human resource developers. *Journal of Career Development, 30*(2), 109–128.

Bonner, F. B. (2001). Addressing gender issues in the historically black college and university community: A challenge and call to action. *The Journal of Negro Education, 70*(3), 176–191.

Brown, W. A. (1997). Increasing power, not just numbers. *Black Issues in Higher Education, 14*(18), 92.

Carroll, C. M. (1982). Three's a crowd: The dilemma of the Black woman in higher education. In G. T. Hull, P. B. Scott, & B. Smith (Eds.), *All the women were White, all the Blacks were men, but some of us were brave: Black women's studies* (pp. 115–128). New York, NY: The Feminist Press.

Collins, P. H. (1986). Learning from the outsider within: The sociological significance of Black feminist thought. *Social Problems, 33*(6) 14–32.

Collins, P. H. (1989). The social construction of black feminist thought. *Signs, 14*(4), 745–773.

Collins, P. H. (2000). *Black feminist thought: Knowledge, consciousness, and the politics of empowerment.* New York, NY: Psychology Press.

Crews, L. C. (2007). *The experiences of African American administrators at predominantly white two-year and four-year institutions* (Doctoral dissertation). Retrieved from Proquest Dissertations and Theses. (Order No. 3354476)

Du Bois, W. E. B. (2007). *The souls of black folk* (B. H. Edwards, Ed.). New York, NY: Oxford University Press.

DuCille, A. (1994). The occult of true black womanhood: Critical demeanor and black feminist studies. *Signs, 19*(3), 591–629.

Etter-Lewis, G. (1991). Black women's life stories: Reclaiming self in narrative texts. In S. Gluck & D. Patai (Eds.), *Women's words: The feminist practice of oral history* (pp. 43–58). New York, NY: Routledge.

Fleming, J. (1984). *Blacks in college: A comparative study of students' success in black and in white institutions.* San Francisco, CA: Jossey-Bass.

Gardiner, M. E., Enomoto, E., & Grogan, M. (2000). *Coloring outside the lines: Mentoring women into school leadership*. Albany: State University of New York Press.

Glass, R. D., & Wong, P. L. (2003). Engaged pedagogy: Meeting the demands for justice in urban professional development schools. *Teacher Education Quarterly, 30*(2), 69–87.

Guido, F. M., Chávez, A. F., & Lincoln, Y. S. (2010). Underlying paradigms in student affairs research and practice. *Journal of Student Affairs Research and Practice, 47*(1), 1–22. doi:10.2202/1949-6605.6017

hooks, b. (1994). *Teaching to transgress: Education as the practice of freedom*. New York, NY: Routledge.

Hurtado, S. (2007). Linking diversity with the educational and civic missions of higher education. *The Review of Higher Education, 30*(2), 185–196.

Jackson, J. F. L. (2004a). Introduction: A crisis at the top: A national perspective. *The Journal of Negro Education, 73*(1), 1–3.

Jackson, J. F. L. (2004b). Introduction: Engaging, retaining, and advancing African Americans in executive-level positions: A descriptive and trend analysis of academic administrators in higher and postsecondary education. *The Journal of Negro Education, 73*(1), 4–20.

James, J., & Farmer, R. (1993). *Spirit, space & survival: African American women in (White) academe*. New York, NY: Routledge.

Johnson-Bailey, J., & Cervero, R. M. (1996). An analysis of the educational narratives of reentry Black women. *Adult Education Quarterly, 46*(3), 142–157.

Lloyd-Jones, B. (2009). Implications of race and gender in higher education administration: An African American woman's perspective. *Advances in Developing Human Resources, 11*(5), 606–618. doi:10.1177/1523422309351820

Loder, T. L. (2005). Women administrators negotiate work-family conflicts in changing times: An intergenerational perspective. *Educational Administration Quarterly, 41*(5), 741–776. doi:10.1177/0013161x04273847

Long-Sutehall, T., Sque, M., & Addington-Hall, J. (2010). Secondary analysis of qualitative data: A valuable method for exploring sensitive issues with an elusive population? *Journal of Research in Nursing, 16*(4), 335–344.

Lorde, A., & Clarke, C. (2007). *Sister outsider: Essays and speeches*. Freedom, CA: Crossing Press Feminist Series.

Moses, Y. T. (1989). *Black women in academe: Issues and strategies* (Project on the Status and Education of Women). Washington, DC: Association of American Colleges.

Mosley, M. H. (1980). Black women administrators in higher education: An endangered species. *Journal of Black Studies, 10*(3), 295–310.

Myers, L. W. (2007). *A broken silence: Voices of African American women in the academy*. Westport, CT: Bergin and Garvey.

National Center for Education Statistics. (2001). Employees in degree-granting institutions, by race/ethnicity etc. [Table 225]. In *Digest of Education Statistics 2001* (Chapter 3). Retrieved from http://nces.ed.gov/pubs2002/2002130.pdf

National Center for Education Statistics. (2010). Employees in degree-granting institutions, by race/ethnicity, sex, employment status, control and type of institution, and primary occupation: Fall 2009 [Table 256]. In *Digest of Education Statistics 2010* (Chapter 3). Retrieved from http://nces.ed.gov/pubs2011/2011015_3a.pdf

Patitu, C. L., & Hinton, K. G. (2003). The experiences of African American women faculty and administrators in higher education: Has anything changed? *New Directions for Student Services, 2003*(104), 79–93. doi:10.1002/ss.109

Perl, E. J., & Noldon, D. F. (2000). Overview of student affairs research methods: Qualitative and quantitative. *New Directions for Institutional Research,* 108, 37–48. doi:10.1002/ir.10803

Stroud, R. S. (2009). *Theorizing African American women's leadership in predominantly white institutions of higher education* (Doctoral dissertation). Retrieved from Proquest Dissertations and Theses. (Order No. 3352309)

Turner, C. S. V. (2008). Women of color in academe experiences of the often invisible. In J. Glazer-Raymo (Ed.), *Unfinished agendas: New and continuing gender challenges in higher education* (pp. 230–252). Baltimore, MD: Johns Hopkins Press.

U.S. Census Bureau. (2010). *Black (African American) history month: February 2011.* Retrieved from http://www.census.gov/newsroom/releases/archives/facts_for_features_special_editions/cb11ff_01.html

Wilson, R. (1989). Women of color in academic administration: Trends, progress, and barriers. *Sex Roles, 21*(1), 85–97.

11

CRITICAL PEDAGOGY AND INTERSECTIONAL SEXUALITY

Exploring Our Oppressions and Privileges Through
Reflexivity, Responsibility, and Resistance

Haneen S. Ghabra, Sergio F. Juarez, Shanna K. Kattari, Miranda Olzman,
and Bernadette Marie Calafell

In the spring of 2014, we came together in a Communication Studies seminar on Critical Sexuality Studies. Coming together as four
PhD students and one associate professor, we brought a unique mix
of privileges and oppressions. We merged collectively as four cisgender
identified females and one cisgender male. Whereas three of us identified
as queer, two of us identified as heterosexual. In addition, ethnically, our
identities brought together two Latin@s and Chican@s, one Kuwaiti-Palestinian, and two White individuals, of varied levels of ability and impair-
ment. Based upon our experiences, varied backgrounds, and identities,
we reflected on inclusive pedagogical strategies that enable spaces of possibility, connection, and resistance in an academy that is often hostile to
Others, such as ourselves. Our use of *Others* is based upon our understandings that our identities are marked as abject and often undesired in
relationship to the White, heterosexual, male norm to whom the academy
caters. We politically and critically embrace our Otherness. Understanding pedagogy and classroom dynamics, driven by ethics of care, responsibility, and love, we reflect on our experiences so we might discuss how
instructors and students can work together to create inclusive educational
environments.

Perspectives on Performance

Our perspectives are guided by an understanding of critical performative pedagogy as a deep interrogative practice that acknowledges education as a form of cultural politics while implicated in power relations (Alexander, 2010). Our writing is influenced by an ethical imperative to acknowledge the body at the center of learning, and through a critical performative pedagogy, we can explore how particular bodies present themselves in the classroom and how inequities of power and privilege impact those bodies (Alexander, 2010). We understand that we learn through the body, through our senses, through our theories in the flesh. Rather than buying into a binary between the mind and the body, we own the knowledges our raced, classed, gendered, impaired, and sexualized bodies provide us. In critical pedagogy, various pieces, such as self-reflexivity, empowering students to talk back, and instructors modeling vulnerability, must come together to create a space for learning in the classroom. These include critical reflexivity of our own experiences, privileges, and beliefs; the centering of voices that are often absent in the world of academia by including their writings, performances, videos, and more; discussion of allyship and how it can be practiced; and use of our own narratives and counternarratives to spark the conversation and dialogue so crucial in critical classrooms. In doing this work, we draw on performative writing as a means of inviting others to the conversation and as a way to implicate their whole selves, bodies, and experiences, while simultaneously challenging the meaning of performative teaching in the academy.

Performative writing attempts to show rather than tell, meaning we craft narratives that not only bring readers into our stories but also affectively implicate them (Madison, 1999; Pollock, 1998; Spry 2011). Though performative writing may be a relatively new tool in academic writing, it owes a great deal to the work of feminists of color, such as Moraga and Anzaldúa (1981), who have introduced the idea of *theories in the flesh*. Anzaldúa (2002) elaborated upon the theory in the flesh through the concept of *concocimento*, which allows us to bring together our senses and experiences to bear upon the social, political, and cultural meanings of subversive knowledges we need to survive as cultural Others. Anzaldúa's (2002) work helps to keep our work critical, political, and accountable to the body. Like Corey (1998), we understand the power of personal narrative to disrupt and rewrite master narratives that govern society. One of the main themes that became apparent when we discussed how to organize this chapter was that each of us wanted to illuminate a better understanding of our own intersectional identities and relate that to how those identities affected our experiences in a course about sexuality. Because of our varying experiences, we begin this chapter with individualized narratives that illustrate how this particular course affected each of us so deeply yet in different ways. We conclude, though, with our voices merged as a way to demonstrate allyship and healing. Thus, we offer these narratives as spaces for new radical possibilities. We also integrate quotations from our course readings that work alongside our narratives to affectively illustrate critical pedagogical practices for the reader.

And So It Begins: Creating Critical Pedagogical Spaces

> *Queerness as it is currently constructed offers no viable political alternatives since it invites us to put forth a political agenda that makes invisible the prominence of race, class, and to varying degrees gender in determining the life chances of those on both sides of the hetero/queer divide.* (Cohen, 2005, p. 35)

Bernadette

I have been teaching a graduate seminar called Critical Sexuality Studies for several years and at two different universities. From the start of envisioning this course, I knew I didn't want it to be a recitation of the queer canon, meaning the delivery of normative scholarship by White queer men. As a queer bisexual woman of color, I never saw myself reflected in that work. I felt alienated by the work not only because it completely ignored my experiences, but also because, more often than not, the level of disembodiment, abstraction, and jargon was simply off-putting. The body and the experiences or theories in the flesh it provides us are often ironically erased, and *identity* seems to be a bad word. I can guarantee that 9 times out of 10, students will read the work of Michel Foucault and Judith Butler in other courses, but they won't read Gloria E. Anzaldúa (2012), Cherríe L. Moraga (2000), José Esteban Muñoz (1999), or Gust A. Yep (2003). As a graduate student, I took two courses on queer theory: One was taught in my home department of Communication Studies, focused on mainstream or canonical queer theory, and the other, housed in English, was focused on queer Latin@ studies. Both courses, along with my own research, helped to shape my approach to teaching Critical Sexuality Studies. In my classroom, difference lives in the center not the margins, meaning that I choose to have students read noncanonical scholarship throughout the course. Difference shapes the course. It is a critical pedagogical perspective that works to create what hooks (1994a) termed *homeplace* for students from historically marginalized communities. I try to teach in a way that speaks to those students who are Others, such as myself, and ask students from dominant groups to be reflexive about their identities, privileges, and histories.

I hope to create a syllabus that allows cultural Others to find a place of possibility and home. As a feminist scholar and teacher, intersectionality frames my understanding of power and its workings. This can be jarring for students who may be more commonly used to courses that offer a week on race, a week on gender, or a week on sexuality rather than a course that does not alienate difference but diffuses it throughout the course schedule.

The fourth time teaching this course, it finally clicked. If I could describe a near-perfect quarter, this was it. I didn't face any outright resistance, which, though sometimes fruitful, can be exhausting for faculty of color. Students loved the material, and it gelled for me as well. The makeup of the class was also different than most, because it was made up largely of students of color rather than White students. Based on my prior experiences at my university with students from outside the department, I am always hesitant to allow those students into my graduate courses. These have been among the worst students I have ever taught, not because of their academic performance but because they often lack a willingness to engage in a critical paradigm, even while they claim to be critical scholars. Once the critical infringes too much on their privileges, they suddenly don't want to be critical anymore. Some of these students have also been among the most violent in using their privilege against me as a woman of color instructor. This violence has ranged from outward hostility in the classroom to slandering me online. The costs are emotional and physical as I deal with what Smith, Yosso, and Solórzano (2006) have termed *racial battle fatigue*. During the course, I could only imagine the resistance I might receive when students who did not know me discovered that we would not be reading the canon, but instead the course would be focused on the experiences of queer people of color. I was, however, pleasantly surprised this quarter to meet Shanna, who is a student in social work. She challenged all my assumptions, and her presence in the class was invaluable. She taught me a great deal, including how to be more accountable to my able-bodied and cisgender privileges.

Enter the Outsider

> *Without community, there is no liberation, only the most vulnerable and temporary armistice between an individual and her oppression. But community must not mean a shedding of our differences, nor the pathetic pretense that these differences do not exist.* (Lorde, 1981, p. 99)

Shanna

As someone with a background in sexuality and sex education, I desperately wanted to have access to the Critical Sexuality Studies class offered through the Department of Communication Studies. I was tired of the Whitewashing of the history of sexuality; I wanted to move away from the White, cisgender canon, and this course seemed exactly what I desired—a more diverse and inclusive view of sexuality from various perspectives. Queer theory isn't always actually very queer; it often relies on the words of White, middle-class, gay, cisgender men (and occasionally women), without ever delving into the experiences of people who live beyond the gender or orientation binary, those whose race automatically draws forth assumptions about their sexuality (Cohen, 2005), or those whose ability relegates them to the construction that they will always be asexual.

However, I was an outsider—an outsider to communication studies, an outsider possessing some pretty apparent oppressive identities. How would I, a White, cisgender, middle-class, social work doctoral student, ever possibly fit in a classroom dedicated to the exploration of critical sexuality studies? I sent an inquiry to the instructor, unsure how to authentically get across my desire to more deeply understand the broad experience of sexuality, without coming across like a White tourist, making a pit stop in the class only to check off authors and theorists of color. The back and forth of e-mails was tough; for once in my academic life, I was (understandably) not just recklessly welcomed with open arms, but was instead asked to prove myself and my interest. At times, it felt as though I was not wanted in this class, and I was requested to really think about my motivations for asking to join it. *Was I willing to do the difficult work of examining my own identities, attitudes, and beliefs, or did I just want another five credits for my transcript?* This demonstration of a critical framework for the class, requiring students to make an intentional choice to join, asking them to be self-reflexive before the first session, only made my interest for it grow; I wanted to be challenged, to be called out, to be asked to think more deeply about each and every one of my experiences and assumptions around sexuality. I wanted this to happen in a way that my Whitewashed master's program, which consisted primarily of White students and professors talking about White sexuality and reading White research, although only focusing on Black/Brown bodies when talking about discrimination or sexually transmitted infection prevention, had never provided. I was hungry for a class that not only included voices so often absent from the academy but that also was actually built around these voices and experiences.

Once the class began, by focusing on my positionality and critically examining my own identities with the help of Bernadette, such as exploring being a Jewish woman who also believes in Palestinian liberation, or recognizing the push and pull of being a White person who struggles with access in the academy as a disabled person, I was able to make room in my own self-awareness for an equilibrium that neither celebrated my privileged identities nor tokenized my marginalized identities. I was offered a reminder that yes, I hold various privileges in many spaces, but at the same time, I also hold my more marginalized identities as a queer, disabled, Jewish woman. Throughout the Critical Sexuality Studies class, I balanced these two sides and became reflexive about how my own Whiteness positioned me in the classroom and what space I took up, while also being able to offer my own unique viewpoints that stemmed from my lived experiences as a woman with disabilities, as a Jew in a Christocentric society, and as a queer woman who is read as heterosexual. Using this balancing mechanism, I was able to closely examine when I could contribute a new lens or framework to the rest of the class and when what I wanted to say was just a reinforcement of the status quo.

I gave push back on ableist words used by other participants and used my identities and experiences to educate and to share the struggles of disabled people having their sexual identities erased and labeled as asexual/hypersexual (Tepper, 2000). I shared my personal tension around being both White (privileged racially) and Jewish (marginalized ethnically/religiously) and was an active part of discussion on what this means for me as an antiracist/anti-oppressive activist struggling with what it means to be Jewish despite not supporting many actions of Israel. By sharing these salient and sometimes conflicting identities, the professor and students in the classroom gave me both support to explore as well as pressure to interrogate my own identities and how they interplay, as well as to begin to examine the various types of allyship I wished to practice more intentionally.

This is what I consider the true meaning of Crenshaw's (1991) intersectionality. Our identities do not exist in a vacuum. My Whiteness is as much a part of me as my queerness, my middle-class status as relevant as my Jewish identity, and sometimes the intersections of my identities create their own issues, such as being queer and a *crip* (a reclaimed term used by some disabled individuals), two identities that have a lot of similarity and interplay, as explored by Sandahl (2003). Given this evidence of intersectionality, one identity cannot be taken and examined in the absence of others. Only in a classroom that supports critical self-interrogation can individuals truly feel the engagement of their own oppressive and marginalized identities and create a space in themselves to be open about the tension that these various identities create.

Critical pedagogy can be defined as a teaching method used in classrooms to introduce and expose students to the dominant, hegemonic culture that is pervasive in our society and encourage the creation of a counterculture (Braa & Callero, 2006). In Critical Sexuality Studies, the emphasis provided by Bernadette was indeed to direct students to take responsibility for reading more closely into every single piece of writing, every in-class interaction, even into every background experience, in order to simultaneously acknowledge and reject the neoliberal hegemonic definitions of *sexuality*. Arguably, this resulted in a classroom space that not only encouraged the creation of a counterculture, but also was itself in fact the embodiment of the rejection of these norms and tokenizations of bodies. This space created a new learning environment, one that lifted up difference and focused on the Other—so unique compared to many of the classrooms in which I had previously participated. This happened by centering the voices and experiences of authors of color, requiring even in the syllabus that students practice critical reflexivity, and by Bernadette herself critically examining her own experiences, as well as guiding others through the process of doing so.

Multiple Equations: Spaces of Antipathy, Resistance, and Belonging

> *Queer theory's promise lies less in identity-based scholarship than in the interrogation of social processes and systems that produce and sustain dominant and marginalized identities. Too narrow a focus on sexuality can mask other social divisions that intersect with—and constitute—sexual identities.* (Chevrette, 2013, p. 180)

Haneen

As I walked into our Critical Sexuality Studies classroom, I quickly scanned the room for any familiar faces. Frantically, I started to calculate my marginalized identities into a math equation: Muslim plus Palestinian plus Kuwaiti times female equals an increase in oppressive incidents. Previous experiences of constantly being disciplined by Whiteness or masculinity in the classroom had left me in a constant state of negation. For instance, I am always corrected for my accent; I am always reminded that Muslim women are oppressed and that White Western feminism is the only feminism that stands as true for the general public. Individuals constantly ask me how I think "we" (as if we are all united) can combat "terrorism" in the Middle East, when they do not realize that terrorism has been inflicted onto the Middle East by Western hegemonic structures. So I wondered, what would be the probability that I would be forced to sit in the pain of my marginalized identity as a woman of color in this specific classroom? How many privileged identities would confine me to this space? How would I resist this space?

I sought refuge in the syllabus, quickly scanning the readings for a familiar author. My heart rate slowed down as I noticed that many of the assigned readings were women of color. It was the very first time that a syllabus had a plethora of authors who were of a minority group in one way or the other. I looked up at our professor in awe and in gratitude. For once, my identities as a Kuwaiti-Palestinian Muslim woman felt in place in the midst of a larger academic institution that remains White-centric. It is through the discomfort in the space of graduate seminar classes that minorities have to grapple with the effects of a number of oppressions while simultaneously working twice as hard to soothe the discomfort and pain associated with discriminations. It is also through the role of the professor that we as students either find spaces of belongingness or spaces of antipathy.

Following Mohanty (2003), women of color are constantly scarred by the burdens of our histories, location, and privileges. Therefore, we need to work through conversations about difference and power. Race, class, gender, sexuality, ability, and body size are constantly in motion and are woven into our lives through experience and history (Mohanty, 2003). I echo Anzaldúa in stating that women of color are always at a loss within mainstream education because we are always in a battle with a more dominant ideology (Anzaldúa & Keating, 2009). The hardest thing for those who are oppressed is to understand our subjugations from our radicalism but also from our pain (Moraga, 2000).

My experience in class opened up a plethora of intersectional possibilities for me. There was a constant battle between my fear of being silenced by forceful White and male privileged colleagues in the classroom and my fear of not being able to speak up and resist that oppression. I found it ironic that even in a classroom with so much possibility for resistance of hegemonic structures and openness to critiquing privilege, I was still in a superior system that neither I, my colleagues, nor my professor could resist by working all together. Whereas I realize that this class exemplifies resistance to an overarching system, I also realize that we need to create more of these moments within pedagogy and within our own scholarship. Although I understand that the scholarship we read paves the pathway that we will take in the future, I also acknowledge that the readings we were assigned in this class would mark me forever. For the very first time, I experienced resistance in various forms through each week's readings. I came to terms with my able-bodied, educational, and class privilege. I worked through the presentation of my privileges like a roller coaster ride. Through disidentification, intersectionality, affect, pain, ethics, and resistant communication, I was able to connect to the readings while finding my own space during classroom discussions. The numerous readings by scholars of color paved an interstice that was ripe with readings that I could relate to. These constitutive measures were further put in place by Bernadette as she facilitated and allowed us to facilitate our own experiences through class discussions. It is through spaces of resistance within the classroom that we find spaces of possibility. It is also through these very same spaces that we find pessimism and disappointment in other classes that remain direct products of larger ideological institutions. It places us in a cycle—continuously perpetuating privilege, racism, and oppression.

I follow Mohanty (2003) in stating that for decades, scholarship has examined women of color and has placed them into a universal category. She argued that today we need to examine pedagogical and institutional practices and how this relates to the scholarship produced. She further explained, "Thus teachers and students produce, reinforce, recreate, resist and transform ideas about race, gender and difference in the classroom" (p. 194). Therefore, we need methods that will decolonize our pedagogical practices. In turn, education can become a form of resistance and a means of liberation for minority groups (Mohanty, 2003).

Delving further, creating cultures of dissent is one method in which academic, institutional, and interpersonal relationships can become more transparent (Mohanty, 2003). Thus, cultures of dissent are also about exposing the academy for the way in which it manages minority groups. Detangling this chaotic web can thus bring about more attention to the overlying liberal and capitalist structures that perpetuate constant discrimination in academia as a whole and especially in the classroom.

Pedagogical strategies of dissent are spaces in which professors and students can create collaborative strategies to resist, reflect, and grow from experience. My experience in the classroom was a pathway to creating more momentum for resistant strategies. Additionally, as Kuwaiti-Palestinian, Muslim, a woman of color, my identity will always be in flux. Hence, writing about marginalization in academia will always be a revolving challenge.

Pedagogy of Revolt: A Struggle Within Myself

> *If the academy, in its very mission, denies the body, except as the object of theoretical disembodied discourse, The Body with a capital "B," then what is the radically thinking "othered" body (the queer, the colored, the female) doing there? What skills does the academy offer for our survival?* (Moraga, 2000, p. 175)

Sergio

Before the class started, I was anxious because I did not believe I would have much input in our class conversations, asking myself, "What does a cisgender heterosexual Mexican have to say about critical sexuality?" Though also identifying as a Chicano, I was and am currently in the process of becoming familiar with intersectionality through Chicana feminist studies. I did not have an understanding of its implications in my life. This goes to show the privileged ignorance I carry with me and my attempt to discard that ignorance. Our classroom was a space where there were little restrictions of ontologies and epistemologies in our collective pursuit of knowledge. Students were able to lead class and to explore knowledge in a pluralistic fashion through a variety of material that could be considered "evidence"—poems, videos of performances, in-class performance exercises, critical dialogue, personal and poetic narratives, and more. We were open to truly critical inquiries, exploring a variety of methods that developed an atmosphere in the classroom that supported difficult dialogue about complex societal issues.

From the moment I engaged our readings of Moraga (2000) and Arrizón (2006), I began to connect intersections of identities that had previously escaped my understanding, a lack of understanding that had been a detriment in my personal life. Moraga wrote of her experience with her brother: "The only thing that earned my brother my servitude was his maleness" (p. 82), going on to describe the inequality between her brother and herself and asking, "Male in a man's world. Light skinned in a white world. Why change?" (p. 84). I saw myself and my sisters in this scenario. Like a ton of bricks, sadness overcame me as I became aware of my privileged position as the firstborn son and having been that tyrant Moraga described. Everyday practices, like being the first to be served at a meal or having critiqued my sisters for not going to college or thinking too much about boyfriends, were damaging. I thought I was helping them but, in turn, only added to the pressure of patriarchal society, and through everyday norms, reified dominant misogynist standards that privilege my cisgender male voice.

In a similar fashion, I was able to relate critical sexuality theories to my family's daily struggles regarding citizenship, documentation, and crossing structural borders. Bernadette facilitated the classroom by sitting with us and telling us of her experiences and the issues she faced as a Latina in the academy and how she has persevered. I call this "keeping it real" with us and not sugarcoating what we may face as faculty members. I felt a connection and a sense of wholeness, a sense that by her disclosing to us as a Latina/Chicana/queer person, we in turn would be valued as whole persons. I could then disclose my experiences with undocumented family members that have given me a firsthand knowledge of fear of crossing border patrol checkpoints along the southern border. I could examine dominant standards that move beyond national borders but also control bodies in a variety of ways. Exploring queer identities within the immigration movement allowed our conversations to illuminate tensions between queer migrants and those leading the political charge. This conflict between groups within the immigration move-ment parallels that of the marriage equality movement, where critique of the policies and practices within the movement raises the issue of homonorma-tivity, which works to exclude certain members within the queer community (Cohen, 2005). Couples with transgender partners, polyamorous partner-ships, as well as unmarried heterosexual people of color are further marginal-ized, although some gain acceptance with the ability to marry. Cohen (2005) described the queering of heterosexual members of communities of color. Being exposed to ideas of queer sexuality and *mestizaje* has been both enlight-ening and liberating, because a body politic of nonnormative sexuality that otherwise might have gone without exploration is addressed.

In this migration movement, we have an opportunity to create a coa-lition between heterosexual undocumented migrants and queer undocu-mented migrants. Cohen (2005) envisioned a politics of transformation, one which is interested in a "new political identity that is truly liberating, transformative, and inclusive of all those who stand outside of the domi-nant constructed norm of state-sanctioned White middle- and upper-class heterosexuality" (p. 22). It is not only individuals with particular identities who suffer but also we all as a community suffer for it. Arrizón (2006) wrote of the importance of a body politic that unsettles hegemonic phases of time and relocates cultural negotiations of hybrid sites—a queer lesbian body is a hybrid site with multiple epistemologies. According to Arrizón,

> The queer-lesbian body revisits the need for agency and accepts different temporalities of subjectivity. The queer-lesbian body marks gender and sexuality together, demanding political representation while insisting on its specificity. This specificity will again be altered when the sites of the brown body, through an understanding of *mestizaje*, joins the processes of "queering." The politic of the racialized body takes on a particular charge. (p. 179, emphasis added)

Our classroom was transformed into a space where lived intersections of race, sexuality, and gender were valid sources of knowledge. Calafell (2010) wrote about the importance of narrative, stating, "[It] does not allow the nuances of intersectionality to be flattened by dry and meaningless num-bers that quickly erase the humanness and complexity of people and their ordinary but extraordinary experiences" (p. 355). This nuanced approach to classroom norms on critical subject matter may be considered critical commu-nication pedagogy (Simpson, 2010). Recognizing that our bodies are vessels of knowledge, we were encouraged to explore knowledge beyond empirical text; our experiences weaved in and out of theory as we co-constructed the classroom to emphasize the importance of lived experiences by allowing us, the students, to tell our stories. We were developing what Arrizón (2006) described as *facultad*, a capacity to uncover deeper realities within our societal structures with an instant quick perception. *Facultad* refers to a space that resists negation and subordination, where bodies "as a border dweller" (Arrizón, 2006, p. 26) construct spaces that challenge colonial patriarchy.

Bernadette's classroom embodied what Moraga (2000) described as a pedagogy of revolt: It is a pedagogy in which one has the ability "to refuse to acknowledge someone or something has authority over you" (p. 185). By allowing students to utilize performance methods, critical scholarship like Chicana feminism, and valuing our lived experiences, our course fostered an ability to revolt against an oppressive educational system that limits the spaces where students of color can question the system itself. The atmosphere created by a pedagogy of revolt could be described as a space of intersectional praxis where my colleagues and I explored the complexities of the issue of migration beyond simplistic binary arguments of race and class (which are very pertinent) but also the intersections of sexuality, gender, and ability.

Balancing Dominance and Marginalization: Exploring Intersectional Pedagogy

> *What I am saying is that the joys of looking like a White girl ain't so great since I realized I could be beaten on the street for being a dyke. . . . In this country lesbianism is a poverty—as is being brown, as is being a woman, as is being just plain poor.* (Moraga, 2000, p. 44)

Miranda

On the first day of our Critical Sexualities Studies course, Bernadette told us her classroom was a space where difference would be centered—that every day would be taught from an intersectional perspective. As a queer, fat, White, Jew, grappling with my own gender-queerness, I was excited to see how this would be executed. Like many, I often focus on my marginalized identities but forget to see the power behind my dominant identities of Whiteness and coming from a wealthy background. I easily see how oppression affects my life, but power often remains invisible. The work of centering difference and working to not recenter dominant ideologies is how I want to teach my own courses—as well as live my life—but I struggle with how to do this well. The way Bernadette facilitated this concept in the classroom was exceptional. Instead of breaking up the class into weeks on race, or a week on queerness in a sexuality course, the multiple identity vectors of authors and ourselves were centered daily. This was clear through the conversations that began to emerge throughout the quarter.

Our conversations ranged from inquiring what an author's responsibility is to live her or his research to the history of the academy, centering Whiteness and heterosexuality in researching sexuality. As we came together at the end of the quarter to write this chapter, I was drawn to writing about responsibility because it is often on my mind in terms of discourse. One of the questions I ask myself regularly since this course is, *What does it mean to be an active ally as a graduate student and as an instructor?* A singular answer to this question does not exist. There are always multiple answers, and they often differ depending on the context. I choose to focus on the liminal space of being a graduate student and a graduate teaching instructor for the purposes of this project. A portion of the funding for my PhD comes from being a graduate teaching instructor. As such, we teach stand-alone courses where we construct our own syllabi and lesson plans. These particular identities are salient to understanding responsibilities in a classroom because I go from a space of being in a classroom as a student to teaching a course as the instructor. Critical Sexualities Studies was my first course with my current adviser, Bernadette. During our quarter together, she demonstrated a clear commitment to intersectional pedagogy and to understanding her students as whole beings. During the quarter, one of the foci was discussing the politics of citation and how many times scholars of color are left uncited. Although I spoke of a deep commitment to this, one of my papers did not demonstrate this. Bernadette and I met and discussed it. She pushed me to become a stronger burgeoning scholar by outing my hypocrisy in my research. This moment is one of the most defining moments of my career as a scholar so far. Because of this experience, I search to see what scholarly voices I am missing or erasing. And my work has become stronger and more diverse because of this. In terms of creating a space where all of our selves are relevant, I cannot help but remember how she treated me when my dog fell ill. I was so distraught, and Bernadette just encouraged me to take her to the vet, to do what I needed to, so to take care of my family. In her class, it is often the small things. She asks how you are doing and waits to hear a full answer. From Bernadette, I learned more of whom I would like to embody as an educator as well as deepening my understanding of what it means to be a student and have access to courses such as this.

Growing up, classrooms were an interesting ground for me. Something always felt uneasy for me in them, and I knew much of that could be explained by what was left out. An attorney-turned-high-school-English-and-history-teacher raised me, and although I studied history in school, he always taught me what was missing. His repeated sentence to me was that "history is written by the winners." Now I view this as "the academy is shaped by the oppressors," as an attempt to resist the narrative of winning, as an acceptable form of oppression. This course demonstrated to me how many authors I missed knowing, even in areas that I thought I knew well. As I devoured Moraga's (2000) *Loving in the War Years*, I asked Bernadette how I could have missed this. She responded, "You have been trained in a White academy." Although I am not Latina, I identify as queer and Jewish, not to mention fat. Reading Moraga felt at many times like reading myself on the page for the first time. I do not wish to appropriate her struggles but to see similarities in some of the spaces we occupy. Bernadette revealed to me the importance of understanding the identities behind the research. There were other pieces of work I did not identify with at all but I knew I had students who were thirsty for these writings. This course taught me how many authors I was missing based on "the canon" of sexualities work, and how biased the development of "the canon" has been.

This section begins to answer the question I ask myself. Being an ally as a student colleague connects to being an ally as an instructor. It requires being able to listen to people and trying to understand their positionality when it differs from my own. It can require silence and stepping down. Yet it can also require speaking up. As a queer, I am tired of often being the lone voice railing against heteronormativity. Yep (2003) stated, "Heteronormativity, as the invisible center and the presumed bedrock of society, is the quintessential force creating, sustaining, and perpetuating the erasure, marginalization, disempowerment, and oppression of sexual others" (p. 18). I choose to speak up actively against heteronormativity but am often disappointed that straight students who identify as allies often choose not to speak up. Yet this quarter through meeting Shanna Katz Kattari and hearing her stories about her disabilities, I realized how often I let ableist discourse pass through me as though nothing oppressive is happening. It demonstrated how narrowly I stick to my own oppressed identity vectors and often (whether consciously or unconsciously) do not stand for others. Through experiences with Bernadette as the instructor and hearing others' experiences in the academy, I turn to syllabus construction and my classroom as a place where I can make an active difference in my own work toward a more substantive allyship.

Being an ally as an instructor means bringing work you may not identify with into a classroom because you may have students who are literally dying to read this work. We have students who have never seen themselves represented in the academy. hooks (1994b) wrote, "To teach in a manner that respects and cares for the souls of our students is essential if we are to provide the necessary conditions where learning can most deeply and intimately begin" (p. 13). Part of my caring for students is meeting with them in my office and checking how their quarters and lives are going. This is where I often learn of family members passing or struggles they are going through. At times, we can piece together what is happening in their lives and how it connects (or does not) to what we are learning in class. The quarter after this course, I was teaching Communication and Popular Culture for the first time. The Critical Sexualities Studies course and our interactions have influenced me to take a more nuanced look at my syllabus construction and lesson planning. How do I attend to intersectionality on a daily basis? What authors am I including as readings? As importantly, what examples do I use in class and how do I facilitate these conversations? To help curb centering myself, this quarter I plan to bring in speakers from different perspectives and positionalities. Lastly, with hooks (1994b) and Calafell (2010) in mind, how do I attend to students as whole people who bring their full lives and experiences into their courses? These questions and answers are the ones that guide me in constructing the courses I am teaching in the future as well as being a more intersectional critical student and burgeoning critical scholar.

> *The danger lies in attempting to deal with oppression purely from a theoretical base. Without an emotional, heartfelt grappling with the source of our own oppression, without naming the enemy within ourselves and outside of us, no authentic, nonhierarchical connection among oppressed groups can take place.* (Moraga, 2000, p. 44)

Conclusions/Beginnings

When we examine these experiences together, through bodies-in-action critical pedagogy, the classroom becomes a space of rehearsing what can be possible (Alexander, 2010). Through a critical performative pedagogy, we ask what our experiences mean in creating a classroom that uses critical pedagogy to challenge both students and instructors, and not only recognize but also truly explore the tensions that happen in the spaces between privileged and marginalized identities. By allowing each individual to explore her or his own experiences, Bernadette privileges the experiences of people with marginalized identities but also opens the possibility to center the experiences of faculty of color and Others while connecting it to the material (Calafell, 2010). The class as a whole can interrogate histories and ideologies of racism, classism, sexism, and ableism, among others, and engage in intersectional reflexivity. Defining *intersectional reflexivity*, Jones (2010) wrote, "Self-reflection might scratch the surface, but self-reflexivity cuts to the bone. It implicates you. Reflexivity is uncomfortable because it forces you to acknowledge that you are complicit in the perpetuation of oppression. . . . Reflexivity has got to hurt. Reflexivity is laborious" (p. 124). Each person holds a host of identities; no one person holds only marginalized or privileged identities—intersectional reflexivity acknowledges this and encourages the individual to examine how these identities interact and what lens(es) they bring to various lived experiences. When instructors model this type of self-awareness of their positionality, it allows students to emulate this reflexivity, creating a more dynamic space. Whereas reflexivity is crucial to critical pedagogy, this should be offered in collaboration with allowing spaces for counternarratives and group dialogue, intentionally centering the voices of marginalized communities by selecting authors with these identities, and engaging in discussion about what allyship might be.

It is important to intentionally create spaces for purposeful allyship. This can be difficult because individuals cannot simply name themselves allies and be rewarded for doing so. That said, the creation of a classroom setting where students feel they can support other students by bringing up issues that affect communities to which they may not belong and showcase writers, theorists, and other names that are traditionally left out of academic discourse allows space for the development of true ally behavior. As an instructor, creating syllabi that include diverse voices and opinions while centering Otherness (including, but not limited to, race, gender, sexual orientation, ability, age, class, and country of origin) rather than privilege is an ideal way of beginning intersectional allyship. Exposure to intersectional identities is not enough; there should be critical discussion of who is and is not in the canon, as well as the inclusivity (or lack thereof) demonstrated in the readings. Students should interrogate their own experiences and how they connect to those of the authors, or separate them further, continuing the conversation.

We see allyship as a roadmap that leads us into what we call *ethical reflexivity and sensitivity.* This assists both the teacher and student to recognize that both privileged and marginalized groups have to be sensitive to the ethical boundaries that surround them. One way to address this is by teaching students to be aware of the harm in speaking for others of different identities. We follow Alcoff (1991) in stating that a privileged person speaking for a person who is less privileged in itself creates an even deeper ground of oppression for the community that is being spoken for. As students, teachers, and scholars, we have an obligation to be ethically sensitive to the various dynamics and power plays that accompany groups of both privileges and oppressions. Thus, we must train our bodies and minds to be culturally aware of the different identities and power structures that surround us in the classroom and beyond. In our class, we were able to explore our positionalities, have conversations about our identities, and ultimately center our experiences to interrogate power, identities, and otherness in the academy (Calafell, 2010). There is never an end to critical pedagogy; it is a process that continues far beyond the boundaries of the classroom and requires a dedication from all those involved in any learning community.

Authors' Epilogue

We came together as people of color with disembodied abstractions, wrapped in White canonical overlays. . . . As heterosexuals, perpetrators of a system in which we hope to practice allyship. . . . As bodies wrapped in bundles of Whiteness, causing agony to communities of color, learning how to navigate and manage our White dominant bodies . . . as male privileged, wondering how to glance back at the past and move forward as a true accomplice, and as able-bodied individuals who can easily fail to recognize our ability privileges. We came together with multiple identities, mingled wounds, and heterogeneous grievances in need of healing. Dominance placed us beyond national borders; it controlled our bodies, gender, sexuality, ability, religion, and body type. In this classroom . . . our identities came together to create spaces of resistance, inclusion, and to begin a long process toward healing.

References

Alcoff, L. (1991). The problem of speaking for others. *Cultural Critique, 20* (Winter), 5–32.

Alexander, B. K. (2010). Critical/performative/pedagogy: Performing possibility as a rehearsal for social justice. In D. L. Fassett & J. T. Warren (Eds.), *The SAGE handbook of communication and instruction* (pp. 315–341). Los Angeles, CA: SAGE.

Anzaldúa, G. (2002). Now let us shift . . . the path of *conocimiento* . . . inner works, public acts. In G. Anzaldúa & A. Keating (Eds.), *This bridge we call home: Radical visions for transformation* (pp. 540–577). New York, NY: Routledge.

Anzaldúa, G. (2012). *Borderlands*/la frontera: *The new mestiza.* San Francisco, CA: Aunt Lute.

Anzaldúa, G., & Keating, A. L. (2009). *The Gloria Anzaldúa reader.* Durham, NC: Duke University Press.

Arrizón, A. (2006). *Queering* mestizaje: *Transculturation and performance.* Ann Arbor: University of Michigan Press.

Braa, D., & Callero, P. (2006). Critical pedagogy and classroom praxis. *Teaching Sociology, 34*(4), 357–369. doi:10.1177/0092055X0603400403

Calafell, B. M. (2010). When will we all matter? Exploring race, pedagogy, and sustained hope for the academy. In D. L. Fassett & J. T. Warren (Eds.), *The SAGE handbook of communication and instruction* (pp. 343–360). Los Angeles, CA: SAGE.

Chevrette, R. (2013). Outing heteronormativity in interpersonal and family communication: Feminist applications of queer theory "beyond the sexy streets." *Communication Theory, 23*(2), 170–190. doi:10.1111/comt.12009

Cohen, C. J. (2005). Punks, bulldaggers, and welfare queens: The radical potential of queer politics? In E. P. Johnson & M. G. Henderson (Eds.), *Black queer studies: A critical anthology* (pp. 22–51). Durham, NC: Duke University Press.

Corey, F. C. (1998). The personal: Against the master narrative. In S. J. Dailey (Ed.), *The future of performance studies: Visions and revisions* (pp. 249–253). Annandale, VA: National Communication Association.

Crenshaw, K. (1991). Mapping the margins: Intersectionality, identity politics, and violence against women of color. *Stanford Law Review, 43(6),* 1241–1299.

hooks, b. (1994a). Homeplace: A site of resistance. In D. S. Madison (Ed.), *The woman that I am: The literature and culture of contemporary women of color* (pp. 448–454). New York, NY: St. Martin's Press.

hooks, b. (1994b). *Teaching to transgress: Education as the practice of freedom.* New York, NY: Routledge.

Jones, R. G., Jr. (2010). Putting privilege into practice through "intersectional reflexivity": Ruminations, interventions, and possibilities. *Reflections: Narratives of Professional Helping, 16*(1), 122–125.

Lorde, A. (1981). The master's tools will never dismantle the master's house. In C. Moraga & G. Anzaldúa (Eds.), *This bridge called my back: Writings by radical women of color* (pp. 98–101). New York, NY: Kitchen Table Press.

Madison, D. S. (1999). Performing theory/embodied writing. *Text and Performance Quarterly, 19*(2), 107–124. doi:10.1080/10462939909366254

Mohanty, C. T. (2003). *Feminism without borders: Decolonizing theory, practicing solidarity.* Durham, NC: Duke University Press.

Moraga, C. (2000). *Loving in the war years:* Lo que nunca pasó por sus labios (2nd ed.). Boston, MA: South End Press.

Moraga, C., & Anzaldúa, G. (Eds.). (1981). *This bridge called my back: Writings by radical women of color.* New York, NY: Kitchen Table Press.

Muñoz, J. E. (1999). *Disidentifications: Queers of color and the performance of politics.* Minneapolis: University of Minnesota Press.

Pollock, D. (1998). Performative writing. In P. Phelan & J. Lane (Eds.), *The ends of performance* (pp. 73–103). New York, NY: New York University Press.

Sandahl, C. (2003). Queering the crip or cripping the queer?: Intersections of queer and crip identities in solo autobiographical performance. *GLQ: A Journal of Lesbian and Gay Studies, 9*(1), 25–56. doi:0.1215/10642684-9-1-2-25

Simpson, J. S. (2010). Critical race theory and critical communication pedagogy. In D. L. Fassett & J. T. Warren (Eds.), *The SAGE handbook of communication and instruction* (pp. 343–360). Los Angeles, CA: SAGE.

Smith, W. A., Yosso, T. J., & Solórzano, D. G. (2006). Challenging racial battle fatigue on historically White campuses: A critical race examination of race-related stress. In C. A. Stanely (Ed.), *Faculty of color: Teaching in predominantly White colleges and universities* (pp. 299–327). Bolton, MA: Anker.

Spry, T. (2011). *Body, paper, stage: Writing and performing autoethnography.* Walnut Creek, CA: Left Coast Press.

Tepper, M. S. (2000). Sexuality and disability: The missing discourse of pleasure. *Sexuality and Disability, 18*(4), 283–290. doi:10.1023/A:1005698311392

Yep, G. (2003). The violence of heteronormativity in communication studies: Notes on injury, healing, and queer world-making. *The Journal of Homosexuality, 45*(2–4), 11–59. doi:10.1300/J082v45n02_02

CONCLUSION

Inclusive Pedagogy 2.0: Implications for Race, Equity, and Higher Education in a Global Context

Frank Tuitt

In 2000, as a part of my dissertation, I set out on an intellectual journey to better understand what it might look and feel like to teach in a manner that respects and cares for the souls of Black graduate students (Tuitt, 2000). Believing in what Lani Guinier and Gerald Torres (2002) identified as the miner's canary, I understood that studying the pedagogical experiences of Black graduate students could provide some insight into what was problematic and yet possible, as it relates to creating inclusive and equitable learning environments in traditionally White institutions (TWIs).[1] The notion of Black graduate students in TWIs serving as a diagnostic tool for what is problematic and possible with education has its roots in *The Miner's Canary* (Guinier & Torres, 2002):

> To the extent that individuals have common experiences of marginalization, those experiences often function as a diagnostic device to identify and interrogate system wide structures of power and inequality. When these experiences converge around a visible group, they can raise our awareness about that collective phenomenon. This consciousness, when it helps us identify structural inequalities, becomes a potential catalyst for changing those structures. (p. 19)

The belief was that by identifying the best pedagogical practices for *educating* Black graduate students in particular, and students of color in general, I would be able to identify best teaching methods that could improve the educational experiences of *all* students (Tuitt, 2003a).

Accordingly, the culmination of my attempt to identify a catalyst for changing those teaching and learning structures (Guinier & Torres, 2002) resulted in the conceptualization of "inclusive pedagogy," which I later featured in an edited book project, *Race and Higher Education: Rethinking Pedagogy in Diverse College Classrooms* (Howell & Tuitt, 2003), as the final chapter, entitled "Afterword: Realizing a More Inclusive Pedagogy" (Tuitt, 2003b). My initial conceptualization of inclusive pedagogy sought to have instructors recognize that "by viewing students as whole human beings with complex lives and experiences, inclusive pedagogy offers some insight into how college educators can create classrooms in which diversity is valued as a central component of the learning process" (Tuitt, 2003b, p. 243). Twelve years later, having taught many classes where I attempted to put inclusive pedagogy theory into practice and after writing several publications about those efforts (Danowitz & Tuitt, 2011a; Tuitt, Agans, & Griffin, in press) and introducing countless others around the nation and across the globe to the concept of inclusive pedagogy, I have the privilege of working with two of my most talented former students on this book project.[2] Collectively, our desire was to produce a volume that could exemplify how the utilization of critical and inclusive pedagogies (CIPs) has and continues to create transformative, affirming, and equitable learning environments for all students, but especially historically marginalized students in a global context. Consequently, this book project and the chapters in it provide compelling insight into the theory, praxis, and outcomes of inclusive pedagogy and offer an enhanced under-standing of how critical and inclusive pedagogical models produce engaging learning environments where all students regardless of their racial and ethnic background have the chance to be the best that they can be.

In this final chapter,[3] I provide a synthesis of lessons learned over the years and combine them with key takeaways gleaned from the various con-tributions in this book. I begin this concluding chapter by reflecting on the current context of race and equity in higher education from a global con-text, reminding us why putting CIPs into practice is still a pressing mat-ter today—and perhaps even more important than 12 years ago. Next, I extrapolate the common core components of critical and inclusive pedagogi-cal models addressed in this volume and identify several implications they have for creating inclusive, affirming, and equitable learning environments.

Race Still Matters

In 2003, I posited that contrary to what the current climate of anti–affirmative action might suggest (*Gratz v. Bollinger et al.*, 2003; *Grutter v. Bollinger et al.*, 2003), race still matters in education. Specifically, I wrote:

To begin with, students who are conscious of their racial background enter the learning environment believing that the color of one's skin—their own as well as their professors'—will be a factor in terms of how they can expect to be treated in the learning environment. . . . They express feelings of distrust toward White faculty members who they assume are not willing to address race related issues or know how to relate to African American students. (Tuitt, 2003a, pp. 288–289)

Not surprisingly, fast forward to 2015, and race and racism (individual and institutional) is still one of the most pressing issues around the globe. Consider that in March of 2004, the United States watched as the junior senator from Illinois gave the keynote speech at the Democratic National Convention, and pundits began to talk about the possibility of the United States of America's first Black president. Since then, the United States has twice elected Barack Obama as the nation's first Black president, and in spite of the myth of a postracial America, race relations in the United States have not mirrored the accomplishment of that moment (Coble, Cobb, Deal, & Tuitt, 2013). In the last few years we have witnessed in the United States a rise in organized race-based hate groups, the Supreme Court's dismantling of the 1965 Voting Rights Act, continual legal assaults on affirmative action such as *Fisher v. University of Texas* (2013) and *Schuette v. BAMN* (2014), increased anti-immigration legislation such as Arizona's Support Our Law Enforcement and Safe Neighborhoods Act (2010) and the Beason-Hammon Alabama Taxpayer and Citizen Protection Act (2011), heated debates as to the continued use of racialized mascots like the Redskins and the Blackhawks, increased anti-Muslim sentiment, 65 Asian American groups suing Harvard University for unfair rejection of Asian American students (DeRuy, 2015), and greater racial wealth and health disparities since the U.S. economic recession of 2009. Moreover, names including Trayvon Martin, Michael Brown, Tamir Rice, Penny Proud, Eric Gardner, and Walter Scott have become known worldwide, begging the question, do Black lives really matter? Only to be followed by the mass shooting at the Emanuel African Methodist Episcopal (A.M.E.) church in Charleston, South Carolina—a location of deep significance in the historical and contemporary march for racial justice.

The year 2015 also marked the 50th anniversary of the historic march on Selma, Alabama, as a part of a voting rights movement to bring about racial justice in the southern United States. And 50 years later, the United States found itself in the midst of another racial justice movement. The activism and protests have emerged out of a larger mobilization of the Black Lives Matter movement in cities throughout the United States and many other parts around the globe. The #BlackLivesMatter movement, which was started by three Black women, Alicia Garza, Patrisse Cullors, and Opal

Tometi, after the acquittal of George Zimmerman in the murder of Trayvon Martin, aims to center and affirm the ways that Black people engage resilience and meaningfully contribute to society, even as policies and practices in the United States "systematically and intentionally [target them] for demise" (Garza, 2014, p. 1). The rallying cry to make all Black lives matter has not been restricted to the streets of major urban cities.

Over the past couple of years many college campuses across the United States have witnessed significant increased activism regarding the range of experiences and conditions facing racially minoritized communities in higher education. Specifically, racially minoritized faculty, staff, and students (and their allies) at some of the United States' finest TWIs, including but not limited to University of Texas–Austin, Emory, University of Virginia, Penn State, and the University of Michigan have been speaking out in resistance to their daily encounters with microaggressions, macroinvalidations, and other not so subtle acts of racial discrimination. Not surprisingly, the increased activism on our college campuses has also been facilitated by a surge in campus racial incidents occurring throughout the nation.[4] And just as race still matters in the United States, it still matters, despite contextual and historical differences, across the globe, producing hostile living and learning environments and reinforcing racial disparities, especially in education (see Andrews, 2015; Barbara, 2015; Rubin & Breeden, 2015; Sanderson, 2015).

In different parts of the world, such as Tokyo, Paris, the Netherlands, Delhi, Canada, the Dominican Republic, and London, to name a few, interracial coalitions have been mobilizing to bring about awareness of racial disparities, racial neglect, and ever-growing encounters with racist individuals, racist institutions, racist policies, and racist systems and structures. Whether it is the killing of three Black boys by police in Brazil (Barbara, 2015), the increase in funding to fight against racism in France (Rubin & Breeden, 2015), children taking it to the streets in Amsterdam to bring an end to racial and ethnic segregation in their schools (Sanderson, 2015), or calls for schools to change a climate that allows racist language and behavior in London (Andrews, 2015), the various global conflicts around race and racism exemplify the glaring need to address racism and racial equity around the world.

In addition to race mattering in communities across the globe, the search for access to inclusive and equitable higher education learning environments remains similarly elusive. Consider that tracking in higher education across the world is still a structural stratification mechanism that uses standardized testing and secondary school affiliation to sort racially minoritized[5] communities into segregated educational environments while providing a gated postsecondary education for the privileged and elite (Maoláin, 2013). Correspondingly, the inability to access high-quality public education leaves racially minoritized communities with very little option but to turn to unreliable alternatives. With the continued emergence of for-profit institutions (Douglass, 2012) and the growing number of so-called private nonprofit institutions with international campuses, corporate connections, and profit aspirations, students generally, and especially racially minoritized students around the globe, are being seduced on false promises of a high-quality education to potentially walk away with no degree and a whole lot of debt (Sheehy, 2013). Finally, although socioeconomic status remains a consistent barrier to postsecondary education access, many higher education institutions around the globe are still not prepared for, and do not know what to do with, the racial diversification of their student base. Overall, the continued significance of race and racism globally suggests that the *browning* of higher education is just not a U.S. phenomenon in that whether students identify as racial and ethnic minority groups, locally defined minority groups, indigenous, and/or "lower caste," they are becoming the majority of students seeking access to postsecondary institutions not designed with them in mind. As a result, these students are running the risk of being subjected to traditional pedagogical practices, unwelcoming campus climates, deficit-based macro and microaggressions, and educators who are not really invested or capable of teaching *other* communities' children. Arguably, the characteristics of educational norms—we know—work together to create inequitable educational environments that collectively punish racially minoritized students who choose not to assimilate. It is in this global, racial context that the need to advance CIPs is more vital than perhaps ever before. The unfortunate reality is that race still matters:

> To act as though race does not matter places professors in the role of being insensitive to students who do not believe in a colorblind society. Electing to pay too much attention to race potentially places faculty members in the role of objectifying their students. This paradox further complicates the art of teaching. Professors need to find a range of pedagogical practices that works best for them. (Tuitt, 2008, p. 191)

Fortunately, the chapters in this volume offer some direction. In the next section, I return to my original concept of inclusive pedagogy and explore how my thinking about it has evolved over time.

Inclusive Pedagogy 2.0

For the last decade I have had the opportunity to provide training to numerous educators around the globe. During these sessions I ask participants to consider the following questions: (a) *How might we rethink our pedagogy in increasingly diverse learning environments?* (b) *How can we create learning environments that respect and care for the souls of our students?* The first question speaks to the reality of recent demographic projections, which in many parts of the world show that the students attending higher education institutions today, and in the foreseeable future, will continue to be increasingly racially diverse. The second question encourages instructors to begin to reconceptualize their teaching in light of the reality that our students come to us as whole human beings (consisting of mind, body, and soul) with complex lives and experiences. Moreover, their ability to create inclusive and equitable learning environments, where *all* students have an environment in which to learn at the highest levels, will require that they realize a more inclusive pedagogy by creating classrooms where diversity is valued as a central component of the learning process (Tuitt, 2003a). In these sessions, I am often surprised by the fact that many of my participants have not thought critically about their approach to constructing the learning environment. Many of them enter their classrooms relying on their talent and the examples of teaching (both good and bad) they experienced as students. Unfortunately, very few doctoral programs require their graduates to take a course on teaching. Consequently, many have not thought critically about their approach to designing the teaching and learning environment, nor have they considered conceptual or theoretical models that could enhance their practice.

Critical and Inclusive Pedagogies Are Guided by Theoretical Models of Teaching

In accordance with CIPs, all of the chapters in this volume identify theoretical and/or conceptual models that inform construction of the teaching and learning environment. For example, Carter Andrews and Castillo (Chapter 7) and Martinez, del Carmen Salazar, and Ortega (Chapter 8) use the concept of *humanizing pedagogy* to inform their approach to creating critical and inclusive learning environments where they seek to build trust and caring relationships with their students. Drawing upon the work of Freire (1993) the authors in Chapter 7 recognize its power:

> These humanizing pedagogies and practices foster inclusion in the classroom and can lead to transformative learning experiences that heighten students' critical consciousness and understanding of the negative systemic effects of bias and discrimination in the lives of historically marginalized people across the globe. (p. 113, this volume)

Similar to their conceptualization of a humanizing pedagogy, many of the other theoretical models of teaching referenced in this volume find their roots in critical pedagogy and the seminal work of Paulo Freire. Correspondingly, Stewart (Chapter 1); Goldstein (Chapter 5); Smith (Chapter 10); and Ghabra, Juarez, Kattari, Olzman, and Calafell (Chapter 11) utilize variations and combinations of critical pedagogy to inform the pedagogical decisions they make. Whether it is Stewart's or Goldstein's combination of critical pedagogy and inclusive pedagogy, Smith's use of engaging pedagogy, or Ghabra and colleagues' discussion of critical performative pedagogy, the teachings of Paulo Freire remind us that when students fully understand their circumstance, and their place in the world, they can be empowered to change that circumstance and place (Stewart, Chapter 1). However, students cannot be encouraged to fully understand their circumstances and their place in the world if they are not allowed to explore their lived experiences in the classroom.

Critical and Inclusive Pedagogies Leverage the Lived Experiences of Students

At the heart of critical and inclusive pedagogical models is a focus on the exploration of lived experiences. For example in Chapter 11, Ghabra and colleagues write:

> Recognizing that our bodies are vessels of knowledge, we were encouraged to explore knowledge beyond empirical text; our experiences weaved in and out of theory as we co-constructed the classroom to emphasize the importance of lived experiences by allowing us, the students, to tell our stories. (pp. 196–197, this volume)

In "Afterword: Realizing a More Inclusive Pedagogy" (Tuitt, 2003b), I posited that life experience should be an important part of the curriculum because when instructors encourage students to personalize subject matter with examples from their own lived experiences, they are better able to make connections between the ideas they are learning in the classroom and the world as they understand it. Similarly, Williams (Chapter 4) sees personal experience and narrative as an important tool for learning. Through her utilization of *radical honesty* she strives to provide a space in her classroom for vocalizing personal truths and leverages her own and her students' truths "to connect the dots between individual and group experiences of (dis)empowerment to institutional and systemic analysis of racism and sexism" (p. 73). Williams's use of radical honesty to invite personal truths and lived experience into the classroom reminds us that we should not ask our students to engage in any pedagogical activity that we as instructors are not prepared to do. Modeling for our students how we make a connection between our own lived experiences and the way we understand complex theories and concepts provides examples on how to bring our whole selves into the learning environment. However, Bolitzer, Castillo-Montoya, and Williams (Chapter 2) caution us that though faculty engaging students' prior knowledge to advance learning of academic subject matter is a good first step in creating equitable classroom environments, introduction of diverse students' multiple experiences and ways of knowing may also conflict with one another. Specifically, they advise that recognizing student diversity as a collective resource and facilitating students' representation of their identities are vital.

Critical and Inclusive Pedagogies Strive to Create Identity Affirming and Socially Just Learning Environments

In some of my earlier writings on inclusive pedagogy I advocated for the creation of identity-safe classrooms (Tuitt, 2003b, 2008). Since that time my thinking about the possibility of creating safe learning environments has shifted in part based on the awareness that for all the years I have spent as a Black male, in predominantly White classrooms, as a student or instructor, I have yet to experience one that was safe. The unfortunate reality is that even with the best intentions, extraordinary skills and talents, and a mastery of critical and inclusive pedagogical practices, no instructor, no matter how great, can control everything that happens in the classroom. Therefore, our classrooms will always be imperfect learning environments filled with imperfect human beings and subject to potential violations of human dignity. Accordingly, I now advocate for the creation of identity-affirming and just learning environments as a goal for which all CIPs should strive. Affirming in the sense, as several of the authors (Bolitzer et al.) in this volume reinforce this notion, that students and their instructors arrive to the classroom with multiple and intersectional aspects of their identity that shape how they experience and behave (as well as the overall sense of belonging) in the learning environment. For example, Bolitzer and colleagues (Chapter 2) suggest that in order to design critical and inclusive learning environments faculty should consider

> how to create opportunities for students to share their own representations of who they are and help students recognize the multiplicity and complexity of their intersecting identities. Students' intersecting identities may include religion, language, gender, sexual identity, or aspects of their identity that do not fit into any preexisting categories. (p. 35, this volume)

Additionally, CIPs are identity affirming in that they enable students to authentically share who they are when instructors (and classmates) provide the necessary "support to explore as well as pressure to interrogate [their] own identities and how they interplay" (Ghabra et al., p. 191, this volume). In this sense the notion of creating identity-affirming classrooms is not simply a matter of reinforcing and/or meeting students where they are, but also involves pushing students to deconstruct and extend their understanding of their individual and group sense of self. Whether instructors realize this or not, we as educators are in the identity-development business in that the pedagogical decisions we make inform how students think about their instructors, themselves, and their overall sense of belonging in the classroom. Accordingly, instructors seeking to create critical and inclusive learning environments need to be very thoughtful and just in their attempts.

In his *Letter from Birmingham Jail,*[6] Martin Luther King Jr. (1992) wrote that "any law that uplifts human personality is just. Any law that degrades human personality is unjust" (p. 7). Correspondingly, in critical and inclusive learning environments, instructors must take great care to ensure that the pedagogical decisions they make are designed to uplift the humanity of their students and avoid activities that "distort the soul" or cause damage to the multiple intersectional aspects of their identity. In following Martin Luther King Jr.'s definition of a *just law*, in just learning environments instructors would not ask their students to engage in any pedagogical activity that they themselves are not willing to model. Moreover, in seeking to create identity-affirming and just learning environments, instructors would keep in mind that "there are some instances when a law (pedagogical decision) is just on its face and unjust in its application" (p. 8) and not only consider the theoretical intention behind their pedagogical decisions but also interrogate its application. Therefore instructors seeking to enact a CIP will draw upon a range of sound and tested instructional activities to create their inclusive and equitable learning environment.

Critical and Inclusive Pedagogies Employ a Variety of Interactive and Dynamic Teaching Practices

Building upon the work of bell hooks (1994), in *Enacting Inclusivity Through Engaged Pedagogy: A Higher Education Perspective* (Danowitz & Tuitt, 2011b) I argued that:

> In addition to being meaningful, education should be exciting. It is rare that any professor, no matter how eloquent, can generate through [their] actions enough energy to create an exciting classroom. Excitement is generated through collective effort. The classroom should be an exciting place, never boring. And if boredom should prevail, have in your teaching repertoire a variety of pedagogical strategies that can intervene, alter, or even disrupt the boring atmosphere. (p. 50)

Throughout this volume, contributors provide examples of different pedagogical practices they employ to create interactive, inclusive, and equitable learning environments. For example, in Chapter 9, Gaitanidis and Shao-Kobayashi write that "it is not difficult to imagine . . . a situation of near-zero interaction between students and instructor during a class on contemporary Japanese culture" (p. 152, this volume). To combat this, they seek to construct engaging and creative learning environments, "in which polyphony and dialogism are orchestrated effectively . . . carefully planned, designed, and implemented" (p. 153, this volume). At the heart of their CIP are group activities, presentations, reflective writing assignments, lectures, readings, public speech critiques, and instructor and peer group feedback sessions. Similarly, in Chapter 5, Goldstein describes his use of the Barnga Card Game Simulation to develop deep cross-cultural thinking and empathy. Recognizing that "genuine learning comes from doing" (p. 84, this volume), Goldstein found that experiential learning activities "help clear the intellectual and emotional path to the deeper understanding" (p. 86, this volume) that CIPs seek to create. Carter Andrews and Castillo (Chapter 7) also use a variety of interactive and dynamic teaching practices to create critical, inclusive, and equitable learning environments. Specifically they utilize writing assignments, group work, ice breakers, discussion-based activities (e.g., K-W-L-H and the Diversity Toss), and field placements to challenge their:

> Students' understandings of normality and privilege, promote marginalized voices and experiences, engage in critical self-reflection, counter [their] inclinations to engage in "othering" individuals and groups, and consider how [they] can be transformative participants in the struggle for educational equity. (p. 119, this volume)

All of the interactive and dynamic practices described in this volume are supported by and grounded in interdisciplinary readings and perspectives with the clear understanding that the content instructors choose signals to students what matters and what does not.

Critical and Inclusive Pedagogies Utilize Diverse and Interdisciplinary Content and Perspectives

In Chapter 11, Ghabra and colleagues describe their instructor's intentionality related to the inclusion of diverse perspectives through interdisciplinary readings. Specifically, their professor writes:

> In my classroom, difference lives in the center not the margins, meaning that I choose to have students read noncanonical scholarship throughout

the course. Difference shapes the course. . . . I hope to create a syllabus that allows cultural Others to find a place of possibility and home. (pp. 188–189, this volume)

For her students, the centering of voices that are often absent in the world of academia by including their writings, performances, videos, and more created a critical and inclusive learning environment "that lifted up difference and focused on the Other" (p. 192, this volume). According to Koshino (Chapter 6) lifting up the *Other* is essential in increasingly racially diverse classrooms "because the Eurocentric values and perspectives embedded in the educational curriculum" (p. 107, this volume) can limit the ability of racially minoritized students to access meaningful learning opportunities.

Carter Andrews and Castillo (Chapter 7) remind us that we must be thoughtful and critical in our consideration of what content and perspectives to include. They contend that in order to create critical, inclusive, and equitable learning environments some ideological perspectives may have to be excluded, such as those "ideas [that] represent deficit orientations about individuals and groups" (p. 121, this volume). They try to navigate the delicate balance between including diverse perspectives and content but not at the expense of any student. They also advise that we should resist the desire to indoctrinate our students for "that indoctrination is not humanizing pedagogy nor does it facilitate the critical awareness" (p. 125, this volume) they seek to develop. Finally, when including diverse content and perspectives, instructors should draw from multiple disciplines. For example, Williams (Chapter 4) contends that "fields and disciplines such as ethnic studies, Africana studies, women and gender studies, and Black feminist anthropology were created to trouble oppressive systems of power and provide tools for changing the ways we experience our lives" (p. 79, this volume). To her these interdisciplinary research areas are "dedicated to connecting praxis and theory and founded on principles of truth-telling, truth-seeking, critique, and transformation" (p. 79, this volume), which is at the center of critical and inclusive pedagogies.

Critical and Inclusive Pedagogies Are Equity Minded

In my own pedagogical praxis, I combine inclusive pedagogy with critical race pedagogy to "challenge students to use the knowledge they acquired to promote equity and social justice for society, in general, as well as for [racially minoritized] groups and communities, in particular" (Danowitz & Tuitt, 2011b, p. 48). Like many of the contributors to this book, my hybridization of inclusive and critical race pedagogy seeks to help students develop a critical [race] consciousness through the intentional facilitation of "teachable moments" that force students to explore their collective lived experience and make connections between their own assumptions related to race and racism, and explore how those assumptions can come to life in their everyday experiences (Yosso, 2002). Similarly, Stewart (Chapter 1), Martinez and colleagues (Chapter 8), and Carter Andrews and Castillo (Chapter 7) advocate for the use of a variety of equity-minded pedagogical practices designed to leverage their students' experiences as individuals and as a community of learners and encourage them to reflect and act. Collectively, by challenging students to move from theory to practice, and vice versa, those who employ CIPs can inspire students to engage in learning for the public good (Bowen & Bok, 1998). This teaching and learning philosophy is based on the premise that the best way for a student to learn how to engage in transformative work is to create opportunities both in and out of the classroom; to recognize that as educators each encounter we have with our students has the potential to profoundly impact their lives, the people they come in contact with, the organizations in which they work, the communities in which they live, and society as a whole; and to reject learning for learning's sake and embrace the notion that education should be used for social and political change.

CIPs Require Courageous and Transparent Instructors

According to Smith (Chapter 10), educators must develop the courage and fortitude to resist the traditional Eurocentric perspective of the role of the administrator (teacher)–student relationship and develop engaged pedagogical relationships with students. Recently, I experienced such a moment in my Diversity in Organization course when I approached a sense of vulnerability and transparency that for a fleeting second had me seriously considering retreating to a less risky zone. In my retelling of yet another encounter with racial microaggression, I was attempting to model for my students how to engage in what Williams (Chapter 4) refers to as radical honesty. Specifically, Williams states:

> Radical honesty emphasizes the significance of personal narratives and opens a space for creating strategies that enable scholars and students to bring their "whole self" to the classroom, while getting rid of the shame that frequently accompanies their bodies in academic settings. (pp. 72–73, this volume)

However, bringing the "whole self"—mind, body, and soul—into the classroom can be risky business, especially for racially minoritized faculty members who dare to "acknowledge the failings of an academic system with which we remain engaged" (p. 81, this volume), as Williams puts it. In that moment, instead of retreating to a less risky form of safety, I remembered that CIPs require that instructors, according to Williams, "acknowledge [their] vulnerabilities, and most importantly, share—with colleagues and students—[their] strategies for self-care and self-love" (p. 81, this volume).

In order to authentically bring our "whole self" into the learning environment, instructors need to critically engage in the self-work of getting to truly know their inner soul. Like Stewart (Chapter 1), the contributors to this book understand that using CIPs require that the instructor engage in critical self-work and be vulnerable in the teaching–learning process. When instructors are successful at bringing their whole self into the learning environment by modeling this type of self-awareness of their positionality, it allows students to emulate their own reflexivity, resulting in a more dynamic space (Ghabra et al., Chapter 11). According to Ghabra and colleagues, CIPs recognized that instructors, like their students, consist of hosts of identities. Modeling "intersectional reflexivity acknowledges this and encourages [our students] to examine how [their multiple] identities interact and what lens(es) they bring to various lived experiences" (p. 201, this volume). Moreover, this type of transparency in the learning environment helps our students to see how our identities inform the pedagogical decisions we make.

de los Reyes and colleagues (Chapter 3) argue that for instructors "to become compassionate and effective agents of change, we need to engage in the process of introspection, reflection, and action" (p. 63, this volume). They define *introspection* as the systematic and careful linking of the personal, the political, and the intellectual in a system of beliefs and values that allows instructors to know who they are, what they are able to do, and what contradicts their deeply held beliefs. Specifically they write:

> By being clear about who we are, what political principles and theories support our vision, and what our dreams are, we insure that we remain firm in our practice and that our principles are not compromised. We believe that to disconnect the practice from theory—the personal from the political and the intellectual—is a very dangerous approach to social change leading to confusion, vacillation, reaction, and mistakes. (p. 63, this volume)

This transparency, like Williams's conceptualization of radical honesty, is not simply about truth-telling for the sake of speaking truths (although this is itself a valuable exercise) but more about the development of a critical eye toward analysis, intention, and authenticity to identify beneficial and effective pedagogical practices for creating inclusive, affirming, and equitable learning environments.

Conclusion

CIPs offer multiple opportunities for creating affirming and equitable learning environments where all students, regardless of their prior lived experiences, can be the best that they can be. In order for that to be actualized, instructors need to be the best they can be. Overall the chapters in this book remind us that teaching and learning are deeply interrelated. To create inclusive, affirming, and equitable learning environments for *all* students, but especially racially minoritized students, educators must reject the temptation to revert back to traditional pedagogical practices and at the same time confront dominant ideologies and conceptualize a pedagogy of hope. Specifically, the authors in this book share a common belief that by utilizing CIPs they are able to engage in a meaningful praxis that empowers them to lift up the souls of their students and engage in what bell hooks (1994) refers to as education as the practice of freedom. This pedagogy requires that educators embrace their students as whole human beings consisting of mind, body, and soul and create interactive and dynamic classroom environments that inspire deep and meaningful transformational learning. The authors in this book also remind us that enacting CIPs can be costly. Whether it is being emotionally drained from frequent expressions of radical honesty, fighting racial battle fatigue from everyday encounters with micro and macro aggressions, teaching in the line of fire as you address attempts to dehumanize you or others in the classroom, and/or dodging the dismissive bricks from oppressive institutional structures like tenure or colleagues and administrators who fail to appreciate your commitment to a liberatory pedagogy—giving up a little piece of your soul in the name of education is a price you must be willing to pay.

In closing, I have come to understand that utilizing CIPs is not a form of praxis that all educators should embrace. In fact, educators who fail to do the self-work may cause more harm than good and, as a result, engage in the creation of unjust learning environments. Although this concluding chapter attempts to lay out a series of pedagogical considerations related to enacting CIPs, potential converts should be wary of trying to put them into practice without careful consideration of their capacity to do the work. Advancing CIPs requires self-awareness, courage, and continuous commitment, and it should, as teaching in racially diverse classrooms is a lot harder than teaching in classrooms where all our students are the same. In that sense, diversity matters, context (both institutional and external) matters, and identity matters in that they all work together to shape how students experience our classrooms. And for those of you who are not new to the praxis of critical and inclusive pedagogies, please keep in mind that we can always do better and that our good intentions in and of themselves will not produce the progressive outcomes we seek. Fifteen years later, after my initial intellectual excursion to imagine a pedagogy of possibilities, I end this volume more convinced than ever before that even with all our limitations, CIPs provide us with potential to create equitable learning environments, to labor for freedom, and to "demand of ourselves and our comrades, an openness of mind and heart that allows us to face reality even as we collectively imagine ways to move beyond boundaries, to transgress" (hooks, 1994, p. 207).

Notes

1. I advocate the use of *traditionally* opposed to *predominantly* White because "PWI [predominantly White institution] would not include those higher education institutions whose campus populations have been predominantly White but now have students of color in the numeric majority. I argue that even though institutions like MIT and Berkeley have more students of color than Whites on campus, the culture, tradition, and values found in those institutions remain traditionally White" (Tuitt, 2008, pp. 192–193).

2. As an aside note, I must share how blessed I am to have former students build upon my original work and in their own scholarship take it to places I never dreamed.

3. I would like to acknowledge and thank my graduate assistants Kristin Deal and Varaxy Yi Borromeo for their research and editing in support of this chapter.

4. See *The Journal of Blacks in Higher Education* at www.jbhe.com/incidents for the most recent list of campus racial incidents.

5. Chase, Dowd, Pazich, and Bensimon (2014) define the term *minoritized* as referring to both the objective outcomes resulting from the historical and contemporary practices of racial–ethnic exclusion as well as the continued social, political, and economic existence of marginality and discrimination though compositional racial–ethnic parity may have been achieved in particular contexts.

6. I would like to thank Dr. Bianca Williams for pointing me to Martin Luther King Jr.'s *Letter from Birmingham Jail* for a way to explain my conceptualization of a just learning environment.

References

Andrews, K. (2015, August 12). Why Britain's schools are failing to tackle racism. *The Guardian*. Retrieved from http://www.theguardian.com/commentisfree/2015/aug/12/racism-schools-government-reforms-targets

Barbara, V. (2015, March 23). In denial over racism in Brazil. *The New York Times*. Retrieved from http://www.nytimes.com/2015/03/24/opinion/vanessa-barbara-in-denial-over-racism-in-brazil.html?_r=0

Beason-Hammon Alabama Taxpayer and Citizen Protection Act, Alabama House Bill, 56. (2011).

Bowen, W. G., & Bok, D. (1998). *The shape of the river. Long-term consequences of considering race in college and university admissions.* Ewing, NJ: Princeton University Press.

Chase, M. M., Dowd, A. C., Pazich, L. B., & Bensimon, E. M. (2014). Transfer equity for "minoritized" students: A critical policy analysis of seven states. *Educational Policy, 28*(5), 669–717.

Coble, B., Cobb, F., Deal, K., & Tuitt, F. (2013). Navigating the space between: Obama and the postracial myth. In D. J. Carter Andrews, & F. Tuitt (Eds.), *Contesting the myth of the "postracial" era: The continued significance of race in U.S. education* (pp. 25–41). New York, NY: Peter Lang Publishing.

Danowitz, M., & Tuitt, F. (2011a). Changing curriculum and changing students' lives. In J. Tienari, S. Katila, & S. Sumerila (Eds.), *Working for inclusion: Positive experiences from across the world* (pp. 33–47). Glos, UK: Edward Elgar Publishing.

Danowitz, M., & Tuitt, F. (2011b). Enacting inclusivity through engaged pedagogy: A higher education perspective. *Equity & Excellence in Education, 44*(1), 40–57.

DeRuy, E. (2015, May 18). Unfairly rejected: Why 65 Asian-Americans advocacy groups are suing Harvard for discrimination. *Fusion.* Retrieved from http://fusion.net/story/136188/why-65-asian-american-advocacy-groups-are-suing-harvard-for-discrimination/

Douglass, J. A. (2012, July 15). The rise of for-profit universities and colleges. *University World News.* Retrieved from http://www.universityworldnews.com/article.php?story=20120710160228719

Fisher v. University of Texas at Austin et al., 570 U.S. (2013).

Freire, P. (1993). *Pedagogy of the oppressed* (Rev. ed.). New York, NY: Continuum.

Garza, A. (2014, October 7). A herstory of the #BlackLivesMatter movement. *The Feminist Wire.* Retrieved from http://www.thefeministwire.com/2014/10/blacklivesmatter-2/

Gratz v. Bollinger et al., 539 U.S. 244 (2003).

Grutter v. Bollinger et al., 539 U.S. 306 (2003).

Guinier, L., & Torres, G. (2002). *The miner's canary: Enlisting race, resisting power, transforming democracy.* Cambridge, MA: Harvard University Press.

hooks, b. (1994) *Teaching to transgress.* New York, NY: Routledge.

Howell, A., & Tuitt, F. (Eds.). (2003). *Race and higher education: Rethinking pedagogy in diverse college classrooms.* Cambridge, MA: Harvard Educational Review.

King, M. L., Jr. (1992). Letter from Birmingham jail. *UC Davis L. Rev., 26,* 835.

Maoláin, A. Ó. (2013, November 2013). Access to higher education must be a global priority. *University World News.* Retrieved from http://www.universityworldnews.com/article.php?story=20131105105454648

Rubin, A. J., & Breeden, A. (2015, April 17). France announces stronger fight against racism and anti-Semitism. *The New York Times.* Retrieved from http://www.nytimes.com/2015/04/18/world/europe/france-announces-stronger-fight-against-racism-and-anti-semitism.html

Sanderson, A. B. (2015, May 25). Children take to Amsterdam streets to demand White classmates. *Breitbart.* Retrieved from http://www.breitbart.com/london/2015/05/25/children-take-to-amsterdam-streets-to-demand-white-classmates/

Schuette v. BAMN, 572 U. S. (2014).

Sheehy, K. (2013, November 13). Undergrads around the world face student loan debt. *US News & World Report.* Retrieved from http://www.usnews.com/education/best-global-universities/articles/2013/11/13/undergrads-around-the-world-face-student-loan-debt.

Support Our Law Enforcement and Safe Neighborhoods Act, Arizona State Senate Bill 1070. (2010).

Tuitt, F. (2000). *Towards a more inclusive pedagogy: Rethinking how we teach racially diverse college classrooms* (Qualifying paper). Harvard Graduate School of Education, Boston, MA.

Tuitt, F. (2003a). *Black souls in an ivory tower: Understanding what it means to teach in a manner that respects and cares for the souls of African American graduate students* (Unpublished doctoral dissertation). Harvard Graduate School of Education, Cambridge, MA.

Tuitt, F. (2003b). Afterword: Realizing a more inclusive pedagogy. In A. Howell & F. Tuitt (Eds.), *Race and higher education: Rethinking pedagogy in diverse college classrooms* (pp. 243–268). Cambridge, MA: Harvard Educational Review.

Tuitt, F. (2008). Removing the threat in the air: Teacher transparency and the creation of identity-safe graduate classrooms. *Journal on Excellence in College Teaching, 19*(2), 167–198.

Tuitt, F., Agans, L., & Griffin, R. (in press). Embracing the tension: Using teachable moments to explore the racialized educational experiences of students in traditionally White classrooms. *Understanding and Dismantling Privilege.*

Yosso, T. J. (2002). Toward a critical race curriculum. *Equity & Excellence in Education, 35*(2), 93–107.

EDITORS AND CONTRIBUTORS

Editors

Frank Tuitt received his doctorate from the Harvard Graduate School of Education. Currently, he is the senior adviser to the chancellor and provost on diversity and inclusion at the University of Denver and associate professor of Higher Education in the Morgridge College of Education. Tuitt's research explores topics related to access and equity in higher education, teaching and learning in racially diverse college classrooms, and diversity and organizational transformation. Tuitt is a coeditor and contributing author of the books *Race and Higher Education: Rethinking Pedagogy in Diverse College Classrooms* (Harvard Educational Review, 2003) and *Contesting the Myth of a Post-Racial Era: The Continued Significance of Race in U.S. Education* (Peter Lang Publishing, 2013).

Chayla Haynes is assistant professor of higher education and student affairs leadership at the University of Northern Colorado. Her research centers on innovations in college teaching, creating transformative and identity affirming learning environments, and applying critical race theory (CRT) to postsecondary contexts and problems. Committed to promoting educational equity among racially minoritized college students, her research agenda has been inspired by findings from her dissertation that explored the influence of racial consciousness on the behaviors of White faculty in classrooms, which was the first of its kind to utilize critical legal scholar Kimberlé Crenshaw's restrictive and expansive views of equality framework to empirically measure and describe excellence in college teaching. Her grant-funded research has been presented at national and international conferences sponsored by the American Educational Research Association (AERA), the Association for the Study of Higher Education (ASHE), and the University of Oxford's Educational Research Symposium, to name a few. Her most recent work is featured in *The SAGE Encyclopedia of Intercultural Competence*, (SAGE Publications, 2015) the *National Association of Student Affairs Professionals Journal,* and includes the coedited volume entitled *Interrogating Whiteness and Relinquishing Power: White Faculty's Commitment to Racial Consciousness in STEM Classrooms* (Peter Lang Publishing, 2015).

223

Saran Stewart is a lecturer of comparative higher education in the Faculty of Humanities and Education at the University of the West Indies, Mona Campus. She is also the coordinator for the MEd in Higher Educational Management program and a research specialist in the Research and Grants Unit in the School of Education. Much of her research critically examines issues of comparative education, postcolonial theories, critical and inclusive pedagogies, and diversity in and outside the classroom. Stewart is devoted to the examination and exploration of topics related to access and equity in education and teaching and learning in developing country contexts. Her recent research comparatively examines the scope and prevalence of private tutoring and its effects on access to higher education in multiple Caribbean countries. Her work has been published in the *Journal of Diversity in Higher Education, Journal of Student Affairs, Postcolonial Directions in Education Journal,* and the *Applied Anthropologist Journal.* Stewart most recently received the International Scholars Award at the Research in Education Symposium from the Government of the Republic of Trinidad and Tobago and the Inter-American Development Bank.

Contributors

Liza Ann Bolitzer is a doctoral candidate and instructor in the Higher and Postsecondary Education Program, Department of Organizational Leadership at Teachers College, Columbia University.

Bernadette Marie Calafell is a professor of communication studies at the University of Denver.

Dorinda J. Carter Andrews is an associate professor of race, culture, and equity in the Department of Teacher Education at Michigan State University.

Bernadette M. Castillo is a doctoral student in the Department of Teacher Education at Michigan State University.

Milagros Castillo-Montoya is an assistant professor in the Higher Education and Student Affairs Program, Department of Educational Leadership, at the University of Connecticut.

Eileen de los Reyes was the former deputy superintendent for academics at the Boston Public Schools.

Maria del Carmen Salazar is associate professor and program coordinator of the teacher education program in the Morgridge College of Education at the University of Denver.

Ioannis Gaitanidis is assistant professor in the Center for International Research and Education at Chiba University, Japan.

Haneen S. Ghabra is a doctoral candidate in the Department of Communication Studies at the University of Denver.

David S. Goldstein is senior lecturer in the School of Interdisciplinary Arts and Sciences at the University of Washington, Bothell.

Yamila Hussein is a clinical teacher educator at the Boston Teacher Residency.

Sergio F. Juarez is a doctoral candidate in the Department of Communication Studies at the University of Denver.

Shanna K. Kattari is a doctoral candidate in the Graduate School of Social Work at the University of Denver.

Kako Koshino is an assistant professor in the Department of Educational Studies at Monmouth College.

Lisa M. Martinez is associate professor and chair of the Department of Sociology and Criminology at the University of Denver.

Miranda Olzman is a doctoral student in the Department of Communication Studies at the University of Denver.

Debora M. Ortega is a professor in the Graduate School of Social Work and the director of the Latino Center for Community Engagement and Scholarship at the University of Denver.

Lori D. Patton joined the faculty at Iowa State University in fall 2005 and is an assistant professor in the Department of Educational Leadership and Policy Studies. Her teaching repertoire includes courses that focus on student development theory, college environments, critical race theory, and African American studies.

Satoko Shao-Kobayashi is assistant professor in the Center for International Research and Education at Chiba University, Japan.

Hal Smith is vice president for education and youth development at the National Urban League.

Stella L. Smith is a postdoctoral fellow in the Division of Diversity and Community Engagement at the University of Texas at Austin.

Bianca C. Williams is an assistant professor at the University of Colorado–Boulder Department of Ethnic Studies.

Leslie A. Williams is a doctoral candidate, teaching assistant, and internship program coordinator in the higher and postsecondary education program, Department of Organizational Leadership at Teachers College, Columbia University.

Tarajean Yazzie-Mintz is a senior program officer for Tribal Colleges and Universities early childhood education initiatives at the American Indian College Fund.

academic advisement, African
Americans, in Midwestern college,
104–7, 109
academic conferences, 19
academic English, 87
academic institutions, 73–75
academic orthodoxy, 13–14
academic persistence, 1
academic spaces, 73–75
academic subject matter, 30–32
academic work, 55
access, 23–24
action, x, 49, 63–65, 73, 217
activation of student voice, 15
activism, college, 208
Adamo-Villani, Nicoletta, 88
administrators, 5, 172–73, 181. *See
also* African American female
administrators
Africa, 89–90
African American female
administrators, 170–71
challenges of, 178–81
data, 174–75
discussion, 181–82
engaged pedagogy perspectives,
175–81
families influenced by, 175
findings, 175–81
implications, 181–82
methodology, 174–75
racism faced by, 178–80
sexism faced by, 178–80
students influenced by, 175–77
work–life balance of, 178, 180, 181
African Americans
administrators, 5

Black person as different from, 71
in executive positions, 171–72
graduate students, 47
liberation struggle, 47
professors, 103–4, 109
at PWIs, 171–72
African Americans, in Midwestern
college
academic advisement, 104–7, 109
context, 100–102
culturally responsive teaching, 107–8
curriculum, 107–8
diversity exposure of, 102–4
expectations, 102–4, 106–7
faculty of color, 102–4
faculty–student interaction, 105–7
findings, 102–10
inclusive learning environment,
109–10
method, 100–102
overview, 98–110
participants, 100–101
procedures, 101
professors as hostile in, 106–7
researcher's identity, 101–2
support, 102–7
African American women, higher
education experiences of, 171–72.
See also African American female
administrators; Black feminist
theory
Africana Studies and Cultural
Anthropology, 71–72
"Afterword: Realizing a More Inclusive
Pedagogy" (Tuitt), 206, 211
Aiden, Emily, 178
Alabama, 207

Alcoff, Linda, 201
alienation, 103
Allen, Walter, 99
allies, 198, 199–200, 201
allyship, 201–2
Alvesson, Mats, 11
AME church. *See* Emanuel African Methodist Episcopal church
American Council on Education, 171
American Indian, 47
Amsterdam, Netherlands, 208
animation, 151
announcements, 61
Anzaldúa, Gloria, 187, 188, 193
Arrizón, Alicia, 195, 196, 197
art, 61, 62
Asian woman scholar, 102
assignments, 17–19, 119–21, 123–25
assumptions, 126–27
Atlantic Slavery, 107
audience, 155–56, 160
autobiography, 63–65, 119–20, 123–25

Bakhtin, Mikhail, 149–50, 152, 154
banking education, 9–10, 12–13, 15
banking method, 48
Barnga, 4, 214
    advantages capitalized on by, 89
    in business course, 93
    debriefing session in, 90–94
    domination relations deconstructed by, 87
    emotional response of, 92–93
    English in, 87
    injustice influenced by, 92–93
    observations, 91–92
    overview, 83–95
    reflection in, 90–94
    subordination relations deconstructed by, 87
Bartolomé, Lilia, 125
Barzilai, Sarit, 92
base groups, 123, 125
beef dish (*sukiyaki*), 162, 164
Bell, Derrick, x

Bensimon, Estela, 221n5
Berk, Rupert, 92
biases, 72, 112–13, 127
big group, 60–62
biology, 166
Black, Nancy, 34–35
Black feminist theory, 173–74
Black History Month, 107–8
Black Lives Matter movement, 207–8
Black people
    academic spaces for, 73–74
    African American as different from, 71
    graduate students, 205
    shame of, 74
    students, 118
Black Women, Popular Culture, and the Pursuit of Happiness, 76–79
Blau, Ina, 92
blind adoption, 125
Blommaert, Jan, 26
Bloom, Benjamin, 93–94
Bloom's Taxonomy, 93–94
Bochner, Arthur, 11
Body, 194–97
Bolitzer, Ann, 212
boredom, 213
Boyle, Elizabeth, 88
Brazil, 208
Brown, Brene, 81
browning, 209
Brynen, Rex, 87, 92
Burbules, Nicholas, 92
Bureau of Census, U.S., 31
business course, 92, 93
Butler, Judith, 188

Calafell, Bernadette, 196, 200
California rolls, 158, 160, 161
campus racial climate, research on, 99. *See also* African Americans, in Midwestern college
campus racial incidents, 208
card game. *See* Barnga
Caribbean University, 9–20, 18–19

Carter, Lily, 180
Carter Andrews, Dorinda, 210, 214, 215
Castillo, Bernadette, 210, 214, 215
Castillo-Montoya, Milagros, 212
CBD. *See* Convention on Biological Diversity
Center for Child and Human Development, 128n2
Center for International Research and Education (CIRE), 150–51
Central Education Council, 152
Charleston, South Carolina, 207
Chase, Megan, 221n5
chat rooms, 152–53
Chen, Yong, 159
Chiba University, 150–51. *See also* Center for International Research and Education
Chicano, 194–97
Christian, Barbara, 74, 80
CIPs. *See* critical and inclusive pedagogies
CIRE. *See* Center for International Research and Education
citizens, 56
classrooms. *See also* simulations; truth-telling
  as boring, 213
  community's relationship with, 80
  as exciting, 213
  professor's role in, 79
Clayton-Pedersen, Alma, 99
cognitive dissonance, 86–87
cognitive domain, 94
Cohen, Cathy, 196
collaborative learning, 15, 152–53, 168n3
collective growth, 27–30
collective power, 52
collective resource, diversity as, 33–35
collectivism, 145
college. *See also* African Americans, in Midwestern college

activism, 208
  intersectionality applying to, 27
  prep programs, 137
  principal on, 141–42
  race in, x
  teacher on, 142–43
college students. *See also* African Americans, in Midwestern college; Barnga; Education for Social and Political Change
  experiential learning influencing, 85–86
  inequities of, 23
  radical honesty demands on, 81
  suicide of, 77–79
Collins, Patricia, 173
colonial era, 10
colorblindness, x, 4, 113
colormuteness, 4, 113, 128n1
Colormute: Race Talk Dilemmas in an American High School (Pollock), 128n1
comforting, 78–79
Communication and Popular Culture, 200
Communication Studies seminar, 186–202
communities, 49, 58–62, 80, 118–19, 133, 189
computer-based games, 88
concocimento. See knowledge
conflict, 32–33
conscientização. See critical consciousness
consciousness, 108. *See also* critical consciousness
Convention on Biological Diversity (CBD), 88
Corey, Frederick, 187
cosmopolitan compass, 28
cosmopolitanism, 28
course management systems, 16
Crenshaw, Kimberlé, 191
Creswell, John, 104

critical and inclusive pedagogies (CIPs),
ix–xi, 206. *See also* Barnga; Critical
Sexuality Studies
applying, 11–19
at Caribbean University, 9–20
communication, 196–97
content utilized by, 214–15
as costly, 218
definition of, 132, 191
dehumanization, 132–33
discovery as crucial to, 86–87
educators embracing, 218
enacting, 218
equity implications, 205–19
experiential learning entailing, 87
framework, 11–20
in global context, 205–19
higher education implications,
205–19
injustice influenced by, 92
instructors required by, 216–17
intersectional sexuality and, 186–202
learning environments created by, 2,
212–13
overview, 1–6, 2, 13–14, 218–19
perspectives utilized by, 214–15
practice implications, 19–20
race implications, 205–19
students influenced by, 18–19,
211–13
teaching influencing, 210–11,
213–14
tenets, 13–14
theoretical framework, 132–36
2.0, 205–19
critical consciousness (*conscientização*),
4, 135
base groups influencing, 125
definition of, 11, 85, 114
developing, 11–13, 215–16
hooks on, 172
humanizing pedagogy necessity of,
114–15
inequity challenge and, 114–15
promoting, 16–18

in simulations, 85
critical dialogues, 121
critical labor, 80–81
critical pedagogical spaces, 188–89
critical performative pedagogy, 187–88
critical reflection, 12, 114
critical self-awareness, x–xi
Critical Sexuality Studies
antipathy spaces, 192–94
beginnings, 188–89, 200–202
belonging spaces, 192–94
critical pedagogical spaces created by,
188–89
dominance, 197–200
intersectional pedagogy, 197–200
marginalization, 197–200
outsider entering, 189–92
overview, 186–202
pedagogy of revolt, 194–97
resistance spaces, 192–94
culinary traditions, 160
Cullors, Patrisse, 207–8
Cultural Autobiography, 119–20,
123–25
cultural clashes, 89–94
cultural competency, 100, 128n2
cultural deficiency, 4
cultural incompetence, 113
culturally diverse curriculum, 108
culturally responsive teaching, 4,
99–100, 107–8
cultural values, 141–42
cultures, 100, 112–27, 165, 166, 194
curriculum, 16–18, 107–8

Dale, John, 134
Danowitz, Mary, 213
Danube, Cinnamon, 85–86
debriefing, 90–94
declarative knowledge, 88
deep democracy, 63–65
dehumanization, 132–34, 144–45
dehumanizing pedagogy, 4–5
Delgado-Gaitan, Concha, 100
de los Reyes, Eileen, 217

democracy, 50–51, 63–65. *See also* radical democracy
democratic classroom, 52–55, 60–61. *See also* Education for Social and Political Change
Democratic National Convention, 207
democratic pedagogy, 49–52. *See also* Education for Social and Political Change
democratic practice, 50–51
de-racializing
    Japaneseness, 149–67
    of *washoku*, 159–65
De Santo, Elizabeth, 87–88
development, 38, 145
Dewey, John, 84–85, 92
dialogical professor–student interaction, 15
dialogical subjects, 57
dialogic course structure, 165–66
dialogic relations, 155
dialogic space, 153
dialogism, 152–53, 154–57
dialogues
    critical, 121
    engaging in, 56–59
    humanizing pedagogy, 121
    knowledge co-constructed through, 56
    as meaningful, 57
    power's connection with, 57–58
    T-128 focusing on, 49, 55–59
Dib, Hazar, 88
disabled woman, 189–92
disciplinary burdens, 79–81
discovery, 86–87
discussion-based teaching, 34–35
dissent, 194
diverse administrators. *See* African American female administrators
diversity
    African Americans, in Midwestern college, exposure to, 102–4
    benefits of, 24
    as collective resource, 33–35

definition of, 24
equitable learning environments
    engaging, 33–38
    equity through, 23–38
    growth fostered by, 27–30
    in higher education, 24
    identities and, 25–27
    as intersection, 25–27
    perspectives on, 24–33, 38
    professors engaging, 37–38
    propositions, 33–38
    students influenced by, 172
    within subject-matter learning, 30–33, 36–38
    super-, 25–26
Diversity in Organization course, 216–17
Diversity Toss, 119
doing, learning from, 84–85
domestication, of students, 50
dominance, 197–200
domination, 87
double-consciousness, 74
Dowd, Alicia, 221n5
Du Bois, William, 74

East Asia, 159
education. *See also* teacher education
    culture's relationship with, 100
    as dehumanization vehicle, 144–45
    as freedom practice, 218
    opportunities afforded by, 124–25
    privileges and, 124
Education for Social and Political Change (T-128)
    action focused on by, 49, 63–65
    analysis of, 47–65, 65–66
    beginnings of, 48
    big group in, 60–62
    communities focused on by, 49, 59–62
    dialogue focused on by, 49, 55–59
    foundation established for, 49–52
    language of democracy proposed for, 49–52

overview, 44–66
power focused on by, 49, 52–56
practice in, 49–52
as radical, 48
reflecting in, 63–65
small groups in, 62
transforming of, 49
educators, x–xi, 218. *See also* critical
    and inclusive pedagogies
Ellis, Carolyn, 11
Emanuel African Methodist Episcopal
    (AME) church, 207
emotional labor, 75, 80–81
emotional response, 92–93
empathy, 83, 84
empowerment, truth-telling as, 75–79
*Enacting Inclusivity Through Engaged
    Pedagogy: A Higher Education
    Perspective* (Danowitz and Tuitt),
    213
engaged pedagogy
    administrators applying, 172–73
    African American female
        administrators' perspectives on,
        175–81
    challenges of, 178–81
    definition of, 172
    hooks on, 181
    overview, 170, 172–73, 181–82
    perspective, 181
English, 87, 151–52
equitable learning environments, 32–38
equity
    CIP implications, 205–19
    through diversity, 23–38
    in global context, 205–19
    overview, ix–xi
Ethan, Olivia, 177–78, 179
Ethical Reflexivity and Sensitivity,
    201–2
excitement, 213
executive positions, 171–72
Experience and Education (Dewey),
    84–85
experiential education, 84–85

experiential learning, 83, 85–87
Exploring American Culture: Race
    Ethnicity, and Immigration
    course, 90

faculty (*facultad*), 197
    of color, 102–4, 109
    democratic classroom role of, 52–55
    development, 38
    mentoring, 109
    White, 109–10
faculty–student interaction. *See also*
    instructor-student interactions
    African Americans, in Midwestern
        college, 105–7
    overview, 14
failure, 62
families, 31–32, 131, 175
fat woman, 197–200
feminism, 46, 81. *See also* Black
    feminist theory; Education for
    Social and Political Change
financial aid, 106
Five Tricks, 90–92. *See also* Barnga
Flores Niemann, Yolanda, 74
Flushing, Queens, New York City,
    25–26
food waste, 160–61
foreign-homeland, 9–10
foreign students, 168n1
for-profit institutions, 209
Foucault, Michel, 188
France, 208
freedom, 218
Freire, Paulo, 2, 9–10, 11, 12–13, 15,
    48, 57, 132, 133, 134, 135, 146,
    210–11. *See also* humanizing
    pedagogy
fried rice, 169n6
fun, 89

Gaitanidis, Ioannis, 214
games, 85–89. *See also* Barnga
gang, 143–44
Garza, Alicia, 207–8

Gay, Geneva, 99–100, 108, 109
gendered oppression, 76–79
Georgetown University, 128n2
Ghabra, Haneen, 211, 214–15, 217
Giroux, Henry, 2, 87, 132
Global Project Work (GPW):
    Presenting About Japan in English,
    149–50, 156–67, 169n4
Goldstein, David, 214
Gonzalez, Carmen, 74
GPW: Presenting About Japan in
    English. *See* Global Project Work:
    Presenting About Japan in English
graduate students, 47, 205. *See also*
    Critical Sexuality Studies
graduation rates, 1
Green, Amanda, 87–88
Group A, 156–67
growth, 27–30
Guinier, Lani, 205
Gumport, Patricia, 1–2
Gutierrez y Muhs, Gabriella, 74

Hansen, David, 28
happiness, 76–79
Hargreaves, Andy, 16–17
Harper, Shaun, x
Harris, Angela, 74
Harris-Perry, Melissa, 74
Harvard Graduate School of Education
    (HGSE), 67n1, 67n2. *See also*
    Education for Social and Political
    Change
HBCUs. *See* historically black colleges
    and universities
Heimann, Beverly, 93
heritage, 160
heteronormativity, 199
HGSE. *See* Harvard Graduate School of
    Education
high-achieving students, 143–44
high-energy democracy, 51, 63–65
higher education. *See also* college;
    universities

African American women's
    experiences in, 171–72
browning of, 209
CIP implications, 205–19
collaborative learning in, 152–53
computer-based games in, 88
dialogism in, 152–53
diversity in, 24
in global context, 205–19
in Japan, 151–53
Japanese policies, 150–51
polyphony in, 152–53
as product, 1–2
tracking in, 208
high-need schools, 120–21
high school, 128n1, 140
historically black colleges and
    universities (HBCUs), 103
history teacher, 36
homeplace, 188–89
homogeneity, 151–52
hooks, bell, 2, 37, 170, 172, 181, 188,
    199–200, 213, 218
Horton, Myles, 52
hospitality, 28, 29
Howell, Annie, 206
Human Diversity, Power and
    Opportunity in Social Institutions,
    115–25
humanization, 133–36, 144–45
humanizing pedagogy, 4–5, 133,
    210–11
    assignments, 119–21, 123–25
    critical consciousness as necessary for,
        114–15
    critical dialogues, 121
    for culture, 112–27
    definition of, 113, 135
    dilemma, 126–27
    employment of, 115–25
    enacting, 126–27
    overview, 112–27, 135
    practices, 118–19, 122–23, 127
    praxis, 120–21

principles of, 135–36, 144–45
for race, 112–27
in teacher education, 112–27
teaching deconstruction, 115–25
tensions, 126–27
Hurtado, Sylvia, 99
Hussein, Yamila, 47
hybrid selves, 133
Hyslop-Margison, Emery, 134

IB program. *See* international baccalaureate program
icebreakers, 122–23
identification, 160
identities, 71–72. *See also* Critical
Sexuality Studies; intersectionality
diversity and, 25–27
learning environments affirming,
212–13
power and, 25–27
prior knowledge based on, 31, 34, 37
privileging of, 34
researcher's, 101–2
self-representation of, 35–36
students', 23, 24–38, 119
imagined audience, 155–56, 160
immigrants, 25–26, 195–96
Imposter Syndrome, 74, 75
inclusive learning environment, 109–10
inclusive pedagogy. *See* critical and
inclusive pedagogies
individual growth, 27–30
inequities, 23, 90–94, 114–15
infinite other, 153
in-group peer feedback, 155
injustice, 92–93
instructors, 169n4, 214–15. *See also*
lecturer; professor; teacher
ally as, 199–200
CIPs requiring, 216–17
as courageous, 216–17
feedback of, 155
Human Diversity, Power and
Opportunity in Social Institutions,
116–22

as inclusive, 109
as oppressor, 12
of preservice teachers, 116–22
as transparent, 216–17
instructor–student interactions, 5. *See
also* dialogical professor–student
interaction
Intangible Cultural Heritage, 163
Integrated Postsecondary Education
Data System, 104
Intercultural Press for the International
Society for Intercultural
Education, Training and Research,
89
interlocking communities, 58–59
international baccalaureate (IB)
program, 138
internationalization, 150–51
international negotiation, 87–88
international peacekeeping, 87
interracial coalitions, 208
intersectionality, 25, 26–27, 38, 191
intersectional pedagogy, 197–200
intersectional reflexivity, 200–201
intersectional sexuality, CIP and,
186–202
Intifada, 47
introductory monologue, 71–72, 75
introspection, 63, 217
Irizarry, Jason, 36
isolation, 137–38, 145
Israel, 191

Jack, Ava, 177
Jackson, Christine, 86
Jacob, Isabella, 176
Jamaica, 9–20
Japan, 5. *See also* Global Project Work:
Presenting About Japan in English
collaborative learning in, 152–53
dialogism in, 152–53
food waste in, 160–61
higher education in, 151–53
orientalist view of, 159
polyphony in, 152–53

race in, 151–52
racialization in, 151–52
university in, 149–67
Japanese, 149, 150–52, 160, 165
Japanese cuisine (*washoku*) (*nihon-ryori*), 156–66
Japaneseness, de-racializing, 149–67
Japanese Studies, 150–51
Jewish woman, 189–92, 197–200
Jones, Richard, 200–201
Journey Up the River: The Struggle Continues, 65
just learning environments, 212–13

K–12 students, 120–21
killing, 208
King, Martin Luther, Jr., 213
knowledge (*concocimento*), 37, 187
    declarative, 88
    dialogue co-constructing of, 56
    elite, 9
    prior, 30–32, 34
    privileging of, 34
know-what-learned-how (K-W-L-H) exercise, 118–19
Koshino, Kako, 215
Krathwohl, David, 93–94
Kuwaiti, 192–94
K-W-L-H exercise. *See* know-what-learned-how exercise

Ladson-Billings, Gloria, 85, 133
Lang, James, 89
language, 49–52, 128n1, 142–43, 152–53, 169n5
Lather, Patti, 46
Latina, 122
Latin@ students, 133, 143–45
Latin@ youth, 4–5
    cultural value emphasis, 141–42
    discussion, 144–45
    expectations, 140–41, 142–43
    findings, 137–44
    humanization, 133–36, 144–45
    isolation, 137–38, 145

lessons from, 131–46
    methods, 136–37
    overview, 131–46
    peer influence, 138–39
    preparation, 140–41
    through P–16 pipeline, 131–46
    teachers influencing, 140
    theoretical framework, 132–36
Leadership in Energy and Environmental Design (LEED), 88
learner, students as, 58–59
learning, 84–85, 216. *See also* experiential learning
learning environments. *See also* collaborative learning
    CIPs creating, 2, 212–13
    equitable, 32–38
    as identity affirming, 212–13
    as inclusive, 109–10
    overview, ix–xi, 218–19
    as socially just, 212–13
lecturer, 20
lectures, 154
lecture-style instruction, 10
LEED. *See* Leadership in Energy and Environmental Design
LePine, Jeffery, 86
LePine, Marcie, 86
lesbian, 196, 197–200
Letter from Birmingham Jail (King), 213
liberation, 47
life environment studies (*seikatsu-ka*), 160
listening, in democratic classroom, 60–61
lived experiences, 211–12
London, UK, 208
Loving in the War Years (Moraga), 199
low-energy democracy, 51
Lummis, Charles, 51

MAFF. *See* Ministry of Agriculture, Forestry and Fisheries
marginalization, 197–200

Martinez, Lisa, 210
Mason, Sophia, 179
mass shooting, 207
McLaren, Peter, 2
McVeigh, Brian, 151–52
medical students, 88
Meet Us at the River: An Anthology in Progress, 64–65
mental health counseling, 87
mentoring, faculty, 109
meritocracy, 117
mestizaje. See miscegenation
meta-awareness, 12, 18
Mexican, 194–97
Mexico, 158
MEXT. *See* Ministry of Education, Culture, Sports, Science and Technology
Michael, Addison, 175, 180
microaggression, 216–17
Middle East, 192
middle school, 140
Midwest College, 176
Midwestern college, 98–110. *See also* African Americans, in Midwestern college
Milem, Jeffrey, 99
Mills, Michael, 34–35
miner's canary, 205
The Miner's Canary (Torres and Guinier), 205
Ministry of Agriculture, Forestry and Fisheries (MAFF), 158, 164
Ministry of Education, Culture, Sports, Science and Technology (MEXT), 150, 152. *See also* Global Project Work: Presenting About Japan in English
minoritized, 221n5
miscegenation (*mestizaje*), 196
misconceptions, 85
modules, 67n2
Mohanty, Chandra, 193, 194
monologue, 71–72, 75

Moraga, Cherrie, 187, 188, 195, 197, 199
Morales, Dianne, 67n1
multilingual repertoires, 25–26
Muñoz, José Esteban, 188
Muslim, 192–94
Myers, Samuel, 104

Napier, Sarah, 67n1
narrative. *See also* personal narratives
    experience, 73
    importance of, 196
    of winning, 199
National Aeronautics and Space Administration (NASA), 140
National Center for Cultural Competence, 128n2
National Center for Education Statistics, 100, 104, 171–72
Navarro, Tami, 82n1
Netherlands, 208
New York City, 25–26, 32
nihon-ryori. See Japanese cuisine
9/11 terrorist attacks, 137
Noah, Emma, 176–77, 179–80

Obama, Barack, 207
obesity, 158
objects, students as, 10
OECD. *See* Organisation for Economic Co-operation and Development
Oliver, Jamie, 160, 162
omelet, 169n6
opportunities, 124–25
oppressed, 18
oppression, 13, 19–20, 74, 76–79
oppressor, 12, 18, 19–20
Organisation for Economic Co-operation and Development (OECD), 1
orientalist view, 159
orientation readings, 55
Ortega, Debora, 210
other, 12, 153
Otherness, 201

Others. *See also* Critical Sexuality
      Studies
   beginnings, 200–202
   examples, 188–202
   lifting up, 215
   overview, 186, 200–202
   on performance, 187–88
   personal narratives of, 188–202
   perspectives of, 187–88
out-group peer feedback, 154–55
outsider, 189–92

Palestinian, 192–94
Palestinian occupied territories, 47
Papastergiadis, Nikos, 28
participation, 52
Pazich, Loni, 221n5
Peake, Leigh, 59–60
pedagogical framework, 154–57
pedagogical strategies, 5, 125
pedagogy, 131, 134. *See also* critical and
      inclusive pedagogies; democratic
      pedagogy; engaged pedagogy
   critical communication, 196–97
   definition of, 132
   games' power of, 85–89
   intersectional, 197–200
   of revolt, 194–97
   simulations' power of, 85–89
Pedagogy of the Oppressed (Freire), 135
peer feedback, 154–55
peer influence, 138–39
performance, 187–88
performative writing, 187–88
person, development of, 145
personal experiences, 73, 124–25
personal narratives, 15, 188–202
philosophy, 17, 20
physical comforting, 78–79
Pittenger, Khushwant, 93
pockets of hope, 47
Poetry and Political Discourse, 64
political autobiography, 63–65
political work, 55
Pollock, Mica, 128n1

polygamy, 31–32
polyphony, 152–53, 154–57, 165–66
Powell, Lewis, 32
power. *See also* collective power
   dialogue's connection with, 57–58
   identities and, 25–27
   rethinking of, 52–56
   sharing, 14–15
   T-128 focusing on, 49, 52–56
power broker, 9
Powers, Richard, 88–89
practices, 49–52, 115–16, 118–19,
      122–23, 127, 217
praxis, 120–21
preconceptions, 85
predominantly White institutions
      (PWIs), 99, 171–72, 221n1. *See
      also* African American female
      administrators; African Americans,
      in Midwestern college
presentation, 158–67, 169n5
preservice teachers, 112–13, 116–22,
      126. *See also* humanizing
      pedagogy
*Presumed incompetent: The intersections
      of race and class for women in
      academia* (Gutierrez y Muhs,
      Flores Niemann, Gonzalez, and
      Harris), 74
principal, 141–42
prior knowledge, 30–32, 34, 37
private nonprofit institutions, 209
privileges, 87, 90–94, 124. *See also*
      White privilege
privileging, 34
problem-posing education, 13
professors, 35, 71–72, 214–15
   African American, 103–4, 109
   African Americans, in Midwestern
      college, hostility of, 106–7
   classroom role of, 79
   diversity engaged by, 37–38
   as inclusive, 109
   race influencing, 209
   speech, 108

Project for Promotion of Global Human Resource Development, 150
project of change, 63, 64–65
P–16 pipeline, 131–46
psychological battering, 74
public speech critiques, 154
Pugh, Greg, 86–87
"Pushing the Boundaries of Educational Change" (Hargreaves), 16–17
PWIs. *See* predominantly White institutions

Queens, New York City, 25–26
queerness, 186–202

race
    CIP implications, 205–19
    in college, x
    conversation, ix–xi
    in global context, 205–19
    humanizing pedagogy for, 112–27
    in Japan, 151–52
    language, 128n1
    as mattering, 206–9
    neutrality, x
    overview, ix–xi
    professors influenced by, 209
Race and Higher Education: Rethinking Pedagogy in Diverse College Classrooms (Howell and Tuitt), 206
raceless persona, 133
racial battle fatigue, 189
racial incidents, 208
racialization, 151–52, 158–59, 162
racialized oppression, 76–79
racial microaggression, 216–17
racism, 61, 74, 117, 178–80, 207
"Racism Is Here to Stay: Now What?" (Bell), x
radical democracy, 51
radical honesty, 4, 71–81, 82n1, 82n2, 82n3, 211
readings, 154
recentering, 126
receptacle approach, 28

reciprocity, 50–51
reflection, 28–29, 63–65, 88, 90–94, 217. *See also* critical reflection
reflexivity, 200–202
re-humanization, 133
research, on campus racial climate, 99. *See also* African Americans, in Midwestern college
researcher's identity, 101–2
Responding to the Realities of Race on Campus (Tuitt and Harper), x
revolt, pedagogy of, 194–97
Ruiz, Adriana, 99

Saint Joseph's College, 35
Salazar, Maria del Carmen, 114, 135–36, 144, 210
Sandahl, Carrie, 191
Sarmiento, Johann, 152–53
Schnurr, Matthew, 87–88
scholars, Asian woman, 102. *See also* women-of-color scholars
seikatsu-ka. See life environment studies
self-awareness, 87
self-perception, 119
self-recorded videos, 155
self-reflexivity, 200–201
self-representation, 35–36
Selma, Alabama, 207
selves, 11–12, 73, 133, 212, 216–17
sensitivity, 201–2
September 11th terrorist attacks, 137
service learning inquiry, 115–16
sexism, 61, 85–86, 117, 178–80
sexuality, 186–202
shame, 73–75, 81
Shao-Kobayashi, Satoko, 214
sharing power, 14–15
Shields, Stephanie, 85–86
Shimomura, Hakubun, 150
silencing, 108
simulations. *See also* Barnga
    in business course, 92
    critical consciousness in, 85
    debriefing as essential to, 92

fun as crucial to, 89
international negotiation taught
    through, 87–88
learning taught by, 84–85
losing at, 88
for medical students, 88
pedagogical power of, 85–89
reflection in, 88
social justice issues confronted
    through, 85
Sister Citizen (Harris-Perry), 74
slavery, 107
small groups, 62
Smith, Hal, 47
Smith, Stella, 216
Smith, William, 189
social change, curriculum innovations
    for, 16–18
social identity markers, 119
social justice, simulations confronting
    issues of, 85
socially just learning environments,
    212–13
social power, 90–94
social work, 55
society, 52
sociology, 31–32
Solórzano, Daniel, 189
South Carolina, 207
South One Public, 175, 176–78, 180
South Two Public, 178
speaking, in democratic classroom,
    60–61
speech critiques, 154
speech professor, 108
Spivak, Gayatri, 9
staff, 109–10
Stahl, Gerry, 152–53
Starpower, 88–89
Steinwachs, Barbara, 89
Stenton, Alison, 153
stereotypes, 112–13
Stewart, Saran, 217
Stokell, Richard, 88
stress, 86

structural discrimination. *See* Barnga
struggle, 194–97
students, 169n4. *See also* African
    Americans, in Midwestern college;
    assignments; Barnga; critical
    consciousness; diversity; Education
    for Social and Political Change;
    graduate students; humanizing
    pedagogy; Latin@ students;
    Latin@ youth; reciprocity;
    university students
administrators influencing, 172–73,
    181
African American female
    administrators influencing,
    175–77
American Indian, 47
assumptions harbored about,
    126–27
Black, 118
Caribbean University framework,
    18–19
chat rooms, 152–53
CIPs influencing, 18–19, 211–13
dialogic relations of, 155
diversity influencing, 172
domestication of, 50
as high-achieving, 143–44
identities of, 23, 24–38, 119
K–12, 120–21
as learners, 58–59
lived experiences of, 211–12
medical, 88
misconceptions held onto by, 85
as objects, 10
as oppressed, 18
preconceptions held onto by, 85
prior knowledge of, 30–32, 34, 37
self-representation of, 35–36
students of color challenged by, 61
as teachers, 58–59
teachers' distance from, 107
voice, 15, 17–18
White, 118, 120, 189
women challenged by, 61

students of color. *See also* African
    Americans, in Midwestern college
    preservice teachers educated by, 126
    students challenging, 61
subject-matter learning, 30–33,
    36–38
subjects, 10, 57
subordination, 87
suicide, 77–79
sukiyaki. *See* beef dish
superdiversity, 25–26
support, African Americans, in
    Midwestern college, 102–7
sushi, 158, 160, 161
sustainability, game about, 88
Swim, Janet, 85–86

taxonomy, 93–94
teachable moments, 215–16
teacher education, humanizing
    pedagogy in, 112–27
teachers. *See also* assignments; critical
    consciousness; humanizing
    pedagogy; reciprocity
    on college, 142–43
    as culturally competent, 128n2
    in experiential education, 84
    history, 36
    Latin@ youth influenced by, 140
    power of, 52–56
    students as, 58–59
    students' distance from, 107
    as subject, 10
    writing encouraged by, 143
"Teach Every Child About Food"
    (Oliver), 162
teaching. *See also* culturally responsive
    teaching
    CIPs influenced by, 210–11, 213–14
    discussion-based, 34–35
    humanizing pedagogy deconstruction
        of, 115–25
    philosophy, 17, 20
    theoretical models of, 210–11

teaching community, power of, 52–56.
    See also Education for Social and
    Political Change
teaching fellows (TFs), 47, 62
*Teaching to Transgress: Education
    as the Practice of Freedom*
    (hooks), 170
Technology, Entertainment, Design,
    talk, 162
technology, immigrants using, 26
TED talk. *See* Technology,
    Entertainment, Design, talk
*Telling histories: Black women historians
    in the ivory tower* (White), 75
tempered radical, 13
tensions, 32–33, 126–27
terrorism, 192
texts, 152–53
TFs. *See* teaching fellows
theories in flesh, 187
Thiagarajan, Sivasailam, 89. *See also*
    Barnga
Tometi, Opal, 207–8
T-128. *See* Education for Social and
    Political Change
Top Global University Project, 168n2
Torres, Gerald, 205
tracking, 208
traditionally White institutions (TWIs),
    205, 208, 221n1
transformative labor, 80–81
Trausan-Matu, Stefan, 152–53
Trueba, Henry, 100
truth-in-action, disciplinary burdens of,
    79–81
truths, 15
truth-telling, 71–72, 73, 75–79. *See also*
    radical honesty
Tuitt, Frank, x, 11, 13, 14, 15, 84, 206,
    211, 213
Turner, Caroline, 104
turning points, 136
TWIs. *See* traditionally White
    institutions

undocumented youth, 4–5, 141–42
unearned privilege, 87
UNESCO. *See* United Nations Educational, Scientific and Cultural Organization
Unger, Roberto, 51, 63
United Kingdom (UK), 208
United Nations Educational, Scientific and Cultural Organization (UNESCO), 158, 159, 163
United States (U.S.), 10, 133–34, 158, 168n1
universities, in Japan, 149–67. *See also* college
university students, Japanese, 151–52. *See also* college students
urgent voices, 61
utilization of personal narratives, 15

Vertovec, Steven, 26
video games, 151
videos, 155
violence, 189
vocational school, 36
voices, 15, 17–18, 126, 154–57, 214–15

WAGES. *See* Workshop Activity for Gender Equity Simulations
washoku. *See* Japanese cuisine
"*Washoku*: Japanese-Style Food" (Group A), 158–59
Wegerif, Rupert, 153
West, Cornel, 51, 63
West Africa, 89–90. *See also* Barnga
White, Deborah, 75
White faculty, 109–10
Whiteness, 64, 107, 126, 133
White privilege, 117, 126

White staff, 109–10
White students, 118, 120, 189. *See also* Jewish woman
White supremacy, 126, 133
White voice, 126
whole selves, 73, 212, 216–17
Williams, Bianca, 211, 215, 216
Williams, Leslie, 212
winning, 199
Wolk, Steven, 59–60
women. *See also* African American women
   Asian, 102
   of color, 192–94
   disabled, 189–92
   fat, 197–200
   Jewish, 189–92, 197–200
   Kuwaiti, 192–94
   Muslim, 192–94
   as oppressive, 13
   Palestinian, 192–94
   queer, 188–92, 197–200
   scholar, 102
   students challenging, 61
women-of-color scholars, 74–75, 80–81
Woodson, Carter, 113
work–life balance, 178, 180, 181
Workshop Activity for Gender Equity Simulations (WAGES), 86
writing, 143

Yang, Yang, 153
Yazzie, Tarajean, 47
Yep, Gust, 188, 199
Yosso, Tara, 133, 189
Young, Iris, 56, 57–58

Zawadzki, Matthew, 85–86

"This . . . brilliant and engaging . . . book has the potential to literally change the face of college teaching and learning from a multicultural perspective. No one who reads this text and reflects on its message can continue to teach in the old monocultural ways of teaching and learning."—*Joseph L. **White**, Professor Emeritus of Psychology and Psychiatry, University of California, Irvine*

Sty/us

22883 Quicksilver Drive
Sterling, VA 20166-2102

Subscribe to our e-mail alerts: www.Styluspub.com

Also available from Stylus

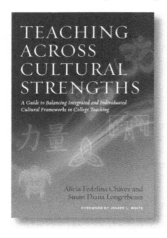

Teaching Across Cultural Strengths
A Guide to Balancing Integrated and Individuated Cultural Frameworks in College Teaching
Alicia Fedelina Chávez and Susan Diana Longerbeam
Foreword by Joseph L. White

"*Teaching Across Cultural Strengths* is a shining star in a night sky of relative darkness on inclusive teaching in the academy. Through their practical yet creative approach, Chávez and Longerbeam make a pivotal impact on the ways culture plays out between and among students and teachers in postsecondary education. Its contribution to students of color and women's learning is substantial, with clear application to these groups as well as others in all academic disciplines. In fact, by placing primary emphasis on culture, this book could bring about a movement to reform the relationship between student and teacher in higher education producing optimal learning in every field. The work presented by these authors can significantly transform teaching on any college campus with a progressive view of learning. Faculty in every academic discipline concerned about student learning and how it occurs through their teaching will find this book practical and insightful. Student affairs educators responsible for professional development, or with deep concern for out of class learning, will find this imperative reading to assist students in their learning, growth, and development. Chávez and Longerbeam get high praise for illuminating the place of culture in post-secondary learning."—*Florence M. Guido, Professor, University of Northern Colorado*

"Every faculty member should read this book. Chávez and Longerbeam provide a richly revised understanding of the dynamics of teaching and of the responsibilities of faculty to learn about this new terrain. They need to do so with the same passion and dedication as they do their area of scholarly expertise. Peppered with a steady range of specific examples of how to create more culturally inclusive pedagogies persuasively supported by faculty testimonies of pleasure at how students are more engaged, no one can pretend it can't be done in their courses. The moving quotes from students threaded throughout the book should prick the conscience of those immobilized into only one form of teaching. Faculty need only to listen to students in this book—and in their own classes—to realize the transformative possibilities they can unleash in their classrooms."
—*Caryn McTighe Musil, Senior Scholar, Association of American Colleges and Universities*

"This book offers a comprehensive set of guidelines based on a sound theoretical foundation, and empirical research that will enable college teachers to narrow the gap in cross cultural teaching and student learning and assist teachers in transforming learning for all students across the many cultures that exist in the classroom. By following the steps outlined in this book, teachers can progressively learn about the role of culture in learning while transforming their teaching through introspection, reflection, practice, and the application of new teaching pedagogies that deepen student learning.

(Continues on previous page)